2/10

My
iPhone™
THIRD EDITION

Brad Miser

Que®

800 East 96th Street
Indianapolis, Indiana 46240 USA

My iPhone™, Third Edition

Copyright © 2010 by Que Publishing

ISBN-13: 978-0-7897-4231-5

ISBN-10: 0-7897-4231-4

Library of Congress Cataloging-in-Publication Data:

Miser, Brad.

My iPhone / Brad Miser. -- 3rd ed.

p. cm.

ISBN 978-0-7897-4231-5

1. iPhone (Smartphone) 2. Cellular telephones. 3. Pocket computers.

4. Digital music players. I. Title.

TK6570.M6M535 2010

621.3845'6--dc22

2009034372

Printed in the United States on America

First Printing: August 2009

Trademarks

Warning and Disclaimer

Bulk Sales

Que Publishing offers excellent discounts on this book when ordered in quantity for bulk purchases or special sales. For more information, please contact

U.S. Corporate and Government Sales
1-800-382-3419
corpsales@pearsontechgroup.com

For sales outside of the U.S., please contact

International Sales
international@pearsoned.com

ASSOCIATE PUBLISHER
Greg Wiegand

ACQUISITIONS AND DEVELOPMENT EDITOR
Laura Norman

MANAGING EDITOR
Patrick Kanouse

PROJECT EDITOR
Mandie Frank

INDEXER
Ken Johnson

PROOFREADER
Jovana San Nicolas-Shirley

TECHNICAL EDITOR
Griff Partington

PUBLISHING COORDINATOR
Cindy J. Teeters

DESIGNER
Anne Jones

COMPOSITOR
TnT Design, Inc.

Contents at a Glance

Chapter 1   Getting Started with Your iPhone **2**

Chapter 2   Connecting to the Internet, Bluetooth Devices, and
iPhones/iPods **28**

Chapter 3   Moving Audio, Video, and Photos onto an iPhone **50**

Chapter 4   Configuring and Synchronizing Information
on an iPhone **80**

Chapter 5   Managing Contacts **98**

Chapter 6   Making, Receiving, and Managing Calls **122**

Chapter 7   Emailing **160**

Chapter 8   Texting **206**

Chapter 9   Managing Calendars and Time **222**

Chapter 10   Surfing the Web **260**

Chapter 11   Listening to Music, Podcasts, and Other Audio **292**

Chapter 12   Watching Movies, TV Shows, and Other Video **332**

Chapter 13   Working with Photos and Video **344**

Chapter 14   Using Preinstalled Applications **372**

Chapter 15   Installing and Maintaining iPhone Applications **388**

Chapter 16   Customizing an iPhone **404**

Chapter 17   Maintaining an iPhone and Solving Problems **432**

Index **453**

Table of Contents

1 Getting Started with Your iPhone **2**

Touring Your iPhone 4

    Getting to Know the iPhone's External Features 4

    Knowing Why It's Called a Multi-Touch Interface 5

Preparing iTunes 16

    Downloading and Installing iTunes on a Windows PC 17

    Updating iTunes 18

    Using an iTunes Store Account 18

Preparing MobileMe 20

    Obtaining a MobileMe Account 20

    Configuring MobileMe on a Windows PC 21

    Configuring MobileMe on a Mac 24

    Managing MobileMe Syncs 25

Using This Book 26

**2 Connecting to the Internet, Bluetooth Devices,
and iPhones/iPods** **28**

Connecting an iPhone to the Internet 30

    Connecting to an Open Wi-Fi Network 31

    Connecting to a Commercial Wi-Fi Network 35

    Connecting to a Closed Wi-Fi Network 36

    Changing Networks 38

    Forgetting Wi-Fi Networks 39

    Connecting to the Internet via a Cellular Data Network 41

Connecting to Other Devices Using Bluetooth 45

Connecting to Other iPhones and iPod touches 47

    Using an Application with Peer-to-Peer Networking by Default 48

    Configuring an Application to Use Peer-to-Peer Networking 49

3   **Moving Audio, Video, and Photos onto Your iPhone** **50**

    Using iTunes to Add Audio and Video Content to the iPhone 52

        Importing Audio CDs to the iTunes Library 52

        Purchasing Audio and Video from the iTunes Store 55

        Renting Movies from the iTunes Store 58

        Subscribing to Podcasts in the iTunes Store 60

        Building Music Playlists 62

        Building Smart Playlists 64

        Moving Audio and Video from the iTunes Library onto an iPhone 67

    Using iTunes to Add Photos to Your iPhone 72

        Moving Photos from a Windows PC onto iPhone 72

        Moving Photos from a Mac to iPhone 74

    Using the iTunes iPhone Application to Add Content to an iPhone 75

4   **Configuring and Synchronizing Information on an iPhone** **80**

    Syncing Information with iTunes 82

        Using iTunes to Sync Information on Macs 82

        Using iTunes to Sync Information on Windows 88

    Syncing Information with MobileMe 92

5   **Managing Contacts** **98**

    Configuring How Contacts Are Displayed on an iPhone 100

    Creating New Contacts While Using an iPhone 101

        Creating a Contact from a Recent Call 102

        Creating a Contact from an Email 104

        Creating Contacts on an iPhone Manually 106

    Using Contacts on an iPhone 115

        Using the Contacts Application 116

        Using Contacts Information in Other Applications 117

    Changing or Deleting Contacts 118

        Changing, Adding, or Removing Information for an Existing
          Contact Manually 119

        Adding Information to an Existing Contact While Using Your iPhone ... 120

        Deleting Contacts Manually 121

    Bonus Web Task: Creating a Contact from a Map

6   **Making, Receiving, and Managing Calls** **122**

Configuring Phone Settings 124

Creating Your Own Ringtones 124

Setting Phone Sounds 128

Configuring Phone Settings 130

Other Phone Settings 132

Making Calls 132

Dialing with the Keypad 133

Dialing with Contacts 134

Dialing with Favorites 135

Dialing with Recents 136

Managing In-Process Calls 138

Receiving Calls 143

Answering Calls 143

Answering Calls When You're Already on a Call 145

Managing Calls 146

Clearing Recent Calls 147

Adding Caller Information to Favorites 148

Using iPhone's Headset for Calls 149

Using Voice Control (iPhone 3GS Only) 149

Using Visual Voicemail 150

Recording a Greeting 151

Listening to and Managing Voicemails 153

7   **Emailing** **160**

Configuring Email Accounts on an iPhone 162

Configuring Gmail, Yahoo! Mail, or AOL Email Accounts on an iPhone
Manually 163

Configuring Exchange Email Accounts on an iPhone Manually 165

Performing Advanced Configuration of Email Accounts on an iPhone ... 170

Configuring General Email Settings 176

Configuring How Email Is Retrieved 176

Configuring Global Email Settings 179

Working with Email 183

Receiving andReading Email 183

Sending Email 189

Replying to Email 194

Forwarding Email 195

Managing Email 197

Bonus Web Task: Managing Email Accounts

Bonus Web Task: Deleting Email Accounts

8   Texting **206**

Configuring the New Text Message Sound 209

Configuring Messaging Preferences 210

Sending Text Messages 211

Receiving and Replying to Text Messages 214

Working with Text Messages 216

Conversing in Text 216

Including Images in Text Conversations 218

Deleting Messages 220

Deleting a Conversation 221

9   Managing Calendars and Time **222**

Configuring an iPhone's Calendar, Date, and Time Settings ... 223

Working with Calendars 232

Viewing Calendars 233

Adding Events to a Calendar Manually 237

Adding Events to the Calendar by Accepting Invitations ... 246

Working with Event Alarms 249

Using an iPhone as a Clock 249

Telling Time with an iPhone 249

Using the Clock Application 250

Bonus Web Task: Using an iPhone as a Stopwatch

10   Surfing the Web **260**

Configuring Safari Settings 262

Browsing the Web on an iPhone 268

Moving to Websites via Bookmarks 268

Moving to Websites by Typing a URL 270

Viewing Websites 272

Searching the Web 274

Returning to Previous Websites 275

Saving and Organizing Bookmarks 277

Creating a Bookmark on the Home Screen 284

Emailing a Link to a Webpage 285

Completing Web Forms 286

Signing In Automatically 288

Opening and Managing Multiple Webpages at the Same Time 289

11 Listening to Music, Podcasts, and Other Audio **292**

Finding and Listening to Music 294

Using the Cover Flow Browser to Find and Play Music 294

Using Playlists to Find Music 298

Using Artists to Find Music 300

Using the Songs Tool to Find Music 304

Using Albums to Find Music 305

Using the More Menu to Find Music 308

Searching for Music 309

Using the Genius to Find Music 310

Finding Music by Shuffling 314

Finding Music by Speaking (iPhone 3GS only) 315

Playing Music 316

Controlling Audio Content with the iPod Control Bar 319

Configure the iPod Control Bar 320

Use the iPod Control Bar 321

Finding and Listening to Podcasts 321

Customizing Your iPhone for Music 324

Building and Editing an On-The-Go Playlist 324

Configuring the iPhone's Music Toolbar 327

Configuring the iPhone's Music Settings 329

12 Watching Movies, TV Shows, and Other Video **332**

Finding and Watching Video 333

Finding Video 334

Watching Video 336

Watching Rented Movies 338

Watching VideoPodcasts 340

Deleting Video 341

Configuring iPhone's Video Settings 342

13 **Working with Photos and Video** **344**

Taking Photos with Your iPhone 346

Taking Video with an iPhone 3GS 349

Viewing and Working with Photos on an iPhone 350

Viewing Photos Individually 350

Viewing Photos as a Slideshow 352

Configure Slideshow Settings 352

Deleting Photos or Video from an iPhone 356

Emailing a Photo 357

Texting a Photo 358

Sending a Photo to MobileMe 359

Assigning a Photo to a Contact 361

Sharing Photos 362

Viewing, Editing, and Working with Video on an iPhone 3GS 363

Watching Video 364

Editing Video 366

Sharing Video 367

Moving Photos from Your iPhone to a Computer 368

Bonus Web Task: Using a Photo as Wallpaper

14 **Using Preinstalled Applications** **372**

Finding Your Way with Maps 374

Finding a Location by Searching 374

Finding a Location with Bookmarks 377

Finding Your Current Location 380

Working with Maps 381

Getting Directions 383

Understanding Other Preinstalled iPhone Applications 387

15 **Installing and Maintaining iPhone Applications** **388**

Using iTunes to Find and Install iPhone Applications 390

Downloading Applications from the iTunes Store 390

Moving Applications from Your iTunes Library onto iPhone 393

Using the App Store to Find and Install iPhone Applications 394

Using iPhone Applications You Install 400

Maintaining iPhone Applications 401

Bonus Web Task: Removing Applications from an iPhone

16 **Customizing an iPhone** **404**

Customizing Your Home Screens 406

Accessing iPhone Settings 408

Using Airplane Mode 408

Configuring General Sound Settings 409

Setting Screen Brightness 410

Setting Wallpaper 412

Configuring Other General Settings 413

Getting Information about an iPhone 413

Securing Your iPhone 414

Configuring the Home Button and Search Options 426

Configuring the Keyboard 428

Setting International Options 429

17 **Maintaining an iPhone and Solving Problems** **432**

Maintaining an iPhone 434

Maintaining iTunes 434

Maintaining an iPhone's Software 436

Maintaining an iPhone's Power 438

Cleaning an iPhone's Screen 443

Solving iPhone Problems 443

Restarting an iPhone 444

Restarting the Computer and iTunes 444

Resetting an iPhone 445

Restoring an iPhone 448

Reinstalling iTunes 451

Getting Help with iPhone Problems 451

Index **453**

About the Author

Brad Miser has written extensively about technology, with his favorite topics being the amazing "i" gadgets, iPhone and iPod touch, that make it possible to take our lives with us while we are on the move. In addition to *My iPhone, Third Edition*, Brad has written many other books, including *My iPod touch; Easy iLife '09; Absolute Beginner's Guide to iPod and iTunes, Third Edition; Special Edition Using Mac OS X Leopard; iPhoto '09 Portable Genius; Teach Yourself Visually MacBook Air; and MacBook Pro Portable Genius*. He has also been an author, development editor, or technical editor on more than 50 other titles.

Brad is or has been a sales support specialist, the director of product and customer services, and the manager of education and support services for several software development companies. Previously, he was the lead proposal specialist for an aircraft engine manufacturer, a development editor for a computer book publisher, and a civilian aviation test officer/engineer for the U.S. Army. Brad holds a Bachelor of Science degree in mechanical engineering from California Polytechnic State University at San Luis Obispo and has received advanced education in maintainability engineering, business, and other topics.

In addition to his passion for silicon-based technology, Brad likes to ride his steel-based technology, aka, a motorcycle, whenever and wherever possible.

Originally from California, Brad now lives in Brownsburg, Indiana, with his wife Amy; their three daughters, Jill, Emily, and Grace; a rabbit; and a sometimes inside cat.

Brad would love to hear about your experiences with this book (the good, the bad, and the ugly). You can write to him at bradmiser@me.com.

Dedication

To those who have given the last full measure of devotion so that the rest of us can be free.

Acknowledgments

To the following people on the *My iPhone* project team, my sincere appreciation for your hard work on this book:

Laura Norman, my acquisitions and development editor, who envisioned the original concept for *My iPhone*. Laura and I have worked on many books together, and I appreciate her professional and effective approach to these projects. Thanks for putting up with me yet one more time!

Griff Partington, my technical editor, who did a great job to ensure that the information in this book is both accurate and useful.

Mandie Frank, my project editor, who skillfully managed the hundreds of files and production process that it took to make this book.

Anne Jones, for the interior design and cover of the book.

Que's production and sales team for printing the book and getting it into your hands.

We Want to Hear from You!

As the reader of this book, *you* are our most important critic and commentator. We value your opinion and want to know what we're doing right, what we could do better, what areas you'd like to see us publish in, and any other words of wisdom you're willing to pass our way.

As an associate publisher for Que Publishing, I welcome your comments. You can email or write me directly to let me know what you did or didn't like about this book—as well as what we can do to make our books better.

Please note that I cannot help you with technical problems related to the topic of this book. We do have a User Services group, however, where I will forward specific technical questions related to the book.

When you write, please be sure to include this book's title and author as well as your name, email address, and phone number. I will carefully review your comments and share them with the author and editors who worked on the book.

Email: feedback@quepublishing.com

Mail: Greg Wiegand
Associate Publisher
Que Publishing
800 East 96th Street
Indianapolis, IN 46240 USA

Reader Services

Visit our website and register this book at www.quepublishing.com/register for convenient access to any updates, downloads, or errata that might be available for this book.

Soon you'll wonder how you
ever got along without one.

In this chapter, you learn how to get going with your iPhone. The topics include the following:

→ Touring your iPhone
→ Preparing iTunes
→ Preparing MobileMe
→ Using this book

Getting Started with Your iPhone

The good news is that getting started with an iPhone is a simple, painless process. You've got your hands on one, so it's time to get going. In this chapter, you get a tour of the iPhone so you can use its controls and work with its interface quickly and easily. You also learn about installing iPhone's required partner, iTunes, which you use to move content onto your iPhone and keep it in sync. Another optional but very valuable partner for your iPhone is Apple's MobileMe service, which we also take a look at. Last, you learn a bit about how you can get the most out of this book.

Touring Your iPhone

You'll find that an iPhone is one of the most amazing handheld devices ever because of how well it is designed. It has only a few external features you need to understand. For most of the things you do, you'll just use your fingers on your iPhone's screen (which just seems natural), and the iPhone provides a consistent interface so you accomplish most tasks with similar steps.

Getting to Know the iPhone's External Features

Take a quick look at the iPhone's physical controls and ports and learn to understand how you move around its screens.

Wake/Sleep button   Press this to lock the iPhone's controls and put it to sleep. Press it again to wake the iPhone from Sleep mode.

Headphone port   Plug the iPhone's earbuds into this port.

Mute Off/On switch
Slide it toward the front of the iPhone to hear sounds; a bell icon appears on the screen to indicate that Mute is disabled. Slide it toward the back of the iPhone to mute all iPhone sounds.

Volume   Press the upper part of the rocker switch to increase volume; press the lower part of the switch to decrease volume.

Camera   The iPhone's camera lens is located on its backside near the top. If you have an iPhone 3GS, you can take video or still photos. With an iPhone 3G, you can take still photos.

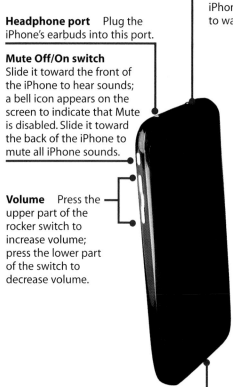

Docking port   Use this port, located on the bottom side of the iPhone, to connect it to a computer or power adapter using the included USB cable.

Home button   Press this button to move to the all-important Home screen. It can also perform other functions, such as displaying iPod controls or moving into Search mode when you press it twice.

Knowing Why It's Called a Multi-Touch Interface

Apple designed the iPhone to be touched. The previous section describes the only physical controls an iPhone has; as you read, there aren't many. Most of the time, you control your iPhone by using your fingers on its screen to tap buttons, select items on lists, scroll, zoom, type text, and so on. After you use it a while, you might want everything to work this way because it's so easy and intuitive.

Application buttons

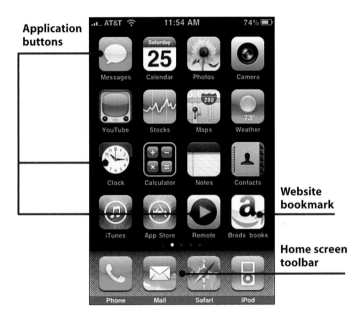

Website bookmark

Home screen toolbar

Going Home

Most iPhone activities start at the Home screen, which you get to by pressing the Home button located at the bottom of the iPhone. Along the bottom of the Home screen, you see the toolbar; this toolbar is visible when you view most of the Home screen's pages so that you have easy access to the buttons it contains (more on the Home screen shortly). Above the toolbar, you see applications on iPhone that do all sorts of cool things; as you install applications, the number of buttons increases. You can also create bookmarks for websites and store them as buttons on the Home screen. As you add applications and bookmarks, the number of pages of the Home screen increases so you can store them all on it. You can organize the buttons on the pages of the Home screen in anyway you'd like.

Touching the iPhone's Screen

The following figures highlight the major ways you control iPhone. A tap is just what it sounds like; you gently press a finger to the iPhone's screen over the item you want to control and then quickly lift your finger up again. To drag, you place your finger on the screen and move it across the screen without lifting it up. (You don't need to apply pressure, just contact.) To pinch or unpinch, place two fingers on the screen and drag them together or move them apart.

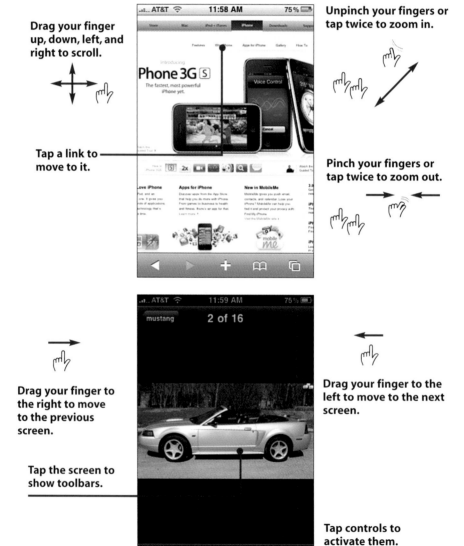

Typing on an iPhone

There are lots of things you do with an iPhone that require you to type, and iPhone's keyboard is pretty amazing. Whenever you need it, whether it's for emailing, entering a website URL, performing a search, and so on, it pops up automatically.

Use the iPhone's virtual keyboard to type.

If you type a word that the iPhone doesn't recognize, it makes a suggestion about what it thinks is the correct word in a pop-up box. To accept the suggestion, tap the Space key. To reject the suggestion, tap the pop-up box to close it and keep what you typed.

To type, just tap the keys. As you tap each key, the character you tap pops up in a small window so you can see what you entered, which is useful feedback for you. (You also hear audio feedback if you haven't disabled it.) The keyboard includes all the standard keys you expect. To change from letters to numbers and special characters, just tap the .?123 key; tap the #+= key to access more special symbols. Tap the ABC key to return to letters. It also has contextual keys that appear when you need them. For example, when you are entering a website address, the .com key appears so you can enter these four characters with a single tap.

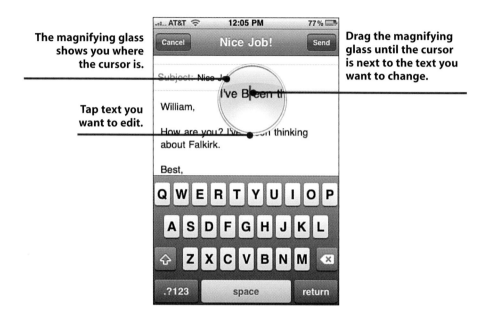

The magnifying glass shows you where the cursor is.

Tap text you want to edit.

Drag the magnifying glass until the cursor is next to the text you want to change.

To edit text, tap and hold on the text you want to edit. A magnifying glass icon appears on the screen, and within it you see a magnified view of the current location of the cursor. Drag the magnifying glass to where you want to make changes and then lift your finger from the screen when the cursor is in the correct location; the cursor remains in that location, and you can use the keyboard to make changes to the text or to add text at that location.

Tap Select to choose a portion of what's in the window.

Tap Select All to choose everything in the window.

Tap where you want to start selecting.

You can also select text or images to copy and paste the selected content into a new location. Tap and hold down briefly where you want to start the selection until the magnifying glass icon appears, and then lift your finger off the screen. The Select menu appears. Tap Select to select part of the content on the screen, or tap Select All to select everything in the current window.

The blue markers indicate where the selection starts and stops.

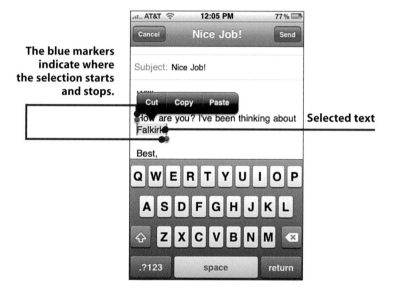

Selected text

You see markers indicating where the selection starts and stops. (The iPhone attempts to select something logical, such as the word or sentence.)

Drag the markers so they enclose what you want to select.

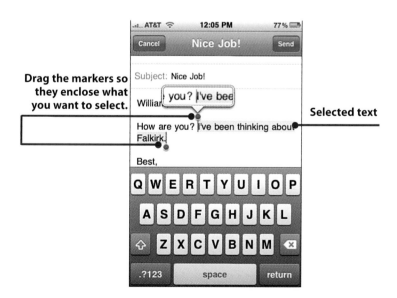

Selected text

Drag the two markers so the content you want to select is between them; the selected portion is highlighted in blue. As you drag, a magnified view of where the selection marker is appears to help you place it more accurately. When the selection markers are located correctly, lift your finger from the screen. (If you tapped the Select All command, you don't need to do this because the content you want to copy is already selected.)

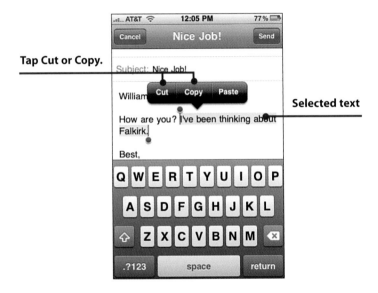

Tap Cut or Copy.

Selected text

Tap Cut to remove the content from the current window or Copy to just copy it.

Tap Paste.

Tap where you want to paste.

Move to where you want to paste the content you selected. Tap where you want the content to be pasted; for a more precise location, tap and hold and then use the magnifying glass icon to move to a specific location. Tap Paste.

Pasted content

The content you copied or cut appears where you placed the cursor.

Using the Home Screens

Tap a dot to move to the corresponding page.

Drag to the left or right to move between Home screen pages.

Earlier, you read that the Home screen is the jumping-off point for many of the things you do with your iPhone because that is where you access the buttons you tap to launch applications, move to website bookmarks you've saved there, and configure your iPhone's settings.

The Home screen actually has multiple pages. To move to a page, drag to the left to move to later pages or to the right to move to earlier pages. Or tap the dot corresponding to the page you want to move to.

Drag all the way to the right or tap the magnifying icon to move to the Search page.

If you move all the way to the "left," you see the Search page. Using this tool, you can search your iPhone. You search different kinds of objects at the same time, such as email, music, and so on.

Search term

Current results

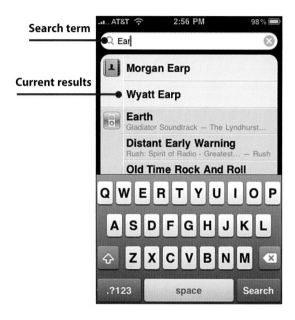

To perform a search, tap in the Search bar and type. As you type, items that meet your search are shown on the list below the Search bar. When you're done typing the search term, tap Search.

Search results

Contacts

Music

The results are organized into sections, which are indicated by icons along the left edge of the screen, such as email, contacts, and so on. To see the detail of an item, tap it. The results remain so that you can always move back to the results screen to work with other items you found.

When you want to clear a search, tap the Clear button (x) at the right end of the Search bar.

Monitoring the iPhone's Status

Cellular phone network   **Wi-Fi or cellular data network**

Cellular phone signal strength

Battery status

Time

At the top of the screen, you see various icons that provide you with information, such as the network and strength of your cellular phone connection, if you are connected to a Wi-Fi or cellular data network, the time, the state of iPhone's battery, and so on. Keep an eye on this area as you use your iPhone.

Sleeping/Locking and Waking/Unlocking

When an iPhone is asleep and you press the Wake/Sleep button or the Home button, the iPhone wakes up, and its screen activates; you see the Unlock slider. Drag the slider to the right to unlock iPhone so that you can work with it. You move to the iPhone Home screen or to the last screen you were using.

Locked

Drag to the right to unlock an iPhone.

The Time Is Always Handy

If you use your iPhone as a watch the way I do, just press the Home button or the Wake/Sleep button. The current time and date appear; if you don't unlock it, the iPhone goes back to sleep after a few seconds.

In most cases, you should just put iPhone to sleep when you aren't using it instead of shutting it off. It doesn't use much power when it sleeps, and it wakes up quickly when you want to start using it again. (In fact, you seldom need to turn iPhone off.)

Shutting Down and Restarting an iPhone

If you want to turn your iPhone off, press and hold the Wake/Sleep button until the red slider appears at the top of the screen. Drag the slider to the right to shut the iPhone down.

To restart iPhone, press and hold the Wake/Sleep button until the Apple logo appears on the screen. In a moment, you see iPhone's Home screen, and it's ready for you to use again.

**Drag to the right to
shut down your iPhone.**

Preparing iTunes

iTunes is the application you use to move content (music, podcasts, movies, and so on) and information (such as email account configurations) onto your iPhone. You need to download and install iTunes on your computer or make sure that you are using the most current version if it's already installed. To get started, jump into any of the following sections that apply to your particular situation.

IPHONE AND ITUNES

This isn't a book about iTunes, so I cover only the details you need to know to use iPhone. iTunes is a powerful application that you can use to manage all your digital entertainment and, of course, to move content onto your iPhone, CD, DVD, iPods, and so on.

You might find yourself in one of two situations on the iTunes front. If you are a Windows user and have never used iTunes, you have to download and install it, which is covered in the next section. (If iTunes is already installed, skip over that section.) If you're a Windows or Mac user and already have iTunes installed on your computer, update it to make sure that you are using the latest version; the section titled "Updating iTunes" covers how to do so.

After iTunes is installed and updated, you should get an account at the iTunes Store, which enables you to purchase content or rent movies. As you might guess, there's a section called "Obtaining and Signing In to an iTunes Store Account" if you don't already have an account there.

>>>step-by-step

Downloading and Installing iTunes on a Windows PC

If your PC doesn't have iTunes installed, perform the following steps.

1. Open a web browser.

2. Move to www.apple.com/itunes/download/.

3. Uncheck the two check boxes.

4. Click Download Now. The installer application starts.

5. Follow the onscreen instructions to open and the run the installer to install iTunes.

Updating iTunes

You should check to make sure you are using the most current version of iTunes.

1. Open iTunes.

2. On a Windows PC, choose Help, Check for Updates. On a Mac, choose iTunes, Check for Updates. The application checks your version of iTunes against the current version.

3. If you are using the current version, click OK to clear the dialog telling you so. If you aren't using the current version, you're prompted to download and install it. Follow the onscreen instructions to download and install the newer version.

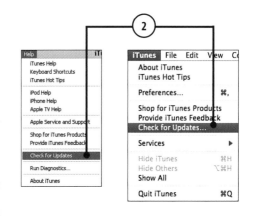

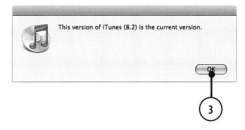

Using an iTunes Store Account

An account on the iTunes Store enables you to purchase audio and video content that is then downloaded to your iTunes Library from where you can move it onto your computer. And you can purchase and download content directly onto your iPhone as well. Even if you don't intend to purchase content or rent movies, you need an account to download and install applications for your iPhone. To obtain and sign into an account, perform the following steps.

1. Open iTunes.

2. Click iTunes Store. You connect to the Internet and move into the iTunes Store.

3. Click Sign In. The Sign In dialog appears. If you see your Apple ID instead of the Sign In button, iTunes is already logged into an iTunes Store account.

Got an iTunes Store Account?
You can log in to an existing iTunes Store account by entering your Apple ID or AOL screen name and password and then clicking Sign In. Skip the rest of these steps.

4. Click Create New Account. You move to the first screen in the account creation process.

5. Read the information and follow the onscreen instructions to create an Apple ID. After you complete the steps, you receive your Apple ID and password.

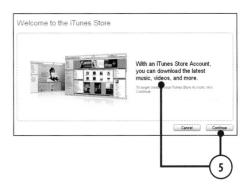

6. Click the Sign In button.

7. Enter your Apple ID and password.

8. Click Sign In. You are logged into your iTunes Store account.

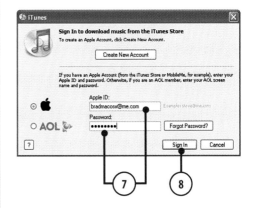

Preparing MobileMe

Apple's MobileMe service provides you with a number of features including online disk space, an email account, an online photo gallery, and more. When it comes to your iPhone, MobileMe offers one primary benefit, and it is a really good one. With MobileMe, you can keep your contacts, calendar, web favorites, and MobileMe email in sync between computers and your iPhone wirelessly. Instead of having to connect your iPhone to a computer to move information over the USB cable, information (such as your email) is moved directly from the Internet onto iPhone via its cellular data or Wi-Fi Internet connection. Not only is this easier, but also your information remains much more current on all your devices.

MobileMe isn't free. Currently, an individual MobileMe account is $99 per year, and the cost of a family account is about $149 per year. However, you can sign up for a free trial account that is available for 60 days. At the end of that period, you can choose to cancel the account if you don't find it valuable.

There are three general steps required to use MobileMe with an iPhone. One is to obtain a MobileMe account. The second is to configure MobileMe on your computers; this task is slightly different on Windows PCs or Macs, so you'll find a section for each kind of computer. The third step is to configure iPhone to access the information provided by MobileMe; these tasks are described in the relevant chapters but are primarily discussed in Chapter 4, "Configuring and Synchronizing Information on an iPhone."

>>>*step-by-step*

Obtaining a MobileMe Account

To begin your free trial MobileMe account, follow these steps.

1. Use a web browser to move to www.apple.com/mobileme/.

2. Click Free Trial.

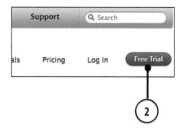

3. Follow the onscreen instructions to obtain your MobileMe account. This involves creating your member name and password and providing contact information and a credit card (which isn't charged until the end of your free trial period). At the end of the process, you'll have a MobileMe member name and password. You use this information to access MobileMe services on all your devices.

Your Member Name Is Important

Be careful about what you choose as your member name; in addition to using this to log in to MobileMe, it becomes part of your email address. You can't change your member name after you've created your account.

Configuring MobileMe on a Windows PC

Use the MobileMe control panel to configure MobileMe syncing on a Windows PC.

1. Open the MobileMe Preferences control panel. (If you don't have this control panel, you aren't using the current version of iTunes. Go back to the "Updating iTunes" section and update iTunes.)

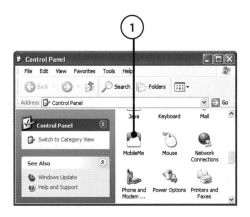

2. Enter your MobileMe member name and password.

3. Click Sign In. Your computer connects to your MobileMe account. In the Account Status section, you see information about your account, such as the amount of disk space you have, when the account expires, and so on.

Exchange Handled Separately

If you have an Exchange account, you don't use MobileMe to sync your calendar or contact information. Instead you configure the Exchange account on iPhone and choose which information to sync with it. (This is explained in Chapter 7, "Emailing.")

4. Click the Sync tab.

5. Check the Sync with MobileMe check box.

6. On the top drop-down menu, choose how frequently the sync happens. Choose from Hourly, Automatically, and Manually. If you select Manually, you must click the Sync Now button to sync iTunes to your iPhone.

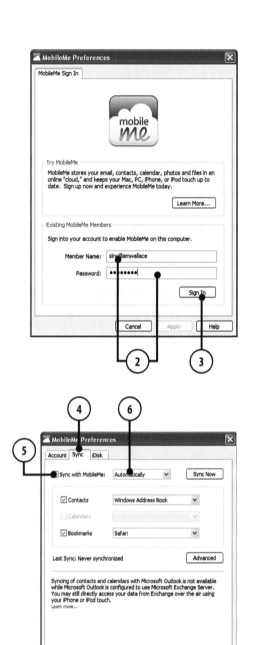

7. If you want your MobileMe contact information to be included in the sync, check the Contacts check box and choose where you want the contact information stored, such as in the Windows Address Book.

8. To include MobileMe calendar information in the sync, check the Calendar check box and choose the location of the calendars to be synced from the drop-down list.

9. To have your bookmarks moved into the MobileMe cloud, check the Bookmarks check box and choose the web browser where the bookmarks you want to sync are maintained (Internet Explorer or Safari).

10. Click OK. If you selected any option but Manually in step 6, the information you selected is copied from the computer to the MobileMe cloud where you can access it on iPhone, and the process is repeated according to the schedule you set. If you selected Manually, click the Sync Now button to move the information.

11. Skip to the section titled "Managing MobileMe Syncs."

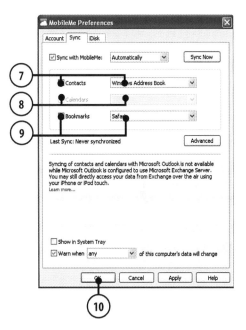

Configuring MobileMe on a Mac

Use the MobileMe pane of the System Preferences application to configure MobileMe syncing on a Mac.

1. Open the System Preferences application and click the MobileMe icon.

2. Enter your member name and password.

3. Click Sign In. Your account information is configured, and the MobileMe pane updates to show that you have configured MobileMe.

4. Click the Sync tab.

5. Check the Synchronize with MobileMe check box.

6. On the pop-up menu, select how you want synchronizations to occur. You can choose Manually to sync manually; choose a time, such as Every Hour, to sync at those times; or choose Automatically to have syncs performed whenever included data changes.

7. Check the check box next to each item you want to include in the syncs.

8. Click Sync Now. The information you selected is copied onto the MobileMe cloud where you can access it from iPhone. Future syncs happen according to the schedule you set, or if you selected Manually, you have to click the Sync Now button whenever you want to sync your information.

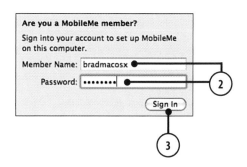

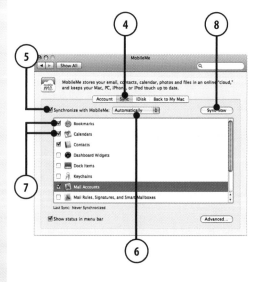

Managing MobileMe Syncs

As information changes on your iPhone or on a computer, that information is synced via the MobileMe cloud. When this happens, the differences between data on each device must be managed. You decide what happens the first time you sync, and you manage the process each time thereafter. Choose Merge Data if you want the data on MobileMe to be merged with the information on your computer. Choose Replace Data on Computer to replace the information on your computer with information stored on the MobileMe cloud. Choose Replace Data on MobileMe to have the information on your computer replace the data on the MobileMe cloud. Choose Ignore for Now if you don't want any action taken.

>>>step-by-step

Syncing for the First Time

The first time you sync information via MobileMe (or if you reset your sync options), you decide how you want information to be moved. You are prompted via the MobileMe Sync Alert dialog.

1. At the prompt, choose how you want information to be moved.

2. Click Allow. The sync proceeds.

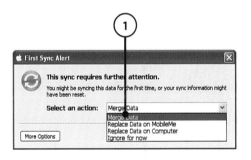

Managing Sync Alerts

During syncs, you are prompted when the amount of data changes beyond the limits you set on the MobileMe Preferences control panel or the MobileMe pane of the System Preferences application. For example, you might choose to be notified when more than 5% of the computer's data will change. When this happens, you see a dialog that enables you to make selections about how data is moved. You can use the controls in this dialog to review the changes and accept or prevent them as you see fit. When you've decided, you click the appropriate Sync button to allow the sync to proceed. If these prompts get too annoying, move back to the MobileMe preferences and increase the percentage of data change that triggers a notification or disable the notifications entirely.

This Isn't a Book on MobileMe Either

If you get a MobileMe account, make sure you explore all it has to offer, including the great web applications for email, contacts, and calendars. You might find that its iDisk online disk space is worth the cost of an account on its own.

Using This Book

This book has been designed to help you transform an iPhone into *your* iPhone by helping you learn to use it easily and quickly. As you can tell, the book relies heavily on pictures to show you how an iPhone works. It is also task-focused so that you can quickly learn the specific steps to follow to do all the cool things you can do with your iPhone.

Using an iPhone involves lots of screen touching with your fingers. When you need to tap part of the screen, such as a button or keyboard, you see a callout with the step number pointing to where you need to tap. When you need to drag or slide your finger along the screen, such as to browse lists, you see the following icon:

The directions you can drag are indicated with arrows.

To zoom in or zoom out on screens, you pinch or unpinch, respectively, your fingers on the screen. These motions are indicated by the following icons:

When you need to tap twice, such as to zoom out or in, you see the following icon:

When you need to rotate iPhone, you see this icon:

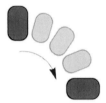

Sometimes you shake the iPhone to activate a control. When you do, you see this icon:

Because iTunes and the iPhone work with both Windows computers and Macs, this book is designed for both platforms as well. When there are significant differences, such as applications you use to store photos, you see task sections devoted to each type of computer. You can safely skip over sections focused on a type of computer you don't use.

Connect a Wi-Fi network for high-speed Internet access.

Go here to connect an iPhone to the Internet and to connect to other devices using Bluetooth.

Use peer-to-peer applications to play games or share information with other iPhones or iPod touches.

In this chapter, you explore how to connect your iPhone to the Internet and to other iPhones and iPod touches. Topics include the following:

→ Connecting to the Internet via Wi-Fi or wireless cellular networks

→ Connecting to other devices using Bluetooth

→ Connecting to other iPhones and iPod touches

Connecting to the Internet, Bluetooth Devices, and iPhones/iPods

Your iPhone has many functions that rely on an Internet connection, with the most obvious being email, web browsing, and so on. However, many default and third-party applications rely on an Internet connection to work as well. Fortunately, you can connect your iPhone to the Internet by connecting it to a Wi-Fi network that provides Internet access. You can also connect to the Internet through a wireless network provided by your cell phone provider.

Using Bluetooth, you can wirelessly connect your iPhone to other devices, such as Bluetooth headsets, headphones, and so on.

With peer-to-peer applications, you can also connect your iPhone to other iPhones and iPod touches to create a local network to exchange information, play games, and so on.

Connecting an iPhone to the Internet

To connect your iPhone to the Internet, you can connect it to a Wi-Fi network that provides Internet access, or you can connect it to a wireless network provided by your cellular provider.

You can use a variety of Wi-Fi networks, including those available in your home, business, or in public places, such as airports, restaurants, and schools. The benefit to Wi-Fi is that the performance of most of these networks is much better than what you will experience with the other options. The downside to a Wi-Fi connection is that you must be in range of one, and in some cases, you need to pay for an account to access a network.

You can also connect to the Internet though wireless data networks provided by your cellular provider. The primary benefits to these cellular networks are that they are typically widely available to you; your iPhone connects to them automatically; and you don't have to pay any additional fees to use them (beyond the data fees associated with your iPhone account). The downside to these networks is that their performance is less than most Wi-Fi networks, but in some cases, they provide more than adequate performance for most Internet tasks you do.

Automatic Prompting to Join Wi-Fi

By default, when you access one of your iPhone's Internet functions, such as Safari, your iPhone automatically searches for Wi-Fi networks to join if you aren't already connected to one. A dialog appears showing all the networks available to you. You can select and join one of these networks similar to how you join one via Settings, as you learn how to do in the following steps. If you don't want your iPhone to do this, use the Settings button to move to the Wi-Fi Networks screen and turn off Ask to Join Networks. When it's off, you need to manually connect to networks each time you want to join as described in the following steps. If you decline to join an available Wi-Fi network, the iPhone attempts to connect to the fastest wireless data network available to you.

Not All Access Is Free

Be aware that some open networks charge access fees for Internet access, especially in public places such as airports; in these situations, you need a username and password to access the Internet over a network you are connected to. Without a username and password, you can connect to the network, but you'll be able to access only the provider's login page to log in or obtain an account that you use to connect to the Internet. Some of these networks provide some information or functions you can access for free without connecting to the Internet, such as a news page.

>>>*step-by-step*

Connecting to an Open Wi-Fi Network

Many Wi-Fi networks broadcast their information so that you can easily see them when searching with your iPhone; these are called open networks because anyone who is in range can attempt to join one because they appear on Wi-Fi devices automatically. These are the easiest to join.

1. On the Home screen, tap Settings. Next to Wi-Fi, you see the status of your Wi-Fi connection, which is Not Connected if you aren't currently connected to Wi-Fi.

2. Tap Wi-Fi.

3. If Wi-Fi is turned off, tap the OFF button to turn it on. Wi-Fi status becomes ON, and your iPhone immediately starts searching for available networks.

4. Review the networks that your iPhone finds. For each network, you see its name, whether it is secure, and its signal strength. (I've found that the signal strength icon on this screen isn't very reliable; you probably won't really know how strong a signal is until you actually connect to the network.)

5. Tap the network you want to join. (If you recognize only one of the networks, you've probably used it before, so it is a good choice.) You also need to consider the security of the network; if you see the pad-lock icon next to the network's name, you need a password to join the network and so the Enter Password screen appears. If the network is not marked with the padlock icon, it is not secure, and you can skip to step 8.

6. Enter the password for the network.

7. Tap Join. If you provided the cor-rect password, your iPhone con-nects to the network and gets the information it needs, including an IP address. If not, you're prompted to enter the password again. After you connect to the network, you return to the Wi-Fi screen.

Typing Passwords

As you type a password, each charac-ter is hidden by dots in the Password field except for the last character you entered, which is displayed on the screen for a few moments. This is helpful even though you see each character as you type it. You always see the most recent character you entered, which can prevent you from getting all the way to the end of a sometimes long password only to discover you've made a mistake along the way and have to start all over again.

Secure network (requires a password)   Signal strength

Network name   Doesn't require a password

Info button

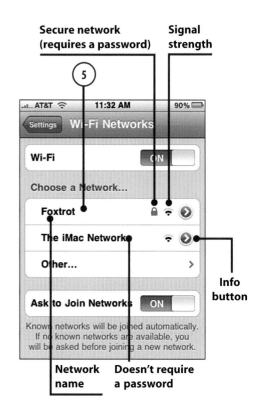

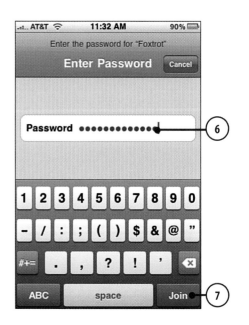

8. Review the network information. The network to which you are connected is in blue and is marked with a check mark. You see the signal strength for that network. (This indication is typically more accurate than the one you see before you are connected.)

9. Tap the Info button for the network to which you are connected. You see the Info screen, which is labeled with the name of the network.

10. Scroll the screen to review the network's information. The most important item is the IP Address. If there is no number here or the number starts with 169, the network is not providing an IP address, and you must find another network. You can safely ignore the rest of the information on the screen in most situations. If you want to access some of the more advanced settings, such as HTTP proxy, you need information from the network administrator to access the network, so you need help to get your iPhone connected.

11. Tap Wi-Fi Networks to return to the Wi-Fi Networks screen.

Was Connected, Not Now

If you've been using a network successfully, and at some point your iPhone cannot access the Internet but remains connected to the network, move to the network's Info screen and tap Renew Lease. This refreshes your iPhone's IP address, sometimes enabling you to access the Internet again.

Connected network

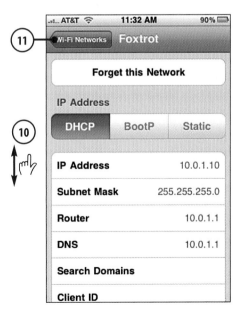

12. Move to the Home screen. You should see the Wi-Fi connection icon at the top of the screen; this indicates that you are connected to a network and also indicates the strength of the signal by the number of waves you see.

13. Tap Safari. Safari opens.

Security Key Index

Some private networks require a key index in addition to a password. Unfortunately, there's no way to enter a specific key on your iPhone. If a network requires this key, check with the administrator to make sure you have the right configuration information and don't need a key index.

14. Try to move to a webpage, such as www.apple.com/iphone/. (See Chapter 10, "Surfing the Web," for details.) If you move to a webpage that is not from a Wi-Fi provider, you're good to go. If you are taken to a webpage for a Wi-Fi provider, you need an account to access the Internet. If you have a username and password for that network, enter them on the login form. If you don't have an account, you must obtain one; use the webpage to sign up. After you have an account with that provider, you can get to the Internet.

Wi-Fi connection

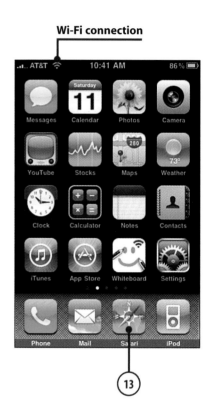

Connecting to a Commercial Wi-Fi Network

Many networks in public places, such as hotels or airports, require that you pay a fee or provide other information to access that network and the Internet. When you connect to one of these networks, you're prompted to log in. Check out these steps.

1. Tap the network you want to join. The iPhone connects to the network, and you see the Log In screen for that network.

2. Provide the information required to join the network, such as a username and a password. In most cases, you have to indicate that you accept the terms and conditions for using the network, which you typically do by checking a check box.

3. Tap the button to join the network. This button can have different labels depending on the type of access, such as Free Access, Login, and so on.

Not Always

Not all commercial networks prompt you to log in as these steps explain. Sometimes, you use the network's homepage to login instead. You join the network as described in the previous section, and when you try to move to a webpage as explained in step 14 in that section, you're prompted to log into or create an account with the network's provider.

Connecting to a Closed Wi-Fi Network

Some networks don't broadcast their names or availability; these are called closed networks because they are hidden to people who don't know they exist. To connect to one of these networks, you must know the network's name because it won't show up on the iPhone's list of available networks. You also need to know the type of security the network uses and its password. You have to get this information from the network's provider.

1. Follow steps 1 through 3 in "Connecting to an Open Wi-Fi Network" to turn Wi-Fi on and to move to the Wi-Fi Networks screen.

2. Tap Other. You see the Other Network screen.

3. Enter the name of the network.

4. Tap Security.

5. Tap the type of security the network uses. The options are None, WEP, WPA, WPA2, WPA Enterprise, or WPA2 Enterprise. You don't need to worry about what each of these options means; you just need to pick the right one for the network. You'll need to get the type of security from the person who manages the network. (The None option is for unsecured networks, but it's unlikely that a hidden network wouldn't require a password.) When you select an option, it is marked with a check mark.

6. Tap Other Network. You move back to the Security screen. In the Security field, you see the type of security you selected, and the Password field appears.

7. Enter the password.

8. Tap Join. If the information you entered matches what the network requires, you join the network and can begin to access its resources. If not, you see an error message and have to try it again until you are able to join. When you successfully join the network, you move back to the Wi-Fi Networks screen.

9. Test the Internet connection as described in step 14 in "Connecting to an Open Wi-Fi Network."

Changing Networks

You can change the network that your iPhone is using at any time. For example, if you lose Internet connectivity on the current network, you can move your iPhone a different network.

1. Move to the Settings screen. The network to which your iPhone is currently connected is shown.

2. Tap Wi-Fi. Your iPhone scans for available networks and presents them to you in the Choose a Network section of the Wi-Fi Networks screen.

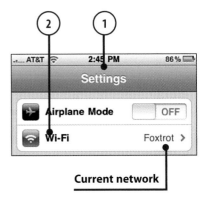

Current network

3. Tap the network you want to join. Your iPhone attempts to join the network. If you haven't joined that network previously and it requires a password, enter it when prompted to do so. After your iPhone connects, you see the new network's name highlighted in blue and marked with a check mark.

Be Known

After your iPhone connects to a Wi-Fi network (open or closed) successfully, it becomes a known network. Your iPhone automatically connects to known networks when it needs to access the Internet. So unless you tell your iPhone to forget a network (explained in the next section), you need to log in to it only the first time you connect to it.

Forgetting Wi-Fi Networks

As you learned earlier, your iPhone remembers networks you have joined and connects to them automatically as needed. Although this is mostly a good thing, occasionally you won't want to use a particular network any more. For example, when moving through an airport, you might connect to a network for which you have to pay for Internet access, but then you decide you don't want to use that network after all. Each time you move through that airport, your iPhone connects to that network automatically, which can be annoying. So you might want your iPhone to forget that network so it doesn't automatically connect to it in the future.

1. Move to the Wi-Fi Networks screen.

2. Tap the Info button for the network that you want your iPhone to forget.

3. Tap Forget This Network.

4. Tap Forget Network in the resulting prompt. Your iPhone forgets the network, and you return to the Info screen. If your iPhone had been getting an IP address from the network, that address is cleared, and your iPhone attempts to connect to a different network automatically.

5. Tap Wi-Fi Networks. You return to the Wi-Fi Networks screen. If a network you've forgotten is still available to your iPhone, it continues to appear in the Choose a Network list, but your iPhone will no longer automatically connect to it. You can rejoin the forgotten network at any time just as you did the first time you connected to it.

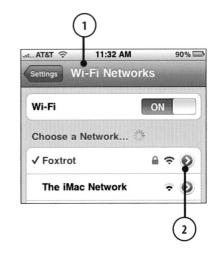

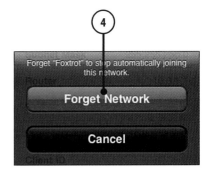

Call Phone Provider Wi-Fi Networks

Many cell phone providers also provide other services, particularly Internet access. In some cases, you can access that provider's Internet service through a Wi-Fi network that it provides; ideally, you can do this at no additional charge. So, you can take advantage of the speed a Wi-Fi connection provides without paying more for it. You start connecting to these networks just like any other by selecting them on the available network list. What happens next depends on the specific network. In some cases, you need to enter your mobile phone number, and then respond to a text message to that phone number. Some providers, such as AT&T, provide an application that enables you to connect to their Wi-Fi networks without going through the confirmation process each time. (The AT&T application is called Easy Wi-Fi for AT&T phones.) After you download and install such an application, you can automatically connect to and use the Wi-Fi network whenever it is available. (See Chapter 15, "Installing and Maintaining iPhone Applications," for help finding and installing applications.)

Connecting to the Internet via a Cellular Data Network

Most cell providers for the iPhone also provide a wireless Internet connection that your iPhone uses automatically when a Wi-Fi connection isn't available. (The iPhone always tries to connect an available Wi-Fi network before connecting to a cellular Internet connection.) These networks are great because the area they cover is large and connection to them is automatic. And access to these networks is typically part of your monthly account fee; ideally, you pay for unlimited data, but check the details of your account to see if you have unlimited access to the Internet through your cellular network or if there is usage-based cost.

Sometimes, the performance offered by these networks is less than ideal; in other cases, the performance is very good. The performance can also vary by your location within the network as well, so you mostly just have to try your Internet applications to see what kind of performance you have in any location.

Some providers have multiple networks, such as a low-speed network that is available widely and a higher-speed network that has a more limited coverage area. Your iPhone chooses the best connection available to you so you don't have to think about this much. However, if you connect to a low-speed network, you might find the performance unusable for web browsing or other data-intensive tasks; in which case, you have to suffer with it or connect to a Wi-Fi network.

In the United States, the exclusive iPhone provider is AT&T; its high-speed wireless network is called 3G. In other locations, the name and speed of the networks available to you might be different.

The following information is focused on the 3G network because I happen to live in the United States. If you use another provider, you are able to access your provider's network similarly, though your details might be different. For example, the icon on the Home screen reflects the name of your provider's network, which might or might not be 3G.

AT&T's 3G high-speed wireless network provides reasonably fast Internet access from many locations. (Note: The 3G network is not available every-where, but you can usually count on it near populated areas.) To connect to the 3G network, you don't need to do anything. If you aren't connected to a Wi-Fi network, you haven't turned off 3G, and your iPhone isn't in Airplane mode, the iPhone automatically connects to the 3G network if it is available in your current location. When you are connected to the 3G network, you see the 3G indicator at the top of the iPhone's screen.

3G network

Whenever you are connected to the 3G network, you can access the Internet for web browsing, email, and so on. While the speed won't be quite as good as with a Wi-Fi network, it is relatively fast, certainly enough to be usable.

While the 3G network is fast, it does come with a price, which is shorter bat-tery life. If you want to disable access to the 3G network to increase the amount of time between charges, perform the following steps.

>>>step-by-step

1. Move to the Settings screen.

2. Tap General.

3. Tap Network. The Network screen appears.

4. Next to Enable 3G, tap ON. The status becomes OFF, and iPhone can no longer access the 3G network. It can still access the EDGE network, which is the topic of the next section.

Managing 3G

To re-enable the 3G network, move back to the Network screen and tap OFF. The status becomes ON, and iPhone can access the Internet quickly via the 3G network. You can also disable 3G access, along with all other receiving and transmitting functions, by placing the iPhone in Airplane mode.

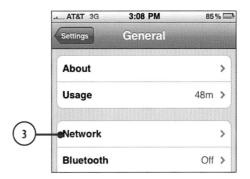

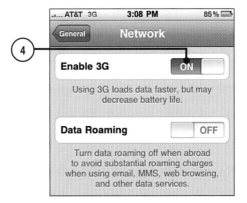

No Roaming Please!

When you move outside of your primary network (such as outside the United States if that is where you live), you are in roaming territory, which means a different provider provides both cellular and data access. Roaming charges can be associated with calls or data exchanges that happen. These charges are often quite expensive. The roaming charges associated with phone calls are easier to manage given that it's more obvious when you make or receive a phone call. However, data roaming charges are much more insidious, especially if the push functionality (where emails are pushed to iPhone from the server) are active. Because data roaming charges are harder to notice, iPhone is configured by default to prevent data roaming.

When you leave your primary network, you no longer are able to access the wireless data networks that you primarily use. (You can still connect to and use Wi-Fi networks.) If you want to allow data roaming, move to the Network screen and tap the Data Roaming OFF button. Its status becomes ON, and when you move outside your primary network, data will come to iPhone via the available roaming network. This can be very, very expensive, so you should disable it again by tapping ON as soon as you're done.

Generally, you should avoid allowing data roaming unless you are sure about its cost. You have no control over this and won't really know how much it will be until you get the resulting bill, which can sometimes be shocking and painful.

When a Wi-Fi or faster network isn't available, you are reduced to using the slower cellular data networks available to you. For AT&T, this is called the EDGE network (the original iPhone could only use Wi-Fi or the EDGE in the United States). When no better network is available (assuming iPhone isn't in Airplane mode), iPhone connects to the slower network automatically so you can still use iPhone's Internet functionality.

There's often a good reason that a slower network, such as the EDGE, is the last resort; the speed is sometimes so slow that you'll need much more patience than I have to use the web.

In the United States, the EDGE network can work okay for email and some of the other less data-intensive functions, however. And sometimes an EDGE connection is better than no connection at all. When iPhone is connected to the EDGE network, the E icon appears at the top of the screen; if you use a different provider, you see the icon for that network instead.

TETHERING

The iPhone (3G and 3GS) supports tethering, which is providing an Internet connection through the iPhone to a computer or other device. This is useful when you are in a location where you can't connect a computer to a network with Internet access (or don't want to spend the money to do so), but can access the Internet with the iPhone's high-speed cellular data connection. The general steps are to turn Internet Tethering on, which you do by tapping that command on the Network screen and then tapping the Internet Tethering OFF button. (If you don't see the Internet Tethering option, your provider currently doesn't offer this service.) Its status becomes ON, and your iPhone shares its Internet connection with a computer connected to it with a USB cord or via Bluetooth.

There are a lot of caveats to this service, including whether your provider offers it, additional costs, and so on. Check with your provider to see if tethering is supported and if there are additional fees to use it. If it is provided and the fees are acceptable, this is a good way to provide Internet access to a computer when a Wi-Fi connection either isn't available or is too expensive.

Connecting to Other Devices Using Bluetooth

An iPhone includes built-in Bluetooth support so you can use this wireless technology to connect to other Bluetooth-capable devices. The most likely device to connect to iPhone in this way are Bluetooth headphones, but you can also use Bluetooth to connect to other kinds of devices, most notably, headphones, computers, and other iPhones and iPod touches. To connect Bluetooth devices together, you pair them.

In Bluetooth, *pairing* is the lingo for connecting two Bluetooth devices. The constant requirement is that the devices can communicate with each other via Bluetooth. There is also a "sometimes" requirement, which is a pairing code, passkey, or PIN. All those terms refer to the same thing, which is a series of numbers that are entered in one or all devices being paired. Sometimes you enter this code on both devices, whereas for other devices you enter the first device's code on the second device. Some devices don't require a PIN at all, in which case you don't even have to think about it.

When you have to pair devices, you're prompted to do so, and you have to complete the actions required by the prompt to communicate via Bluetooth.

The next task demonstrates pairing an iPhone with a Bluetooth headset; you can pair it with other devices similarly.

>>>*step-by-step*

1. Move to the Settings screen.

2. Tap General.

3. Tap Bluetooth.

4. Tap OFF. Bluetooth starts up, and the status becomes ON, and the Bluetooth icon appears next to the battery icon. The iPhone immediately begins searching for Bluetooth devices.

5. Turn on the Bluetooth headset and put it in Discoverable mode (see the instructions provided with the device). The two devices find each other. On iPhone, the headset is listed but shown as not paired.

6. Tap the name of the headset to pair it. The status becomes paired as the iPhone starts communicating with the device and you return to the Bluetooth screen. The devices to which the iPhone is connected are shown on the Devices list. When the iPhone and another device are communicating successfully, the Devices list shows them as paired.

PIN Required?

For most Bluetooth headsets, you can pair the headset with iPhone just by tapping the headset on the Bluetooth screen. Some devices require a PIN to pair the device with iPhone. If this is the case, you'll be prompted to enter the device's PIN. Do so, and the device will be paired with the iPhone.

7. Tap General. You're ready to use the Bluetooth headset.

When you make a call, the iPhone prompts you to use the Bluetooth headset. Tap the headset you want to use; if you don't choose, the iPhone uses whichever device is marked with the speaker icon, which indicates it is the default device. (If you don't see the Bluetooth device, it isn't paired properly so you need to try to set up iPhone to access it again with the previous steps.)

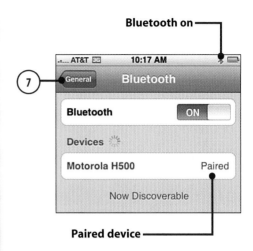

Bluetooth on

Paired device

Connecting to Other iPhones and iPod touches

With version 3.0 of the iPhone operating system, Apple introduced peer-to-peer connectivity, which is an overly complicated way of saying that these iPhones and iPod touches (which also run on the iPhone operating system) can communicate with one another. Developers can take advantage of this in their applications to enable great functionality, especially multiplayer gaming, information sharing, and other collaborative activities.

Unlike Internet or Bluetooth connections, you don't access the peer-to-peer configuration directly. Instead, you use applications that have this capability built into them.

There are two ways that iPhones or iPod touches can communicate with each other: via a Wi-Fi network or via Bluetooth. The method you use in any specific situation depends on the application you are using.

If the application you want to use communicates over a Wi-Fi network, such as a network you use to access the Internet, all the devices with which you want to communicate must be on that same network. If the application uses Bluetooth, you must enable Bluetooth on each device and configure them so they can communicate with one another.

Also each device that will be communicating via the application must have the application installed on it. (See Chapter 15, "Installing and Maintaining iPhone Applications" for help finding and installing applications.)

>>>*step-by-step*

Using an Application with Peer-to-Peer Networking by Default

Some applications are designed to primarily function via communication with other iPhones and iPod touches. These applications typically prompt you to connect to other devices as soon as you launch them.

1. Launch the application on your iPhone.

2. Have the other people launch the application on their devices.

3. At the prompt, tap the device to which you want to connect. The other user will be prompted to allow your connection request. If he does so, you see a notification on your device.

4. Tap Continue.

5. Use the application. (This example is an application called Whiteboard that enables each user to write or scrawl on a shared whiteboard. Of course, the writing might not be legible, but that isn't the iPhone's fault.)

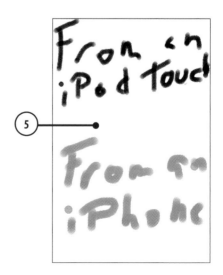

Configuring an Application to Use Peer-to-Peer Networking

Some applications need to be configured to communicate with other devices. This is typical of games that offer both single- and multi-player options. Before you can play, you need to configure the application to communicate on each device.

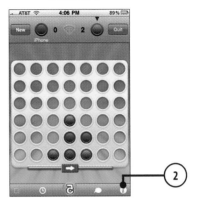

1. Launch the application.

2. Open the application's configuration menu.

3. Tap the communication option you want to use.

4. Select the player you want to be for the game. (Some games will prompt you for a name as soon as you choose a communication option.)

5. Tap Done.

6. Have the other players perform steps 1 through 5 on their devices.

7. Start the game by making a move or whatever else is appropriate. You see the results of what other people do on their devices while they see the results of what you do on your iPhone in real time.

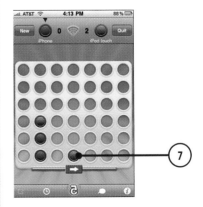

View and work with
photos and video.

Download
content
from the
iTunes Store
onto your
iPhone.

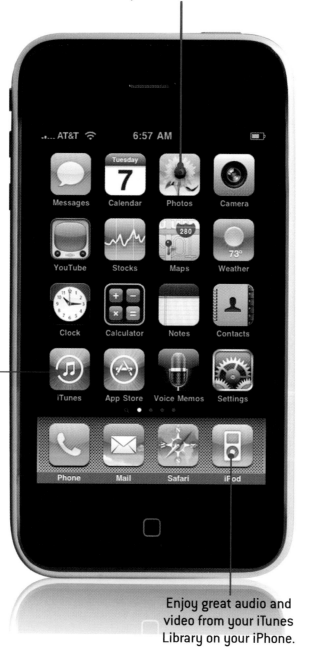

Enjoy great audio and
video from your iTunes
Library on your iPhone.

In this chapter, you learn how to stock your iPhone with audio, video, and photos. The topics include the following:

→ Moving audio and video content from your iTunes Library onto the iPhone
→ Using iTunes to move photos and video onto your iPhone
→ Using the iPhone's iTunes application to download content directly from the iTunes Store

Moving Audio, Video, and Photos onto Your iPhone

One of the best things about an iPhone is that you can use it to listen to audio content of various types (see Chapter 11, "Listening to Music, Podcasts, and Other Audio"). You can also watch video on the iPhone's high-resolution screen (see Chapter 12, "Watching Movies, TV Shows, and Other Video"). You can view and work with photos stored on it, too (see Chapter 13, "Working with Photos and Video").

However, before you can do all these things, you must move content with which you'll work onto your iPhone. There are two basic ways to do this. One is to move content from your iTunes Library onto the iPhone; you can also use iTunes to move photos from a photo application onto your iPhone. The second method is to move audio and video content directly from the iTunes Store onto your iPhone.

Using iTunes to Add Audio and Video Content to the iPhone

iTunes is a great application you can use to store, organize, and enjoy all sorts of audio and video. It's also the primary way to move audio and video content onto your iPhone. You first add the content to your iTunes Library and then move that content onto the iPhone through the sync process.

The most common ways to add content to the iTunes Library are by importing audio CDs or purchasing content from, renting movies from, and subscribing to podcasts in the iTunes Store.

After you have stocked your iTunes Library, you can create playlists to organize content and move it onto your iPhone.

When your content is ready, sync your iPhone with your iTunes Library so the content you want to be available is moved from your computer onto your iPhone.

>>>*step-by-step*

Importing Audio CDs to the iTunes Library

Importing audio CDs is one of the most useful ways to get music and other audio content into your iTunes Library.

1. Launch iTunes by double-clicking its application icon, choosing it on the Windows Start menu, or clicking it on the Mac's Dock.

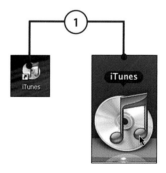

Only the First Time
You need to perform steps 2 through 10 only before the first time you import CDs or when you want to change settings.

2. Choose Edit, Preferences (Windows) or iTunes, Preferences (Mac). The Preferences dialog appears.

3. Click the General tab.

4. On the When you insert a CD menu, choose Import CD and Eject.

5. Click Import Settings.

6. On the Import Using drop-down menu, choose AAC Encoder.

7. On the Setting drop-down menu, choose iTunes Plus.

8. Click OK.

9. Check Automatically retrieve CD track names from Internet.

10. Click OK.

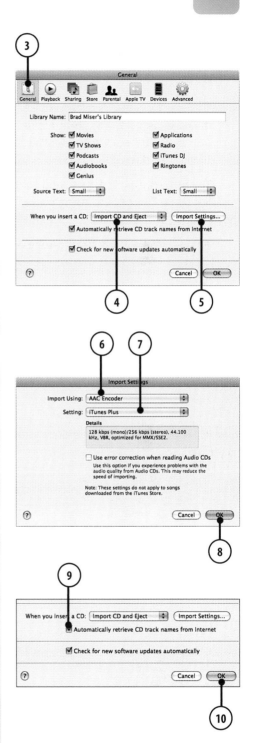

11. Insert a CD into the computer. iTunes connects to the Internet and identifies the CD. When that's done, the import process starts. You don't have to do anything else because iTunes manages the import process for you. When the process finishes, iTunes plays an alert sound and ejects the disc.

12. Insert the next CD you want to import. After it has been ejected, insert the next CD and repeat the process until you've added all the CDs you want to listen to on your iPhone to your iTunes Library.

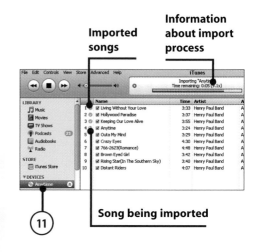

Imported songs

Information about import process

Song being imported

No Duplicates Please

After you've imported a CD, you won't likely ever need to use it again on your computer. So after you import all your CDs, change the iTunes When you insert a CD setting to Ask to Import CD so you don't accidentally import multiple copies of the same CD (in the rare case when you do insert the CD into your computer again).

TAGGING YOUR MUSIC

>>> Go Further

To browse and find music in your iTunes Library, you must tag (label) the tracks you import. When iTunes finds a CD's information on the Internet, it takes care of this for you, including the album artwork associated with that CD (as long as the music is available in the iTunes Store).

If iTunes doesn't find information for CD content you import, you should add tags manually. Do this by selecting a track and choosing File, Get Info. Use the Info dialog to update the track's tags, including name, album, artist, and even artwork. If you select multiple tracks before you open the Info dialog, you can update the tags on the selected tracks at the same time.

>>>*step-by-step*

Purchasing Audio and Video from the iTunes Store

The iTunes Store has a very large selection of music, movies, TV shows, and other content that you can preview, purchase, and download to your iTunes Library. To do this, you must have an Apple Store account, also known as an Apple ID. (You can preview content without an Apple ID.) If you have an AIM/AOL screen name, you can also use that to sign into the store. (You have to provide credit card information to use an AIM/AOL account to make purchases.) For the steps to obtain an Apple ID and log in to the iTunes Store, see Chapter 1, "Getting Started with Your iPhone."

Sign Me In!

If you see the Sign In button instead of your Apple ID in the upper-right corner of the iTunes window, click that button and sign in to your account.

1. Click iTunes Store on the source list. iTunes connects to the iTunes Store, and you see the Home page.

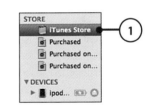

2. Click the Power Search link in the QUICK LINKS section located along the right side of the Home page. You move to the Search screen.

3. To limit your search to a specific kind of content, choose it on the pop-up menu. For example, choose Music Videos to search for music videos.

This Store Is Made for Browsing

The iTunes Store is designed to be browsed. Just about every graphic and almost all the text you see are linked to either categories of content or to specific content. You can browse the store just by clicking around. For example, you can click the Music link to browse music, or you can click any of the other links you see on the Home page to browse some other type of content. There are numerous ways to browse, but all of them involve just clicking around. If you don't have something specific in mind, browsing is a great way to discover and purchase content.

4. Enter the information for which you want to search, such as Artist, Song, Genre, and such.

5. Click Search. Items that meet your search are shown in the lower parts of the window. The center pane is a summary view while the lower pane shows the details.

6. To preview content, double-click it. A 30-second preview plays.

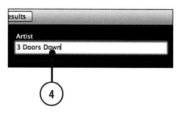

HD Movies and TV

Some movie and TV content is available in HD format. Your iPhone can't play this content. However, when you purchase HD content, you actually get two versions. Along with the HD version that you can play on a computer or a home entertainment system, you get an iPhone-compatible version that you can move onto and watch on your iPhone.

7. If you selected video, watch the video in the iTunes window.

8. Continue previewing content.

9. When you want to purchase and download content, click the BUY button. For example, when you are viewing music, this is the BUY SONG or BUY ALBUM button. When you are viewing TV shows, it is the BUY EPISODE or BUY SEA-SON button. In other cases, it might be BUY VIDEO.

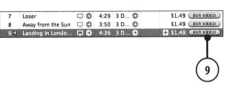

10. If prompted, enter your account's password and click Buy. The content you purchase is downloaded to your computer and added to your iTunes Library.

11. Click the Purchased playlist on the iTunes Source list to see content you've downloaded from the iTunes Store.

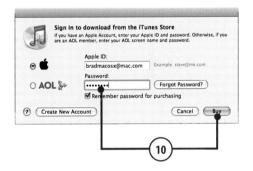

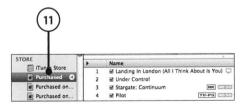

>>> Go Further

BUY NOW OR BUY LATER

You can buy with one click, meaning that you can click the BUY button to immediately purchase or download content. iTunes also enables you to shop with a shopping cart into which you place all the content you are interested in. When you are ready to buy, you move to your shopping cart and check out.

A preference setting determines which method you use. To configure your iTunes shopping experience, use the Store pane of the iTunes Preferences dialog. When you use the shopping cart method, you see ADD buttons instead of BUY buttons. After you add content to the shopping cart, select the cart on the iTunes Source list to complete the purchase and download process.

Renting Movies from the iTunes Store

You can also rent movies from the iTunes Store. When you rent a movie, you can watch it as many times as you'd like within a 24-hour period (starting when you play the rented content) within a 30-day rental window. After either the 24-hour viewing or 30-day rental period expires (whichever comes first), the rented movie is removed from iTunes (or from your iPhone) automatically. To rent a movie, follow these steps.

1. Move into the iTunes Store and click the Movies link.

2. Browse or search for movies in which you might be interested.

3. Click a movie's link to see detailed information about it, including the cost to rent it.

4. To watch the movie's trailer, click the VIEW TRAILER button.

5. To rent the movie, click the RENT MOVIE button. If you've configured your account to remember your password for purchasing, you see a dialog warning you that you are about to rent a movie. If not, you are prompted to provide your password.

6. Click Rent or enter your Apple ID password and click Rent. The movie is downloaded to your iTunes Library.

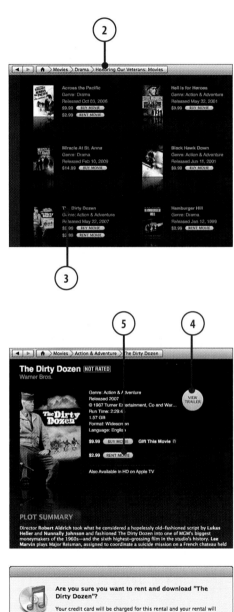

7. To access movies you've rented, click the Rented Movies source. (You have 30 days to watch the movie, but be sure not to play a rented movie until you're sure you will watch all of it within 24 hours because the viewing period starts as soon as you play it.)

>>> Go Further

ONE PLACE ONLY

Unlike other content you get from the iTunes Store, rented movies can be on only one device at a time. So when you move a rented movie from the iTunes Library onto the iPhone, it disappears from the iTunes Library. (You can move it between devices as many times as you'd like by moving from one device back to your iTunes Library and moving it from there onto another device.)

Subscribing to Podcasts in the iTunes Store

Podcasts are radio-like audio or video episodes you can subscribe and listen to or watch. Even better, most podcasts are free.

1. Click iTunes Store. The iTunes Store fills the Content pane.

2. Click Podcasts. The Podcasts Home page appears.

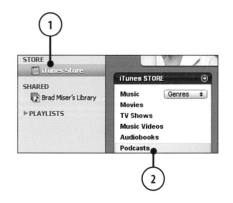

3. Click a category you are interested in, such as Business.

Searching

You can search for podcasts using the Power Search tool and choosing Podcasts on the Power Search pop-up menu. You can also type the podcast name in the Search iTunes Store bar in the upper-right corner of the screen; when you do this, you search across all content so you might see music, movies, and so on in addition to podcasts.

4. Browse the results.

5. Click a podcast to get more information about it.

6. Read about the podcast.

7. Double-click an episode to preview it.

8. Click SUBSCRIBE.

Settings

Click the Settings button to configure how your podcasts are managed by iTunes, such as when it checks for new episodes, if new episodes are downloaded automatically, how episodes are kept, and so on.

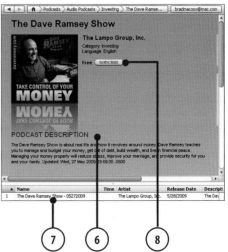

9. Click Subscribe again at the prompt. Under the iTunes Store, you see the Downloads icon that displays the progress of file downloads, including the number of episodes being downloaded.

10. Click Podcasts in the source list. (The number you see indicates how many episodes have been downloaded, but that you have not listened to yet.) You see all the podcasts to which you've subscribed. Under each podcast's name, you see the episodes that have been downloaded. The blue dot next to episodes indicates you haven't listened to them yet.

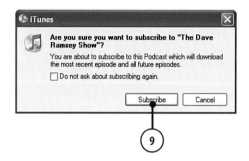

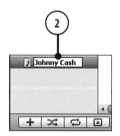

Building Music Playlists

One of the best ways to collect content that you want to place on your iPhone is to create a playlist and manually place content onto it.

1. Click the New Playlist button. A new playlist is created with its default name selected for you to change.

2. Rename the new playlist and press Enter (Windows) or Return (Mac).

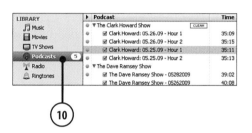

3. Select Music on the iTunes source list.

4. Browse or search for songs you want to add to the playlist.

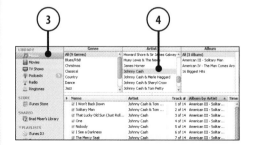

Playlists for All

These steps explain how to create playlists for music, but they work just as well for any content in your Library, including audiobooks, movies, TV show episodes, and so on. Just find the content you want to add and drag it onto the playlist's icon. You can mix types together, such as songs and movies, in the same playlist, too.

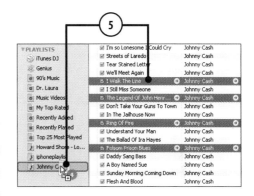

5. Drag songs from the Content pane onto the playlist you created.

6. Repeat steps 3–5 until you place all the songs you want the playlist to contain. You can place any combination of songs in a single playlist.

7. Select the playlist. Its contents appear in the Content pane.

8. Drag songs up and down the playlist until they are in the order in which you want them to play.

iTunes Folders

Over time, you are likely to create a lot of playlists. You can use folders to store playlists in on the source list to make them easier to work with. To create a folder, choose File, New Playlist Folder. Name the folder and then drag playlists into it to store them there. You can expand or collapse a folder by clicking the triangle next to its name. You can place folders within other folders, too. The content in your folders can be moved easily onto your iPhone by syncing an entire folder.

Building Smart Playlists

A smart playlist does the same basic thing as a playlist, which is to collect content you want to listen to or watch and move onto your iPhone. However, instead of placing content in a playlist manually, a smart playlist adds content automatically based on criteria you define.

1. Select File, New Smart Playlist. The Smart Playlist dialog box appears.

2. Select the first tag on which you want the smart playlist to be based on the Tag menu. For example, you can select Artist, Genre, My Rating, or Year, among many others.

3. Select the operand you want to use on the Operand menu. For example, if you want to match data exactly, select Is. If you want the condition to be looser, select Contains.

4. Type the condition you want to match in the Condition box. The more you type, the more specific the condition is.

5. To add another condition to the smart playlist, click the Add Condition button. A new, empty condition appears. At the top of the dialog box, the All or Any menu appears.

6. Select the second tag on which you want the smart playlist to be based in the second condition's Tag menu.

7. Select the operand you want to use in the Operand menu.

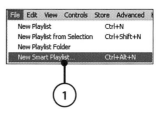

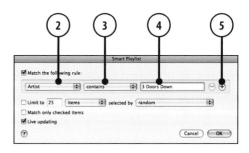

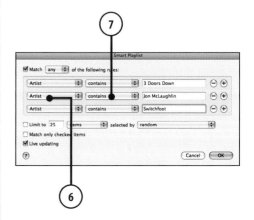

8. Type the condition you want to match from the Condition box.

9. Repeat steps 5–8 to add more conditions to the playlist until you have all the conditions you want to include.

10. Choose all on the menu at the top of the dialog if all the conditions must be met for a track to be included in the smart playlist or choose any if only one of them must be met.

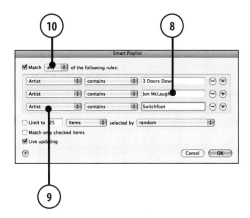

iTunes Is Helpful

As you make selections on the Tag menu and type conditions in the Condition box, iTunes attempts to automatically match what you type to tags in your Library. For example, if your Library includes music by Elvis Presley and you use Artist as a tag, iTunes will enter Elvis Presley in the Condition box for you when you start typing Elvis.

11. If you want to limit the playlist, check the Limit to Check box. If not, uncheck the check box and skip to step 15.

12. Select the parameter by which you want to limit the playlist in the first menu; this menu defaults to Items. Your choices include the number of items, the time the playlist will play (in minutes or hours), or the size of the files the playlist contains (in MB or GB).

13. Type the data appropriate for the limit you selected in the Limit to box. For example, if you selected minutes in the menu, type the maximum length of the playlist in minutes in the box.

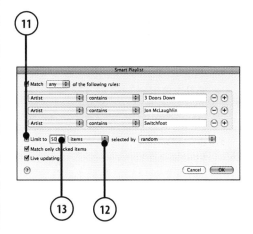

14. Select how you want iTunes to choose the songs it includes based on the limit you selected by using the selected by menu. For example, to have iTunes include tracks you've added to the Library most recently, select Most Recently Added.

15. If you want the playlist to include only songs whose check boxes in the Content pane are checked, check the Match only checked items check box.

16. If you want the playlist to be dynamic, meaning that iTunes updates its contents over time, check the Live updating check box. If you uncheck this check box, the playlist includes only those songs that meet the playlist's conditions when you create it.

17. Click OK. You move to the Source list; the smart playlist is added and selected, and its name is ready for you to edit. Also the songs in your Library that match the criteria in the playlist are added to it, and the current contents of the playlist are shown.

18. Type the playlist's name and press Enter (Windows) or Return (Mac).

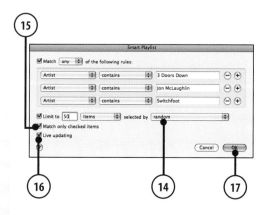

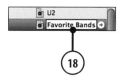

Check Please!

Each item in iTunes has a check box. You use this to tell iTunes if you want it to include the item (such as a song or podcast) in whatever you happen to be doing. If you uncheck this box, iTunes ignores the item when the related option is selected, such as the Match only checked items check box when you create a smart playlist.

Moving Audio and Video from the iTunes Library onto an iPhone

To move audio and video content onto your iPhone, you need to choose the content you want to move there and then synchronize it. You can set up the iPhone so that content is moved automatically or manually.

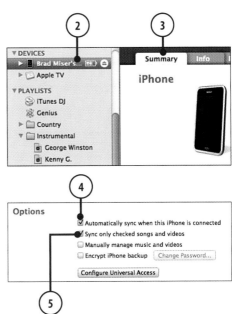

1. Connect the iPhone to your computer using its USB cable. The iPhone is mounted on your computer and appears in the iTunes Source list.

2. Click the iPhone icon. The iPhone synchronization screen appears.

3. Click the Summary tab.

4. Check the Automatically sync when this iPhone is connected check box if you want your iPhone to be synced automatically each time it is connected; uncheck this check box if you want to start syncs manually.

5. To prevent items you've unchecked in iTunes from being moved onto the iPhone, check Sync only checked songs and videos. (If this check box is not checked, all content in the selected sources will be synced.)

It's Not All Good

The iPhone's storage capacity has improved over time; the model with the most storage currently has 32GB of space. Although this is very impressive for such a small device, it might not be adequate to store all the content in large iTunes libraries, especially when a library includes lots of movies and other video content. The only way to deal with this limitation is to pick and choose the content you want to be available on your iPhone through the synchronization process. This isn't hard, but it is a bit of a nuisance. Hopefully, future iPhone versions will include even more storage capacity, such as the 160GB available on the current generation of iPod classic. It's good to be able to store as much of your iTunes content on your iPhone as possible, so more memory is always better.

Options, Options

If you check the Manually manage music and videos check box, you can place content on the iPhone by dragging songs, movies, and other content onto the iPhone icon on the Source list. To protect the backup of your iPhone's data (used to restore your iPhone) with encryption, check Encrypt iPhone backup, create and verify a password, and click Set Password; this password will be required to restore the backed up information onto the iPhone.

6. Click the Music tab.

7. Check the Sync music check box.

8. Select the Selected playlists radio button.

9. Check the check box next to each playlist that you want to move to the iPhone.

10. To expand or collapse a folder to see or hide the playlists it contains, click its triangle.

11. To move an entire folder of playlists onto the iPhone, check its check box.

12. Check Include music videos if you want music videos in your collection to be moved onto the iPhone.

13. Check Include voice memos if you use the Voice Memos application to record audio notes and want those memos to be moved from the iPhone into your iTunes Library.

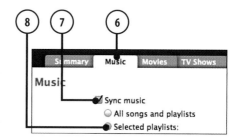

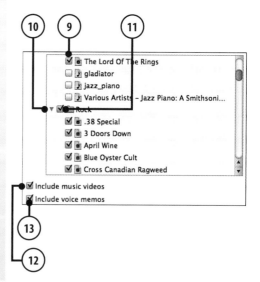

Move All Content

To move all of any type of content, including music, movies, TV shows, and podcasts onto the iPhone, select the related All option, such as All songs and playlists. If your iTunes Library's content will fit in your iPhone's storage capacity, you'll have everything in the library available on your iPhone. These steps assume you have more content in iTunes than can fit on your iPhone, which is the more complicated, and more likely, situation.

14. Click the Video tab. In the Rented Movies section, you see the movies you are currently renting.

15. Click a rented movie's right-facing Move button to move it from the iTunes Library onto the iPhone. The movie's icon moves to the right pane of the window, which indicates it will be moved onto the iPhone during the next sync.

16. To move a rented movie from the iPhone back into the iTunes Library, click the left-facing Move button next to the movie you want to move. During the next sync, it is removed from the iPhone and placed back into the iTunes Library.

17. Scroll down until you see the Movies section.

18. Check the Sync check box to move TV shows onto the iPhone.

19. Choose the number of episodes that should be moved using the pop-up menu. One useful option here is all unwatched, which moves all episodes that you haven't yet watched onto the iPhone. You can also choose a specific number of unwatched episodes or number of shows you've recently added to the library, whether you've watched them or not.

20. Choose the Selected radio button.

21. On the pop-up menu, choose playlists to choose content by playlist or TV shows to choose content by TV series.

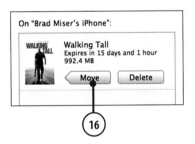

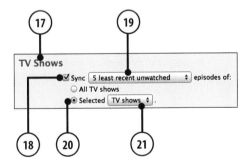

22. Check the check box next to each playlist or TV show you want to move onto the iPhone; if you uncheck a check box, the playlist or TV show is removed from the iPhone.

23. Scroll down until you see the Movies section.

24. Check the Sync movies check box.

25. Check the check box next to each movie you want to add to the iPhone.

26. To remove a movie from the iPhone, uncheck its check box.

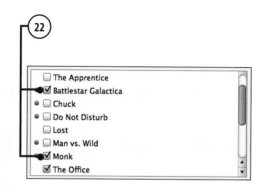

Can't Select a Movie?

If a movie is grayed out and you can't select it, it isn't in a format that is compatible with the iPhone. You can convert movies into the correct format by selecting them in the Content pane and choosing Advanced, Create iPod or iPhone Version.

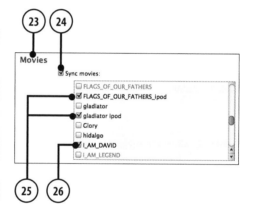

27. Click the Podcasts tab.

28. Check the Sync check box.

29. Choose how many and what type of episodes you want to move onto the iPhone. For example, to move 10 episodes you downloaded recently, but haven't yet listened to, select 10 most recent unplayed. You can choose other numbers of unplayed, numbers of recently downloaded, or numbers of new episodes.

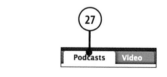

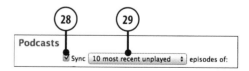

30. Choose Selected podcasts.

31. Check the check box next to each podcast that you want to move onto the iPhone.

32. Uncheck a podcast's check box to remove it from the iPhone.

33. Click Apply. iTunes starts the sync process and moves the selected content from the iTune's Library to the iPhone. You see the progress of the sync in the Information area at the top of the iTunes window. If there's enough space on the iPhone, then the process continues until all the content has been moved, and you can skip steps 34 and 35. If you've selected more content than there is room for on the iPhone, you see a warning dialog explaining how much content you selected versus how much is available.

34. Click OK. The dialog closes.

35. Use the information in steps 6–33 to decrease the amount of content you are moving from the library to the iPhone, such as by including fewer movies, and perform the sync again by clicking Apply. When the sync is complete, you see the The iPhone sync is complete message in the Information area. At the bottom of the window, you see how the iPhone's memory is being used. The Apply button becomes the Sync button; it becomes Apply again whenever you make changes to the content you've selected to sync.

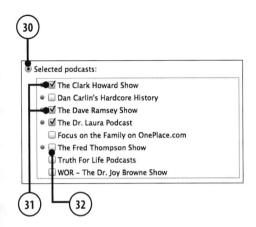

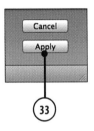

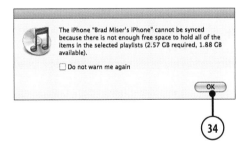

iPhone's memory usage

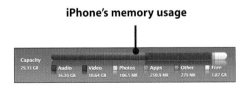

Check First, Then Unplug

Wait until the The iPhone sync is complete message appears in the Information area located at the top of the iTunes window before disconnecting the iPhone from the computer. If you remove it during the sync process, some of the content might not be moved onto the iPhone correctly. While the sync is in process, you also see the Sync in Progress message on the iPhone's screen. Wait until this disappears before disconnecting the iPhone.

Using iTunes to Add Photos to Your iPhone

As you learn in Chapter 13, your iPhone is a great way to view your photos while you are on the go. You can move photos from a computer onto iPhone so you can view them individually and as slideshows. The steps to move photos from a computer to iPhone are slightly different between Windows PCs and Macs. See the section that applies to your computer.

>>>step-by-step

Moving Photos from a Windows PC onto iPhone

You can use iTunes to move photos you're storing on your PC using Adobe Photoshop Album 2.0 or later or Adobe Photoshop Elements 3.0 or later.

1. Connect the iPhone to your computer and open iTunes (if it doesn't open automatically).

2. Click the Photos tab.

3. Check the Sync photos from check box.

4. On the pop-up menu, choose the application containing the photos you want to move onto iPhone, such as Photoshop Elements.

5. If you want all the photos in the selected source to be moved onto iPhone, click the All photos and albums radio button and skip to step 8.

6. If you want only selected albums to be moved onto iPhone, click the Selected albums radio button.

7. Check the check box next to each photo album that you want to sync with iPhone.

8. Click Apply. The photos you selected move onto the iPhone. If you make changes to the photo albums or to the photos you selected, the updates move onto your iPhone the next time you sync it.

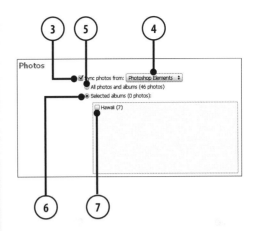

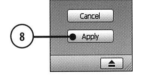

Other Sync Options

If you choose My Pictures on the Sync Photos From pop-up menu, you can move photos stored in your My Pictures folder onto the iPhone. If you select Choose Folder, you are prompted to select a folder of photos that you want to move onto your iPhone. Depending on the option you choose, you might or might not be able to select specific photo albums to move onto the iPhone.

Moving Photos from a Mac to iPhone

iTunes is designed to work seamlessly with iPhoto. You can move all your photos or selected photo albums from iPhoto to iPhone by using iTunes' syncing. You can also move photos you've stored in a folder on your Mac almost as easily.

1. Connect the iPhone to your computer and open iTunes (if it doesn't open automatically).

2. Click the Photos tab.

3. Check the Sync photos from check box.

4. On the pop-up menu, choose iPhoto.

5. If you want all the photos in iPhoto to be moved onto iPhone, click the All photos and albums radio button and skip to step 9.

6. If you want to move specific events (which are collections of photos based on when those photos were taken), click the middle radio button and choose All on the pop-up menu to move all events onto iPhone or choose the number of recent events you want to move, such as 5 most recent to move the most recent five events onto iPhone; skip to step 9.

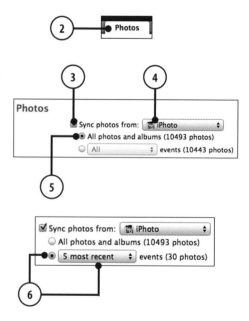

7. If you want only selected albums to move onto the iPhone, click the Selected albums radio button.

8. Check the check box next to each photo album that you want to sync on iPhone (uncheck an album's check box to remove it from the iPhone).

9. Click Apply. The photos you selected move onto the iPhone. If there's not enough memory to store the photos you selected, you're warned; you'll need to remove some of the photos from the sync or remove other kinds of content to make more room.

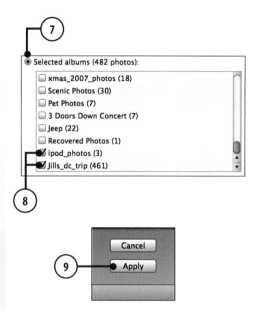

Other Sync Options

If you choose Pictures on the Sync photos from the pop-up menu, you can move photos stored in your Pictures folder onto iPhone. If you select Choose Folder, you are prompted to select a folder of photos that you want to move. Depending on the option you choose, you might or might not be able to select specific collections of photos to move into iPhone. For example, if you select a folder that contains other folders, you can select the contents of each folder individually (which is similar to selecting a photo album to sync).

Using the iTunes iPhone Application to Add Content to an iPhone

You can use the iTunes Store application to download audio and video content from the iTunes Store directly onto your iPhone, where you can play it just like content you've moved onto the iPhone by syncing it with iTunes.

In the iTunes application on your iPhone, you can use the following options that appear at the bottom of the app's screen:

- Music enables you to browse for music.

- Videos provides tools you can use to find and download movies, TV shows, and music videos.

- Podcasts enables you to find and download episodes of audio and video podcasts.

- Search makes it possible for you to search the iTunes Store for any type of content.

- More presents other tools to you: Audiobooks provides tools you use to find audiobook content, iTunes U takes you to tutorials, Download moves you to the Downloads screen where you see the progress of your downloads, and Redeem enables you to redeem codes for iTunes content.

The next time you sync the iPhone after downloading content from the iTunes Store, the content you downloaded is moved into your iTunes Library so you can enjoy it on a computer, too. (This also backs up the content you purchased.)

>>>step-by-step

1. On the iPhone's Home screen, tap iTunes. You move to the iTunes Store application. At the bottom of the screen, you choose how you want to look for content by tapping one of the buttons. The rest of these steps explain how to use the Search tool, however, using other options is similar.

2. Tap Search. The Search tool appears.

3. Tap in the Search box. The keyboard appears.

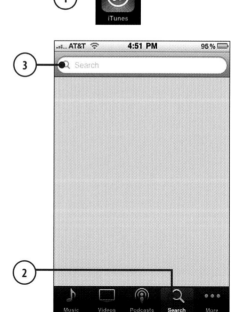

Reconfiguring the iTunes App Toolbar

To change the buttons shown at the bottom of the iTunes app's screen, tap Edit. Then drag the buttons you want to see from the Configure screen down to the location on the toolbar where you want to place them, and then tap Done. The only button you can't replace on the tool-bar is the More button, which is what you tap to see the buttons that cur-rently aren't on the toolbar.

4. Type the search criterion, such as an artist's name or movie title. As you type, content that matches your search appears under the Search bar.

5. When you see something of inter-est on the results list, tap it. For example, tap an artist's name. You see a list of content related to your search, organized by albums or songs when you tap an artist. You see different results and options when you select movies or other types of content, but the general process you use to pre-view and purchase content is the same.

6. Drag your finger up or down the screen to browse the search results, which are organized into categories, such as Top Results, Songs, Albums, Music Videos, and so on.

7. To explore the contents of an album or category, tap it. When you tap an album, at the top of the screen, you see the album's general information, such as when it was released and how many songs it contains. In the lower part of the window, you see the tracks on that album. If you tap a different kind of content, such as a music video, you see options that are appropriate for that type. The rest of these steps focus on an album, but you can download other types of content using similar steps.

8. If you tapped an album, drag your finger up or down the screen to browse the entire list of tracks.

9. To preview a track, tap it. A 30-second preview plays. While it's playing, the track's number is replaced by the Stop button, which you can tap to stop the preview.

10. To buy an album, tap its BUY button, which also shows the price of the album. The button becomes the BUY ALBUM button.

11. To buy a song, tap its Buy button, which shows the price of the song. The button becomes the BUY NOW button.

Previewing and Buying Songs

You can preview and buy songs directly from the results screen, too.

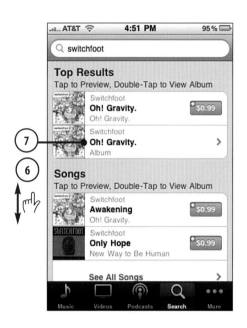

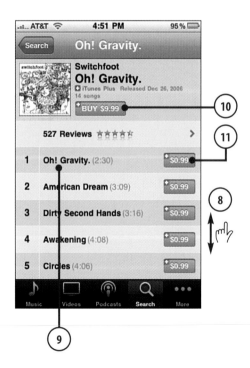

12. Tap the BUY ALBUM or BUY NOW button. You see the iTunes Password prompt.

13. Enter the password for your iTunes Store account and tap OK. A flashing red indicator appears over the More button to show you how many tracks are being downloaded to the iPhone.

Move from Song to Album

When you are browsing a list of songs, tap a song twice to move to the album that the song comes from.

14. Tap More. (If you've moved the Downloads button onto the tool-bar, as described in the sidebar "Reconfiguring the iTunes App Toolbar," you can skip this step.)

15. Tap Downloads. You move to the Downloads screen where you see the details about the tracks you are purchasing, including the amount of time the downloads will take to finish.

   When the process is complete, the Downloads screen becomes empty. This indicates that the content you purchased has been added to the iPhone and is ready for you to listen or watch.

The Next Time You Sync

The next time you sync after purchasing content from the iTunes Store on the iPhone, that content is moved into your iTunes Library. It is stored in a playlist called Purchased on *iPhonename* where *iPhonename* is the name of your iPhone.

Number of items to be downloaded

Download progress

Number of items waiting

Tap to use information
that's been synced.

Tap to
set up
MobileMe
or
Exchange
accounts
for
syncing.

In this chapter, you learn how to get information onto an iPhone and keep it in sync with computers and other devices. The topics include the following:

→ Syncing with iTunes
→ Syncing with MobileMe
→ Syncing with Exchange

Configuring and Synchronizing Information on an iPhone

In later chapters, you learn how you can use your iPhone for email, contacts, calendars, web browsing, and, of course, making phone calls and texting. These tasks are easier and better when you sync information that you have on a computer with your iPhone. That's because when synced, you don't have to configure the same information on your iPhone that you already have on your computer. More important, you'll always have the same information available to you on your computer and your iPhone.

There are three ways you can sync an iPhone with your computer. You can sync with iTunes, MobileMe, or Exchange, and you can use one, two, or all three of these techniques simultaneously.

Syncing Information with iTunes

In Chapter 3, "Moving Audio, Video, and Photos onto Your iPhone," you learned how to move audio and video content from your iTunes Library onto an iPhone. Using a similar process, you can move email accounts, calendars, contacts, and bookmarks from your computer onto your iPhone. This information gets synced each time you connect to the computer, so any changes you make on the iPhone move back to the computer and vice versa.

The only downside to syncing with iTunes is that you have to physically connect the iPhone to a computer, but that usually isn't too big of a deal. The primary benefit is that you don't need any special accounts to be able to sync this information.

Go Wireless

Using MobileMe or an Exchange account are better ways to sync information because you don't have to connect an iPhone to a computer.

As with some other tasks, the details to use iTunes to sync information are slightly different on a Mac than they are on a Windows PC, so read the section that applies to the kind of computer you use.

>>>*step-by-step*

Using iTunes to Sync Information on Macs

To set up information syncing on a Mac, perform the following steps.

1. Connect the iPhone to your Mac.

2. Select the iPhone on the Source list.

3. Click the Info tab.

4. To sync your Address Book contacts, check Sync Address Book contacts; if you don't want to sync this information (such as if you use MobileMe), skip to step 11 instead.

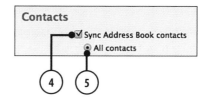

5. To sync all contact information, click All contacts and skip to step 8.

No Duplicates Please

You don't need to set up the same information to sync in more than one way. For example, if you have a MobileMe account, use that to sync your contact and calendar information rather than iTunes because with MobileMe, your information is synced wirelessly. Some information, such as gmail and other email accounts that aren't provided via MobileMe or Exchange, can be synced only via iTunes.

---

6. If you organize your contact information in groups and want to move only specific ones onto the iPhone, click Selected groups.

7. Check the check box next to each group you want to move to the iPhone. If you leave a group's check box unchecked, the contacts it contains will be ignored during the sync process.

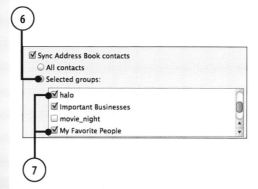

It's Not All Good

iCal for calendars, Mail for email, or Address Book for contact information are the only Mac applications that you can directly sync with the iPhone via the iTunes sync process. If you use Entourage, a tip later in the chapter helps you sync your information.

8. If you want contacts you create on the iPhone to be moved into a specific Address Book group when you sync, check the Put new contacts created on this iPhone into the Group check box and select the group on the pop-up menu. If you don't want them placed into a specific group, leave the check box unchecked.

9. To sync with your contacts stored on Yahoo!, check Sync Yahoo! Address Book contacts, click Agree, and follow the onscreen prompts to log in to your Yahoo! Address Book.

10. To sync with your contacts stored in your Google account, check Sync Google Contacts, click Agree, and follow the onscreen prompts to log in to your Google account.

11. Scroll down until you see the Calendars section.

12. Check Sync iCal calendars; if you don't want to sync calendar information (such as if you use MobileMe), skip to step 17 instead.

13. If you want all the calendars you access in iCal to be synced on the iPhone, click the All calendars radio button and skip to step 16.

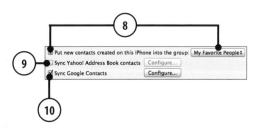

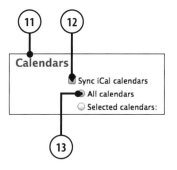

How Am I Syncing?

When you are syncing information via MobileMe or Exchange, you see a text message saying so in the related section. For example, if you use Exchange to sync your calendar information, you see the text, "Your calendars are being synced with Microsoft Exchange over the air." This message doesn't stop you from also syncing the same information using iTunes, but you should be thoughtful about this so you don't sync the same information twice.

Syncing Entourage

If you use Entourage, you can sync its information with your iPhone indirectly by syncing its information with Address Book and iCal, which in turn are synced with your iPhone via iTunes. Open Entourage's Preferences and configure the Sync Services preferences to synchronize contacts with Address Book and events with iCal. Then, configure Address Book and iCal syncing in iTunes as described in these steps. To sync your Entourage email, simply manually configure your email account on the iPhone, as described in Chapter 7, "Emailing."

14. If you want only selected calendars to move onto the iPhone, click the Selected calendars radio button.

15. Check the check box next to each calendar that you want to sync on the iPhone.

16. If you want to prevent older events from syncing, check the Do not sync events older than check box and enter the number of days in the box.

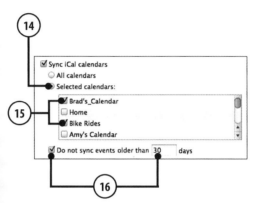

17. Scroll down until you see the Web Browser section.

18. Check the Sync Safari bookmarks check box if you want to move your Safari bookmarks, so you can use them with the iPhone's Web browser; if you don't want this, skip this step.

19. If you want any notes you create with the iPhone's Notes application to be moved onto the computer, check the Sync Notes check box; if not, skip this step.

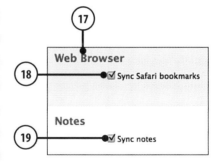

It's Not All Good

If you prefer Firefox as your web browser, you can't sync your bookmarks via iTunes. That's really too bad and is quite annoying for those of us who use Firefox regularly. There's currently no simple way to move bookmarks to or from an iPhone from or to Firefox. (There are ways to do this, but they are clunky and require more room to explain than I have here.) Hopefully, Apple will remove this web browser discrimination in an update to its software soon.

Locating Synced Notes?

When you sync notes, they are stored in the Mail application under the Notes sub-section of the Reminders section shown in the mailbox pane on the left side of the window. If you don't see your notes, expand the Notes item and select On My Mac. You should see your notes in the List pane at the top of the Mail window. Select a note on the list to read it in the Reading pane at the bottom of the window.

20. Scroll down until you see the Mail Accounts section.

21. Check Sync selected mail accounts if you want to configure email accounts that are config-ured in Mail on the iPhone; skip to step 23 if you don't want them configured (such as for MobileMe or Exchange accounts).

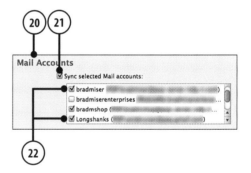

22. Check the check box for each account you want to move onto iPhone. You can choose to move any or all of your email accounts to the iPhone.

23. Scroll down to the Advanced section.

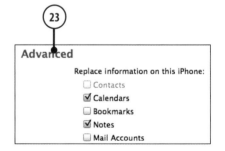

24. Check the check boxes next to any information that you want to be replaced on the iPhone with information from the computer. If you don't check a check box, its information will be merged with that information on the iPhone instead. (If information is grayed out, you aren't syncing that information with iTunes so it isn't an appropriate choice.)

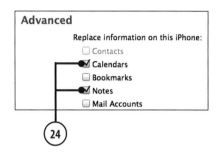

Sync Versus Apply

Whenever you make changes to the sync settings for the iPhone, the Apply button appears. When you click this, the new settings are saved and used for subsequent syncs, a sync is performed, and the button becomes Sync. Click Sync to perform a sync using the current settings.

25. Click Apply. A sync is performed, and the information you selected is moved onto the iPhone.

Each time you sync the iPhone (automatically when you connect the iPhone to your Mac), any updated information included in the sync settings on the computer is moved to the iPhone, and updated information on the iPhone is moved onto the computer.

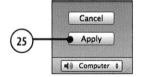

Syncing with More Than One Source

If you configured your iPhone to sync with more than one source of contact information, perhaps Outlook on a Windows PC and Address Book on a Mac, when you sync, you're prompted to replace or merge the information. If you select Replace Info, the existing information in whatever you are syncing with replaces all the information on your iPhone. If you choose Merge Info, the information you are syncing moves onto your iPhone and merges with the existing information.

Using iTunes to Sync Information on Windows

You can sync information on a Windows PC with an iPhone by performing the following steps.

1. Connect the iPhone to your computer.

2. Select the iPhone on the Source list.

3. Click the Info tab.

4. To sync your contacts, check Sync contacts with and choose the application containing the contact information you want to sync on the drop-down list. The options are Windows Address Book, Yahoo! Address Book, Google Contacts, or Outlook. If you choose Yahoo! or Google, log in to your account at the prompt. If you don't want to sync contact information stored on your computer (such as if you use MobileMe), skip to step 9 instead.

5. To sync all contact information, click All contacts and skip to step 8.

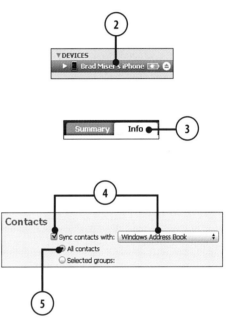

No Duplicates Please

You don't need to set up the same information to sync in more than one way. For example, if you have a MobileMe account, use that to sync your contact and calendar information rather than iTunes because with MobileMe, your information is synced wirelessly. Some information, such as email accounts that aren't provided via MobileMe or Exchange, can be synced only via iTunes.

---

6. If you organize your contact information in groups and want to move only specific ones onto the iPhone, click Selected groups.

7. Check the check box next to each group you want to move into the iPhone. If you leave a group's check box unchecked, the contacts it contains will be ignored during the sync process.

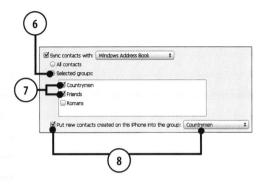

8. If you want contacts you create on the iPhone to be moved into a specific contact group when you sync, check the Put new contacts created on this iPhone into the Group check box and select the group on the pop-up menu. If you don't want them placed into a specific group, leave the check box unchecked.

9. Scroll down until you see the Calendars section.

10. Check Sync calendars with and choose the calendar application that contains the calendars you want to sync with; if you don't want to sync calendar information (such as if you use MobileMe), skip to step 15.

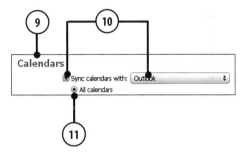

11. If you want all the calendars you access in the application you selected to be synced on the iPhone, click the All calendars radio button and skip to step 14.

12. If you want only selected calendars to move onto an iPhone, click the Selected calendars radio button.

13. Check the check box next to each calendar that you want to sync on the iPhone.

14. If you want to prevent older events from syncing, check the Do not sync Events older than check box and enter the number of days in the box.

15. Scroll down until you see the Web Browser section.

16. Check the Sync bookmarks with check box if you want to sync your bookmarks so you can use them with the iPhone's web browser; if you don't want this, skip to step 18.

17. Select Safari or Internet Explorer on the drop-down list to choose the browser containing the bookmarks you want to sync.

18. If you want any notes you create with the iPhone's Notes application to be moved onto the computer, check the Sync notes with check box and select the application where the synced notes should be stored on the drop-down list; if you don't want to move your notes onto the computer, skip this step.

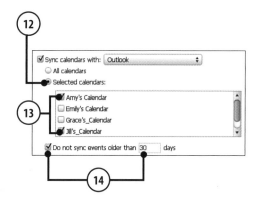

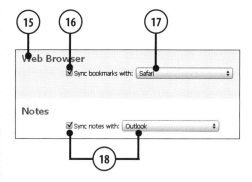

It's Not All Good

If you prefer Firefox as your web browser, you can't sync your book-marks via iTunes. That's really too bad and is quite annoying for those of us who use Firefox regularly. There's currently no simple way to move bookmarks to or from an iPhone from or to Firefox. (There are ways to do this, but they are clunky and require more room to explain than I have here.) Hopefully, Apple will remove this web browser discrimina-tion in an update to its software soon.

Synced Notes?

In the current version of iTunes, Outlook is the only Windows applica-tion that supports notes syncing. When you sync notes, they are stored in the Notes area, which you can access by clicking the Notes icon.

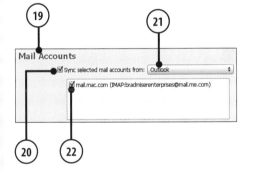

19. Scroll down until you see the Mail Accounts section.

20. Check Sync selected mail accounts from if you want to con-figure email accounts that are configured on your computer on the iPhone; skip to step 23 if you don't want them configured (such as if you use MobileMe or Exchange email accounts).

21. Select the email application con-taining the accounts you want to sync on the drop-down list.

22. Check the check box for each account you want to move onto iPhone. You can choose to move any or all of your email accounts to the iPhone.

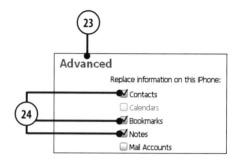

23. Scroll down to the Advanced section.

24. Check the check boxes next to any information you want to replace on the iPhone with information from the computer. If you don't check a check box, that information will be merged with the information on the iPhone instead. (If a check box is grayed out, that information isn't included in the sync so that option doesn't apply.)

25. Click Apply. A sync is performed, and the information you selected is moved onto the iPhone.

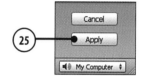

Each time you sync the iPhone (automatically when you connect the iPhone to your computer), any updated information included in the sync settings on the computer is moved to the iPhone, and updated information on the iPhone is moved onto the computer.

Syncing Information with MobileMe

One of the great things about a MobileMe account is that you can sync email, contacts, calendars, and bookmarks wirelessly. Whenever your iPhone can access the Internet via a cellular connection or Wi-Fi network, no matter where you are, the sync process can occur.

Of course, to be able to sync information with MobileMe, you must have a MobileMe account. See Chapter 1, "Getting Started with Your iPhone," for information about obtaining a MobileMe account.

If you have a MobileMe account, it is very simple to access your MobileMe information on your iPhone by configuring the account on the iPhone and configuring its sync options. Here's how.

>>>step-by-step

1. On the Home screen, tap Settings.
2. Tap Mail, Contacts, Calendars.
3. Tap Add Account.
4. Tap mobileme.

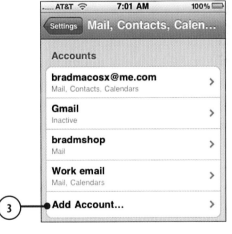

5. Enter your name.

6. Enter your MobileMe email address.

7. Enter your MobileMe account password.

8. Change the default description, which is your email address, if you want to. This description appears on various lists of accounts.

9. Tap Save. Your account information is verified. When that process is complete, you see the MobileMe screen that you use to choose which elements of your MobileMe account are going to be synchronized on iPhone.

10. Tap OFF next to each kind of information you want to sync on the iPhone; its status becomes ON to show you that information will be synced. If you leave a type's status set to OFF, that information is ignored during the sync.

11. Tap Done. The account is synced to the iPhone. You return to the Mail, Contacts, Calendar screen where you see your account on the Accounts list. The account is ready to use. Configure how and when informaton is synced.

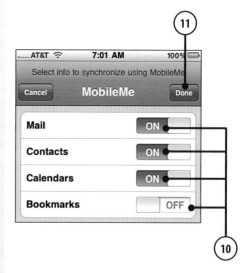

12. Scroll down the screen.

13. Tap Fetch New Data.

14. To enable information to be synced with your iPhone whenever there are updates and the iPhone is connected to the Internet, ensure the Push status is ON (if it isn't, tap OFF to turn it on); or to disable Push to extend battery life, tap ON so the status becomes OFF.

15. Tap the amount of time when you want an iPhone to sync information when Push is OFF and for those accounts that don't support Push; tap Manually if you want to sync manually only.

16. Scroll down the screen.

17. Tap Advanced. You see a list of all your active accounts. Next to each account, you see if it is configured to use Push, Fetch, or Manual. MobileMe accounts are listed twice. One instance is for just email and is labeled Mail on the list. The other listing is for contacts and calendars. You can configure how new data is retrieved for each of these independently.

18. Tap the Contacts, Calendars instance of the MobileMe account.

19. Tap the option you want to use for contact and calendar syncing; the options are Push or Manual. If you choose Push, syncing will occur when the iPhone is connected to the Internet and there is new information on the iPhone or in the MobileMe cloud. If you choose Manual, information is synced only when you manually start the process.

20. Tap Advanced.

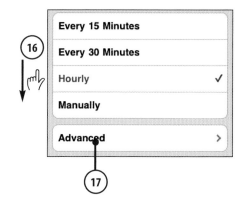

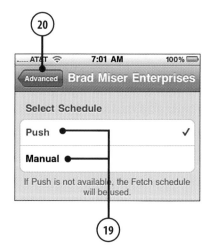

21. Tap the mail instance of the MobileMe account.

22. Tap the option you want to use for email syncing; the options are Push, Fetch, or Manual. If you choose Push, syncing will occur when the iPhone is connected to the Internet and there is new information on the iPhone or in the MobileMe cloud. If you choose Fetch, email syncing will occur according to the time you selected in step 15. If you choose Manual, emails are synced only when you manually start the process. The MobileMe account sync settings are complete.

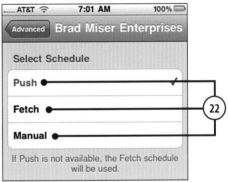

Tap here to work with contact information. ———

Use your contact information in many activities.

Use Settings to configure how contacts are displayed.

In this chapter, you learn how to make sure that your iPhone has the contact information you need when you need it. Topics include the following:

→ Configuring how contacts are displayed
→ Creating contacts on an iPhone
→ Using contacts on an iPhone
→ Changing or deleting contacts

Managing Contacts

Contact information, including names, phone numbers, email addresses, and physical addresses, is very useful to have on your iPhone. For example, when you send email, you want to select the appropriate email addresses rather than having to remember them and type them in. When you want to call someone, you don't have to have to remember a phone number, instead, just choose the person you want to call. Likewise, you might want to pull up addresses on a map in the Maps application.

Configuring How Contacts Are Displayed on an iPhone

Before you start using contacts, make sure that contact information displays according to your preferences. You can determine how contacts are sorted on lists by first or last name, and you can choose which of those appears first on lists.

>>>*step-by-step*

1. On the Home screen, tap Settings.

2. Scroll down until you see Mail, Contacts, Calendars.

3. Tap Mail, Contacts, Calendars.

4. Scroll down until you see the Contacts section.

5. Tap Sort Order. The Sort Order screen appears.

6. To have contacts sorted by first name and then last name, tap First, Last.

7. To have contacts sorted by last name and then first name, tap Last, First.

8. Tap Mail.

Bonus Task

Please go to this book's website at www.informit.com/title/9780789742315 and click the Downloads tab to find an additional task titled, "Creating a Contact from a Map."

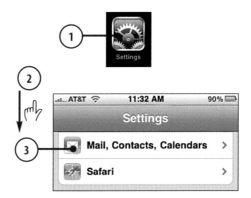

9. Tap Display Order. The Display
   Order screen appears.

10. To show contacts in the format
    first name, last name, tap First, Last.

11. To show contacts in the format last
    name, first name, tap Last, First.

12. Tap Mail.

SIM Contacts

Your iPhone stores data, such as contact information, about your wireless
account on a SIM (Subscriber Identity
Module) card. To import contacts from
a SIM card, insert the card containing
the data you want to import and tap
the Import SIM Contacts button.

Creating New Contacts While Using an iPhone

You can create new contacts on your iPhone in a number of ways. You can
start with some information, such as the phone number from a recent call,
and create a contact from it, or you can create a contact manually "from
scratch." In this section, you learn how to create a contact from a recent
phone call, an email message, a location on a map, and manually.

Creating by Syncing

In most cases, the primary way you'll create contacts is on a computer. You can
sync contacts with a computer using iTunes or wirelessly using MobileMe to
move that contact information onto your iPhone. See Chapter 4, "Configuring
and Synchronizing Information on an iPhone," to learn how to configure syncing. By the way, the process works in the other direction, too. Any new contacts
you create or any changes you make to existing contact information on your
iPhone move back to the computer through the sync process.

Creating a Contact from a Recent Call

You can capture a phone number associated with a recent call to add to an existing contact or to create a new one.

1. On the Home screen, tap Phone.

2. Tap Recents.

3. Tap All to see all recent calls or Missed to see only those calls you didn't answer.

4. Tap the Info button for the number from which you want to create a contact. The Info screen appears; the label on the screen depends on the kind of call you select. For example, if you select a missed call, the screen label is Missed Call.

5. To add the number to an existing contact, tap Add to Existing Contact, and the All Contacts screen appears; skip to step 7. Or, to create a new contact, tap Create New Contact. The New Contact screen appears. The iPhone adds the number you selected and labels it, such as mobile.

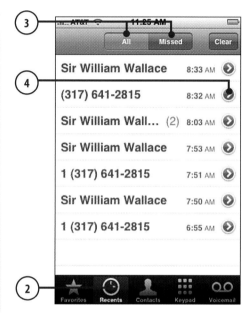

6. Use the New Contact screen to configure the new contact. This works just like when you create a new contact manually, except that you already have some information (in this example, a phone number) for the new contact. See "Creating Contacts on an iPhone Manually" later in this chapter for details. Skip the rest of these steps.

7. Browse the screen or use the index to find the contact with which you want to associate the phone number.

8. Tap the contact. You see the Add Phone screen with the information you're adding, in this example, a phone number.

9. Tap the Label field, which is mobile by default. You see the Label screen.

10. Tap the label for the new information.

11. Tap Add Phone. You return to the Add Phone screen.

12. Tap Save. You see the contact's Info screen, which now contains the phone number you added.

Creating a Contact from an Email

When you receive an email, you can easily create a contact to capture the email address. (To learn how to work with the iPhone's email application, see Chapter 7, "Emailing.")

1. On the Home screen, tap Mail. The Mail screen appears.

2. Use the Mail application to read an email message (see Chapter 7 for details).

3. Tap the email address from which you want to create a new contact. The Info screen appears; the label of the screen depends on the type of email address you tapped. For example, if you tapped the address from which the email was sent, the screen is labeled From. You see as much information as your iPhone can discern from the email address; this is typically the sender's name and email address.

4. Tap Create New Contact. The New Contact screen appears. iPhone adds the name and email address of the new contact you selected. The email address is labeled with iPhone's best guess, such as other or home.

5. Use the New Contact screen to enter more contact information and save the new contact. This works just like when you create a new contact manually, for details, see "Creating Contacts on an iPhone Manually" later in this chapter.

Add to Existing Contact

You can add an email address to an existing contact by tapping the Add to Existing Contact command. You then search for and select the contact to which you want to add the email address. Once saved, that information is associated with the contact. You can also use this command with the Maps application as shown in the next task. For example, suppose you have a contact for a company, but all you have is its phone number. You can quickly find the address using the Maps application and add it to the company's existing contact information without retyping it.

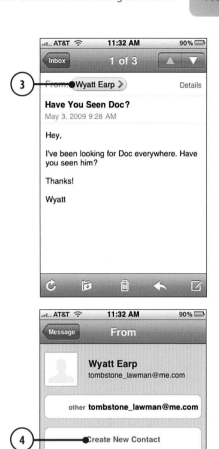

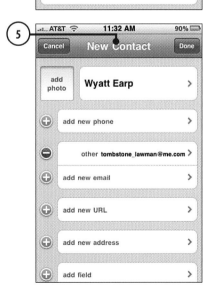

Creating Contacts on an iPhone Manually

Most of the time, you'll manage contact information on a computer and move it to your iPhone. Or you'll use information on the iPhone to create new contacts so you don't have to start from scratch. When you do have to start from scratch, you can create contacts manually and add all the information you need to them.

1. On the Home screen, tap Contacts.

2. Tap Add. The New Contact screen appears. You see the information you can include for a contact. You can add more fields as needed using the add field command.

3. To associate a photo with the contact, tap Add Photo. You are prompted to use an existing photo stored on the iPhone or to take a new photo with your iPhone's camera.

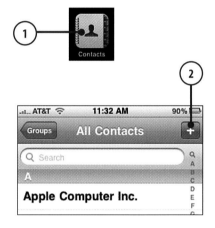

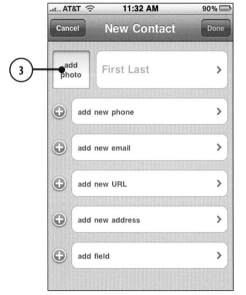

4. To take a photo of the contact, press Take Photo, and skip to step 8.

5. To choose an existing photo stored on iPhone, press Choose Existing Photo. The Photo Albums screen appears.

6. Use the Photo Album tools to move to, select, and configure the photo you want to associate with the contact (see Chapter 13).

7. Tap Choose. iPhone configures the photo and saves it to the contact. You return to the New Contact screen and see the photo you selected.

8. Or, use the iPhone camera to capture the photo you want to associate with the contact.

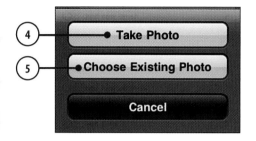

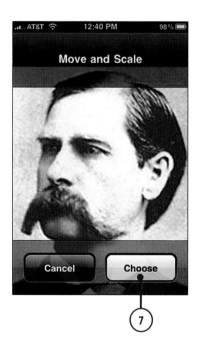

9. Use the Move and Scale screen to configure the photo. (Chapter 13 explains how to use this screen.)

10. Tap Choose. The iPhone saves the photo. You return to the New Contact screen and see the photo you captured and configured.

11. Tap First Last (or it could be Last First). The label you see depends on the display preference you set earlier. The Add Name screen appears.

12. Enter the first name.

13. Enter the last name.

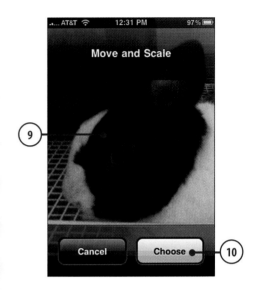

Company Contact

If you're creating a contact for a company or other organization, leave the first and last fields empty. If you don't want to associate a contact with an organization, leave the company field empty.

14. Enter the company for the contact, if applicable.

15. Tap Save. You return to the New Contact screen and see the information you entered.

16. Tap add new phone. The Add Phone screen appears.

17. Enter the phone number, including area code.

18. Tap the Label bar. The Label screen appears.

19. Tap the label you want to associate with the phone number. You return to the Add Phone screen, and iPhone displays the label you selected.

Custom Labels

You can create custom labels for various kinds of contact information. On the Label screen, scroll down the screen and tap the Add Custom Label option. The Custom Label screen appears. Create the label and tap Save. You can then choose your custom label for the new contact you are creating as well as for contacts you create or change in the future.

20. Tap Save. You return to the New Contact screen and see the number and label you entered.

21. To add another number, tap add new phone and repeat steps 17 through 20.

22. Tap add new email. The Add Email screen appears.

23. Enter the email address for the contact.

24. Tap the Label bar.

25. Tap the label you want to associate with the email address. You return to the Edit Email screen.

Edit Labels

If you tap the Edit button on the Label screen, you can delete custom labels or add them.

26. Tap Save.

27. To add another email, tap add new email and repeat steps 23 through 26.

28. To associate a website with the contact, tap add new URL. The Edit URL screen appears.

29. Enter the URL.

30. Tap the Label bar. The Label screen appears.

31. Tap the label you want to associate with the URL. You return to the Edit URL screen.

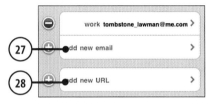

32. Tap Save.

33. To add another URL, tap the add new URL button and repeat steps 25 through 28.

34. Scroll down the screen.

35. To add a new physical address to the contact, tap add new address. The Add Address screen appears.

36. If the address is not in the default country shown, such as the United States, tap the Country button. The Country screen appears.

37. Scroll the screen to find the country for the address you are creating.

38. Tap the country for the address. You return to the Edit Address screen. The data for the address depends on the country you selected. For example, if the country uses state information, you see a State field. If it uses postal codes, you see the Postal Code field.

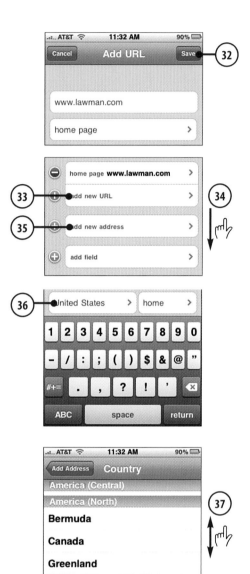

39. Tap the first element of the address, such as Street, and enter the information for that element.

40. Repeat step 39 until you've entered all the address' information.

41. Tap the Label. The Label screen appears.

42. Tap the label you want to apply to the address.

43. Tap Save.

44. To add another address, tap add new address and repeat steps 36 through 43.

45. To add more fields to the contact, tap add field. The Add Field screen appears. On this screen, you see all possible data that you can add to a contact.

46. Scroll the screen to see the types of data you can add to contacts.

47. Tap the data you want to add. The related Add field appears. For example, if you selected Nickname, the Add Nickname field appears.

48. Use the Add screen to enter information for the field you selected. The tools on the Add screen depend on the kind of information you added.

49. Tap Save.

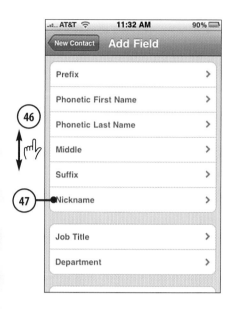

More on More Fields

When you add more fields to contact information, those fields appear in the appropriate context on the Info screen. For example, if you add a nickname, it is placed at the top of the screen with the other "name" information. If you add an address, it appears with the other address information.

50. To add more fields to the contact, tap add field and repeat steps 46 through 49.

51. When you finish adding information, tap Done. The new contact is created and is ready for you to use, and you see the information you entered on the Info screen. It also is included in the next sync so it will be added to your contact information on your computer.

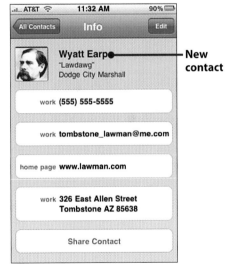

New contact

Using Contacts on an iPhone

There are many ways to use contact information stored on your iPhone. You can access your contact information from the Contacts application and from within other applications that use that information, such as Mail, Phone, and so on.

>>>step-by-step

Using the Contacts Application

Using the Contacts application, you can search or browse for a contact and then view the detailed information for the contact in which you are interested. From the Info screen for a contact, you can perform actions using the contact's information.

1. On the Home screen, tap Contacts. You see the All Contacts screen with the contacts listed in the format you selected, such as last name, first name.

2. Drag your finger up or down to scroll the screen to browse for contact information; flick your finger up or down to scroll rapidly.

3. Tap the index to jump to contact information organized by first letter of the selected format (last name or first name, depending on the preference you set).

4. Use the Search tool to search for a specific contact.

5. To view a contact's information, tap the contact. The Info screen appears.

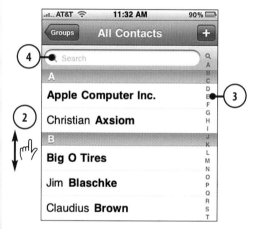

6. Scroll up and down the screen to view all the contact's information.

7. Tap the data and buttons on the screen to perform actions (the actions you see for a contact depend upon the kind of information available for that contact).

8. To return to the All Contacts list without performing an action, tap All Contacts.

Using Contacts Information in Other Applications

You can also access contact information in the context of another application. For example, you can use a contact's email address when you create an email message. When you perform such actions, you use the All Contacts screen to find and select the contact whose information you want to use. The following example shows using contact information to send an email message.

1. Open the application from which you want to access contact information. (This example uses Mail.)

2. Tap the Add button. The All Contacts screen appears.

3. To search for a contact, tap in the Search bar. (As you learned earlier, you can also browse the list or use the index to find a contact.)

4. Enter the search text.

5. Tap the contact whose information you want to use. You move back to the application, and the appropriate information is entered.

Multiple Fields

If you tap a contact who has more than one entry for a type of information, you move to the contact's info screen and then tap on the specific entry you want to use. For example, if a contact has more than one email address, when you tap the contact, you move to the Info screen where you see all the contact's email addresses. Tap the email address to which you want to send the message.

Email address for the contact

Changing or Deleting Contacts

When you sync contacts with a computer via iTunes or MobileMe, the changes go both ways. For example, when you change a contact on an iPhone, the synced contact manager application, such as Outlook, makes the changes for those contacts on your computer. Likewise, when you change contact information in a contact manager on your computer, those changes move to the iPhone when you sync it. If you add a new contact in a contact manager, it moves to the iPhone during a sync operation and vice versa.

>>>step-by-step

>>>step-by-step

Changing, Adding, or Removing Information for an Existing Contact Manually

You can change any information for an existing contact on your iPhone; when you sync, the changes you make are moved into your contact manager, such as Outlook or Address Book.

1. View the contact's Info screen.

2. Tap Edit. The Info screen moves into Edit mode, and you see Unlock and Add buttons.

3. Tap a field to change its informa- tion. The related Edit screen appears, and you can make or save your changes. These Edit screens work just like when you create a new contact. (See "Creating Contacts on an iPhone Manually" earlier in this chapter.)

4. To add more fields, tap the related add command. These also work just like when you are creating a contact manually.

5. To remove a field from the con- tact, tap its Unlock button. The Delete button appears.

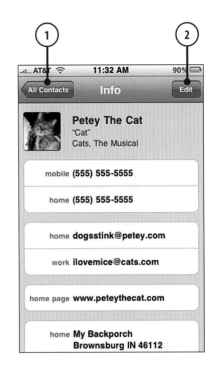

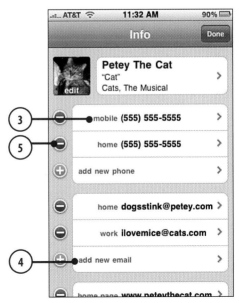

6. Tap Delete. The information is removed from the contact.

7. To change the contact's photo, tap the current photo (which contains the text edit) and use the resulting tools to select a new photo or change the scale or position of the existing one.

8. When you finish making changes, tap Done. Your changes are saved, and you return to the Info screen.

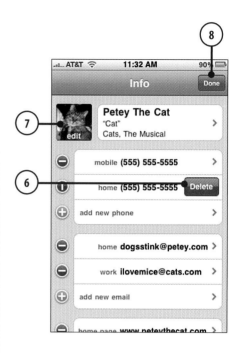

Adding Information to an Existing Contact While Using Your iPhone

As you use your iPhone, you'll encounter information related to a contact but that isn't part of that contact's information. For example, a contact might send you an email from a different address than you entered in that contact's information. When that happens, you can easily add the additional information to an existing contact.

1. Locate the information you want to add to an existing contact, such as a physical address, email address, or website.

2. Tap Add to Contacts or tap Add to Existing Contact (which you see depends on the type of information you are working with).

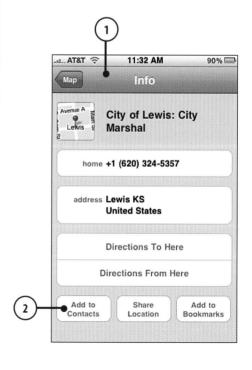

3. Tap Add to Existing Contact (skip this step if you tapped Add to Existing Contact in the previous step). The All Contacts screen appears.

4. Locate and tap the contact to which you want to add the information. The new information is saved to the contact and is highlighted in blue. To change the information, such as its label, tap Edit and follow the steps in the previous section.

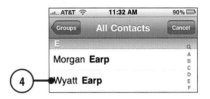

Deleting Contacts Manually

To get rid of contacts, you can delete them from the iPhone.

1. Find and view the contact you want to delete.

2. Tap Edit.

3. Scroll to the bottom of the Info screen.

4. Tap Delete Contact.

5. Tap Delete Contact again to confirm the deletion. iPhone deletes the contact, and you return to the All Contacts list. The next time you sync, iPhone prompts you to approve the deletion on the computer's contact manager, just like other changes you make (again, depending on the level of change that you've set to trigger these notifications).

Tap here to make calls, listen
to voicemail, and more.

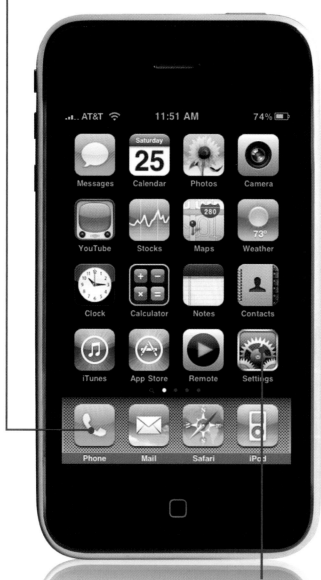

Tap here to configure phone settings.

In this chapter, you'll explore all the cell phone functionality that your iPhone has to offer. The topics include the following:

→ Configuring phone settings
→ Making calls
→ Receiving calls
→ Managing calls
→ Using visual voicemail
→ Getting information about your cell account

6

Making, Receiving, and Managing Calls

Although it's also a lot of other great things, such as an iPod, web browser, email tool, and such, there's a reason the word *phone* is in your iPhone's name. It's a feature-rich cell phone that includes one of the iPhone's best features, which is visual voicemail. Other useful features include a speaker phone, conference calling, and easy-to-use onscreen controls. Plus your iPhone's phone functions are integrated with its other features. For example, when using the Maps application, you might find a location, such as a business, that you're interested in contacting. You can call that location just by tapping the number you want to call directly from the Maps screen. No need to fumble around switching to phone mode and dialing the number manually. The iPhone makes your mobile phone use quicker, easier, and smarter in so many ways, as you'll see in the pages that follow.

Configuring Phone Settings

Before jumping into iPhone calling, take a few minutes to configure your iPhone's phone functions to work the way you want them to. Of course, we all know that your ringtone is the most important setting, and you'll want to make sure your iPhone's ringtone is just right. You can create custom ringtones in iTunes and move them onto your iPhone. Then, use the iPhone's Sound settings to configure custom or standard ringtones and other phone-related sounds. There are some other less fun, but still valuable, settings you should configure to tune your iPhone phone calls to your preferences.

Creating Your Own Ringtones

One of the most fun phone settings are the ringtones you hear when you receive calls. The iPhone includes quite a collection of ringtones from which you can choose. To customize your ringtones, you can create them from selected songs that you can purchase in the iTunes Store. There are two steps to this: create the ringtone and then move it onto your iPhone.

iTunes Store Info

You can find out how to access the iTunes Store to buy and download music in Chapter 3, "Moving Audio, Video, and Photos onto Your iPhone."

Creating a Ringtone in iTunes

To use custom music as a ringtone, you must purchase a ringtone-enabled song from the iTunes Store. In the iTunes Store, songs that are ringtone-enabled are marked with the ringtone icon, which is a bell. After you've purchased a ringtone-enabled song and downloaded it, you can convert it into a ringtone; note there is an additional charge of $0.99 to do this (in addition to the cost of the song itself so your total cost for a custom ringtone is the cost of the song plus $0.99 to create a ringtone).

Ringtone-enabled songs

>>>*step-by-step*

Here's how to create a ringtone from a ringtone-enabled song in your iTunes library.

1. In iTunes, select a song that you want to use as a ringtone by searching or browsing your library. Ringtone-enabled songs are marked with the same bell icon that they are in the iTunes Store. You can easily find all your ringtone-enabled music by selecting Music on the iTunes Source list and ensuring All is selected in each column of the Browser. Then sort the list by the Ringtone-enabled column.

2. Right-click (or Control+click) the song you want to use as a ring-tone.

3. Select Create Ringtone. The Ringtone tool appears at the bottom of the iTunes window, and the song you selected is added to it. By default, the first 15 seconds of the song is selected; the part that is the ringtone is highlighted in the blue select box. You can create a ringtone of up to any 30 seconds of the song.

4. Click Preview. The selected ring-tone plays and loops as you work on it.

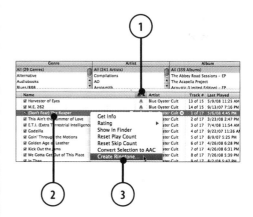

5. Drag the left edge of the selection box until it is at the start of your ringtone.

6. Drag the right edge of the selection box until it is at the end of the ringtone. The length of the ringtone is shown at the bottom of the selection box; you can select up to 30 seconds at any point in the song. The ringtone plays and repeats as you make changes.

7. Repeat steps 5 and 6 until the selection box contains exactly what you want to use as a ringtone.

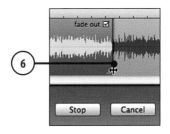

8. Use the Looping pop-up menu to determine the amount of gap between the loops of the ringtone when it rings. The default is .5 seconds, but you can increase this if you want more of a pause between repetitions.

9. When the ringtone is right, click Buy. If you aren't logged into your iTunes Store account, you are prompted to do so. The ringtone you created is saved to the Ringtones area within your library.

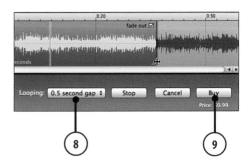

Moving Ringtones onto Your iPhone

After you've created a ringtone using iTunes, you can move it onto your iPhone.

1. Connect your iPhone to your computer and select it on the iTunes Source list.

2. Click the Ringtones tab. The ringtones you've created are shown in the box below Selected Ringtones.

3. Check the Sync ringtones check box.

4. To move all your ringtones onto your iPhone, select All ringtones and skip to step 7.

5. To move only selected ringtones onto your iPhone, select Selected ringtones.

6. Check the check box next to each ringtone you want to move onto your iPhone.

7. Click Apply. A sync is performed, and the ringtones are moved onto your iPhone where you can use them.

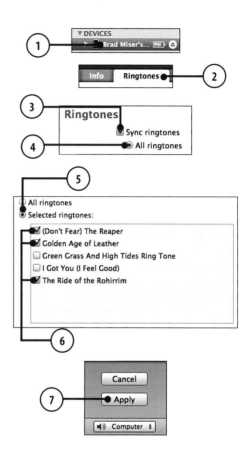

NO LIMITS

>>> Go Further

Creating ringtones from iTunes Store music is good, but it is somewhat limiting because you can only use tunes that are ringtone-enabled. And you have to pay $0.99 for each ringtone (on top of what you've already paid to purchase the song). If you want to use any song or audio as a ringtone, you need an application that provides this capability. Do a web search to find one. One of my favorites for Macs is iToner by Ambrosia Software (www.ambrosiasw.com/utilities/iToner/). With this application, you can use any part of any song or other sound in your iTunes Library as a ringtone.

Setting Phone Sounds

You can set your iPhone to play specific sounds for various events, such
as a ringtone, receiving a voicemail
message, and so on.

1. Tap Settings on the Home screen.

2. On the Settings screen, tap
   Sounds. The Sounds screen
   appears.

3. To prevent your iPhone from
   vibrating when you've silenced
   the ringer, tap the upper Vibrate
   ON button. The status becomes
   OFF, and your iPhone won't
   vibrate when you have silenced it
   using the Mute switch. Tap OFF to
   re-enable vibration.

4. To prevent your iPhone from
   vibrating when the ringer is
   enabled, tap the lower Vibrate ON
   button. The status becomes OFF,
   and your iPhone won't vibrate
   when the ringer sounds to indicate you're receiving a call or
   when some other action for
   which sound is enabled occurs.

5. To increase the volume level of
   ringer sounds, drag the slider to
   the right; drag it to the left to
   lower the volume of ringer sounds.

6. Tap Ringtone or tap the name of
   the current ringtone. The
   Ringtone screen appears. In the
   Custom section, you see ringtones
   you've created in iTunes and
   moved onto your iPhone. In the
   Standard section, you see the
   iPhone's default ringtones.

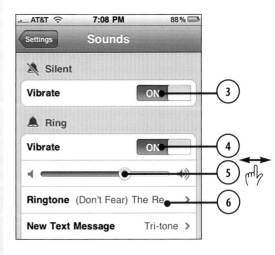

7. Listen to a ringtone by tapping its name. The ringtone is marked with a check mark to show you that it is the active ringtone, and it plays.

8. Browse the screen and keep trying sounds until you find the one you want to use as the ringtone.

9. Tap Sounds. You move back to the Sounds screen, and the sound you selected is shown as the Ringtone.

10. If you don't want to hear a sound when you receive a new voice-mail, tap New Voicemail ON. Its status becomes OFF, and you won't hear a sound when you receive voicemail.

11. Tap Settings. You move back to the Settings screen.

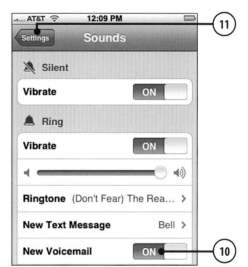

Hearing Things

If you want to hear any of the action sounds, such as New Voicemail, Tap ON to turn that sound off and then tap OFF to turn it back on. When you do, you hear the sound that plays when the related event occurs. (If your iPhone is muted with the Mute switch, you don't hear these sounds regardless of the status of the sounds on the Settings screen.)

Configuring Phone Settings

There are a number of settings you can use to configure the way the phone functions work.

1. Move to the Settings screen.

2. Drag down the Settings screen until you see Phone.

3. Tap Phone. Your number is shown at the top of the screen in case you ever forget it. (Yes, I have forgotten my own number.)

5. If you don't want the correct prefixes added to U.S. phone numbers when you dial them from outside the United States, tap ON next to International Assist. It becomes OFF to show you that you have to add any prefixes manually when dialing a U.S. number from outside the United States. (This step is specific to the iPhone in the United States with service provided by AT&T. If you have your iPhone from a different provider, this function might perform a different action.)

6. To forward your calls to another number, perform steps 7 through 11; if you don't want to forward calls, skip to step 12.

7. Tap Call Forwarding. The Call Forwarding screen appears.

8. To forward calls, tap OFF. It becomes ON to show you that call forwarding is active. The Forwarding To screen appears.

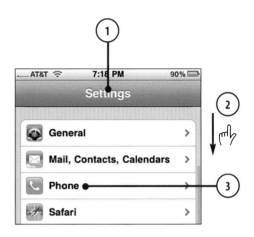

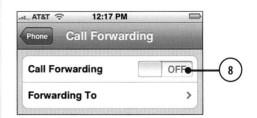

9. Enter the number to which you want to forward calls. Include the number's area code. You can use the special symbols located in the lower-left corner of the keypad to enter pauses and such.

10. Tap Call Forwarding. The iPhone saves the number, and you return to the Call Forwarding screen. The number to which your iPhone will forward calls shows next to the Forwarding To text.

11. Tap Phone.

12. To disable call waiting, tap Call Waiting, and the Call Waiting screen appears; to leave Call Waiting active, skip to step 15.

13. To disable call waiting, tap ON. Its status becomes OFF. When call waiting is turned off and you receive a second call while you're already on another call, the second call immediately goes to voicemail.

14. Tap Phone.

15. To hide your information when you make calls, tap Show My Caller ID; to leave it showing, skip the rest of these steps.

16. Tap ON. The status becomes OFF to show you that your information won't be transmitted when you make a call.

17. Tap Phone. You return to the Phone screen and are ready to use your iPhone to make and receive calls.

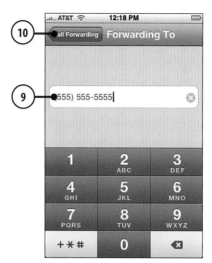

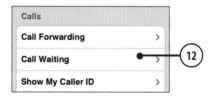

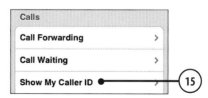

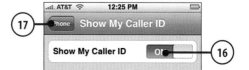

Other Phone Settings

TTY devices enable hearing-impaired people to use a telephone. To use TTY with your iPhone, you need an adapter to connect your iPhone to a TTY device. You also need to turn TTY support on by tapping the TTY OFF button, which becomes ON to show you that TTY support is active.

The Change Voicemail Password command enables you to reset your voice-mail password; this is covered at the end of the chapter.

The SIM (subscriber identity module) PIN setting enables you to associate a personal ID number, or PIN, with the SIM card in iPhone. You can remove this card from your iPhone and install it in other phones that support these cards to use your account with a different phone. If you set a PIN, that PIN is required to use the card in a different phone.

The AT&T Services option (in U.S. markets) enables you to get information about your account. This is covered at the end of this chapter.

Which Network?

When you leave the coverage area for your provider and move into an area that is covered by another provider that supports roaming, your iPhone automatically connects to that network. (In some cases, your provider might send you a text message explaining the change in networks, including information about roaming charges.) While the connection is automatic, you need to be very concerned about roaming charges, which can be significant depending on where you use your iPhone and what your default network is. Before you travel outside of your default network's coverage, check with that network to determine the roaming rates that apply to where you are going. Also, see if there is a discounted roaming plan for that location. If you don't do this before you leave, you might get a nasty surprise when the bill comes in and you see substantial roaming charges.

Making Calls

There are a number of ways to make calls with your iPhone, but after a call is in progress, you can manage it in the same way no matter how you started the call.

Dialing with the Keypad

The most obvious way to make a call
is to dial the number.

1. On the Home screen, tap Phone.
   You move to the Phone screen.

2. If you haven't made a call from
   your current location before,
   check the signal strength to make
   sure you can reach the network.
   As long as you see at least one
   bar, you should be able to make
   and receive calls.

3. Tap the Keypad button. The keypad appears if your iPhone isn't
   already displaying it.

4. Tap numbers on the keypad to
   dial the number you want to call.
   If you dial a number associated
   with one or more contacts, you
   see the contact's name just under
   the number.

5. Tap Call. The iPhone dials the
   number, and the Call screen
   appears.

6. Use the Call screen to manage the
   call; see "Managing In-Process
   Calls" later in this section for the
   details.

Number being dialed

**Name of
contact if
number is
associated
with one**

Dialing with Contacts

As you saw in Chapter 5, "Managing Contacts," iPhone has a complete contact manager so you can store phone numbers for people and organizations. To make a call using a contact, follow these steps.

1. On the Home screen, tap Phone.

2. If you haven't made a call from your current location before, check the signal strength to make sure you can reach the network. As long as you see at least one bar, you should be able to make and receive calls.

3. Tap the Contacts button.

4. Browse the list or use the index.

5. When you see the contact you want to call, tap it. The contact's Info screen appears.

6. Tap the number you want to dial. The iPhone dials the number, and the Call screen appears.

7. Use the Call screen to manage the call; see "Managing In-Process Calls" later in this section for the details.

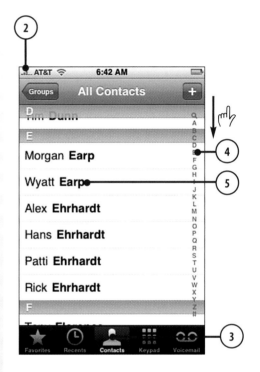

Dialing with Favorites

You can save contacts and phone numbers as favorites to make dialing them even simpler. (You learn how to save favorites in various locations later in this chapter and in Chapter 5.)

1. On the Home screen, tap Phone.

2. If you haven't made a call from your current location before, check the signal strength to make sure you can reach the network. As long as you see at least one bar, you should be able to make and receive calls.

3. Tap the Favorites button. The Favorites screen appears.

4. Browse the list until you see the favorite you want to call.

5. Tap the favorite you want to call. The iPhone dials the number, and the Call screen appears.

6. Use the Call screen to manage the call; see "Managing In-Process Calls" later in this section for the details.

Dialing with Recents

As you make, receive, or miss calls, your iPhone keeps tracks of all the numbers for you. You can use the recent list to make calls.

1. On the Home screen, tap Phone.

2. If you haven't made a call from your current location before, check the signal strength to make sure you can reach the network. As long as you see at least one bar, you should be able to make and receive calls.

3. Tap the Recents button.

4. Tap All to see all calls.

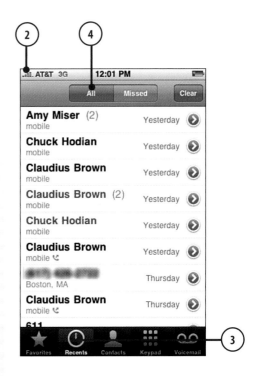

Info for Recents

If you have a contact on your iPhone associated with a phone number, you see the person's name and the label for the number (such as mobile). If you don't have a contact for a number, you see the number itself. If a contact or number has more than one call associated with it, you see the number of recent calls in parentheses next to the name or number. If you initiated a call, you see the receiver icon under the contact's name next to the contact's label.

5. Tap Missed to see only calls you missed.

6. If necessary, browse the list of calls.

7. To call the number associated with a recent call, tap the title of the call, such as a person's name. The iPhone dials the number, and the Call screen appears. Skip to step 11.

8. To get more information about a recent call, tap its Info button. The Info screen appears, labeled with the type of call, such as Outgoing or Missed.

9. Read the information about the call. For example, if the call is related to someone in your Contacts list, you see detailed information for that contact. The number associated with the call is highlighted in red. If there are multiple recent calls, you see information for each call, such as its status (missed, for example).

10. Tap a number on the Info screen. The iPhone dials the number, and the Call screen appears.

11. Use the Call screen to manage the call; see Managing In-Process Calls later in this section for the details.

Going Back

To return to the Recents screen without making a call, tap Recents.

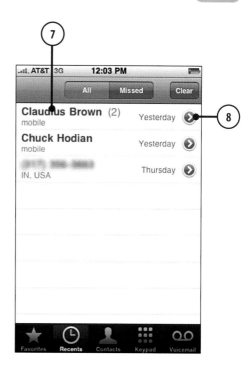

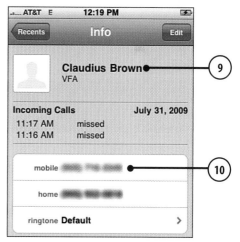

Managing In-Process Calls

When you place a call, there are several ways to manage it. The most obvious is to place your iPhone next to your ear and use your iPhone like any other phone you've ever used. As you place your iPhone next to your head, its screen becomes disabled so you don't accidentally tap onscreen buttons. When you take your iPhone away from your ear, the Call screen appears again, and your iPhone enables its controls.

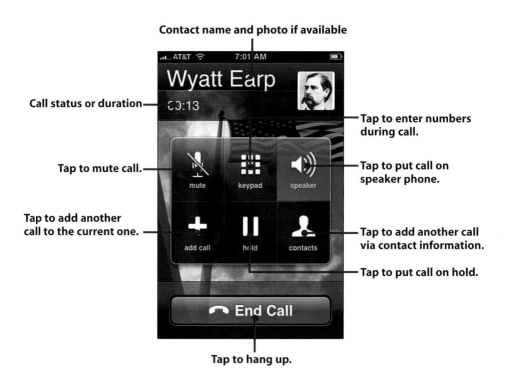

Contact name and photo if available

Call status or duration

Tap to mute call.

Tap to add another call to the current one.

Tap to enter numbers during call.

Tap to put call on speaker phone.

Tap to add another call via contact information.

Tap to put call on hold.

Tap to hang up.

Nobody's Perfect

If your iPhone can't complete the call for some reason, such as not having a strong enough signal, the Call Failed screen appears. Tap Call Back to try again or tap Done to give up. When you tap Done, you return to the screen from which you came.

When you are in a call, press the Volume buttons to increase or decrease its volume. Some of the other things you can do while on a call might not be so obvious, as you'll learn in the next few tasks.

Entering Numbers During a Call

You often need to enter numbers during a call, such as to login to a voice mail system, access an account, and so on.

1. Place a call using any of the methods you've learned so far.

2. Tap the Keypad button.

3. Tap the numbers.

4. When you're done, tap Hide Keypad. You return to the Call screen.

Making Conference Calls

Your iPhone makes it easy to talk to multiple people at the same time. You can have two separate calls going on at any point in time. You can have more calls going on by merging them together.

1. Place a call using any of the methods you've learned so far.

2. Tap add call.

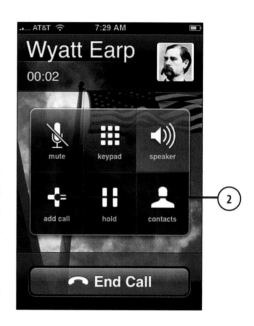

Similar but Different

If you tap contacts instead of add call, you move directly into the Contacts screen. This might save you one screen tap if the person you want to add to the call is in your contacts list.

3. Tap the button you want to use to place the next call. Tap Favorites to call a favorite, tap Recents to use the Recents list, tap Contacts to place the call via contacts, or tap Keypad to dial the number. These work just as they do when you start a new call.

4. Place the call using the option you selected in step 3. Doing so places the first call on hold and moves you back to the Call screen while your iPhone makes the second call. The first call's information appears at the top of the screen, including the word HOLD so that you know the call is on hold. The iPhone displays the second call just below that, and it is currently the active call (marked with the receiver icon).

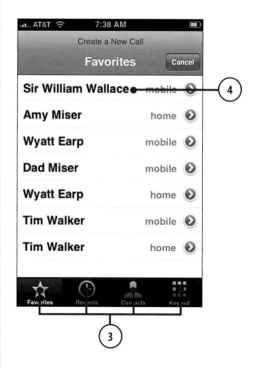

5. Talk to the second person you called; the first remains on hold.

6. To switch to the first call, tap it on the list. This places the second call on hold and moves it to the top of the call list, while the first call becomes active again.

7. To join the calls so all parties can hear each other, tap merge calls. The iPhone combines the two calls, and you see a single entry at the top of the screen to reflect this.

Merging Calls

As you merge calls, your iPhone attempts to display the names of the callers at the top of the Call screen. As the text increases, your iPhone scrolls it so you can read it. Eventually, iPhone gives up and replaces the names with the word Conference.

8. To add another call, repeat steps 2 though 4. Each time you merge calls, the second line becomes free so you can add more calls.

9. To manage a conference call, tap Conference or the names shown at the top of the screen. The Conference screen appears.

10. To speak with one of the callers privately, tap Private. Doing so places the call on hold and returns you to the Call screen showing information about the active call. You can merge the calls again by tapping merge calls.

11. To remove a call from the conference, tap the unlock button. The END CALL button appears.

12. To remove a caller from the call, tap END CALL. The iPhone disconnects the caller from the conference call. You return to the Call screen and see information about the active call.

13. To move back to the Call screen, tap Back. You move to the Call screen and can continue working with the call, such as adding more people to it.

Swap 'em Out

You can also swap calls by tapping the Swap button.

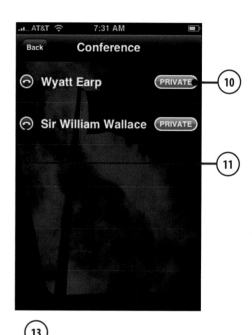

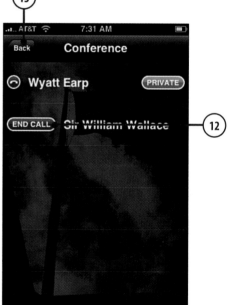

14. To end the call for all callers, tap End Call.

Time Multiplier

When you have multiple calls combined into one, the minutes for each call continue to count individually. So if you've joined three people into one call, each minute of the call counts as three minutes against your calling plan.

Receiving Calls

Receiving calls on your iPhone enables you to access the same great tools you can use when you make calls, plus a few more for good measure.

Answering Calls

When your iPhone rings, it's time to answer the call—or not. If you configured the ringer to ring, you hear your general ringtone or one associated with the caller when a call comes in. If vibrate is turned on, your iPhone vibrates whether the ringer is on or not. And if those two ways aren't enough, a message appears on iPhone's screen to show you information about the incoming call. If the number is in your contacts, you see the contact with which the number is associated, the label for the number, and the contact's image if there is one. If the number isn't in your contacts, you see the number only.

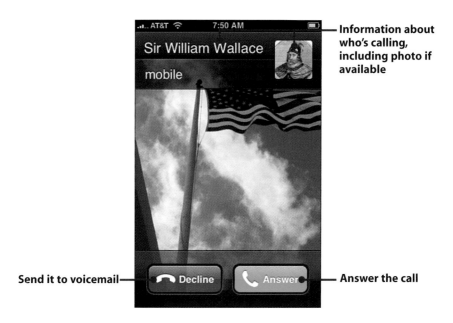

Information about who's calling, including photo if available

Send it to voicemail

Answer the call

If your iPhone is locked when a call comes in, drag the slider to the right to answer it.

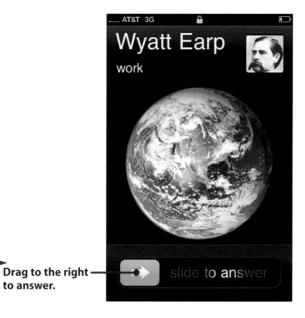

Drag to the right to answer.

Earbuds

If you are wearing your earbuds when a call comes in, press the center part of the switch on the right earbud cable to answer the call. Press it again to hang up. If you have an iPhone 3GS, you can press the upper-part or lower-part of the switch to change a call's volume while it is active.

When you receive a call, you have the following options:

- **Answer**   Tap Answer (if the iPhone is unlocked) or drag the slider to the right (if the iPhone is locked) to take the call. You move to the Call screen and can work with the call like one you placed. For example, you can add a call, merge calls, place the call on hold, end the call, and so on.

- **Decline**   If you tap Decline (when the iPhone is unlocked), the iPhone immediately routes the call to voicemail. You can also decline a call by quickly tapping the Sleep/Wake button twice.

- **Silence the ringer**   To silence the ringer without sending the call to voicemail, tap the Sleep/Wake button or tap either the upper or lower part of the Volume button. The call continues to come in, and you can answer it even though you shut the ringer off.

Silencio!

To mute your iPhone's ringer, slide the Mute switch located above the Volume switch toward the back so the red dot appears. The Mute icon (a bell with a slash through it) appears on the screen to let you know you turned the ringer off. To turn it back on again, slide the switch forward. The bell icon appears on the screen to show you the ringer is active again. To set the ringer's volume, use the Volume controls when you aren't in a call and aren't listening to an iPod function.

Answering Calls When You're Already on a Call

As you saw earlier, your iPhone can manage multiple calls at the same time. If you are on a call and another call comes in, you have a number of ways to respond.

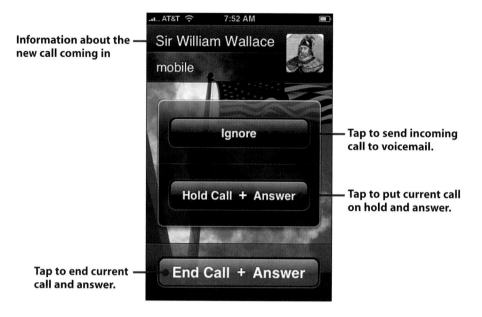

Information about the new call coming in

Tap to send incoming call to voicemail.

Tap to put current call on hold and answer.

Tap to end current call and answer.

- **Decline**   Tap Ignore to send the incoming call directly to voicemail.

- **Place the first call on hold and answer the second**   Tap Hold Call + Answer to place the current call on hold and answer the second one. After you do this, you can manage the two calls just as when you called two numbers from your iPhone. For example, you can place the second call on hold and move back to the first one, merge the calls, add more calls, and so on.

- **End the first call and answer the second**   Tap End Call + Answer to terminate the active call and answer the incoming call.

Auto-Mute

If you are listening to music or video when a call comes in, the iPod function automatically pauses. When the call ends, the music or video picks up right where it left off.

Managing Calls

You've already learned most of what you need to know to use your iPhone's cell phone functions. In the following sections, you learn the rest.

>>>*step-by-step*

Clearing Recent Calls

Earlier, you learned about the Recents tool that tracks call activity on your iPhone. As you read, this list shows both completed and missed calls; you can view all calls by tapping the All tab or only missed calls by tapping Missed. Missed calls are always in red. You also saw how you can get more detail about a call, whether it was missed or made.

Over time, you'll build a large list, which you can easily clear.

1. Tap Phone.

2. Tap Recents.

3. To clear the list, tap Clear.

4. Tap Clear All Recents. The Recents list is reset.

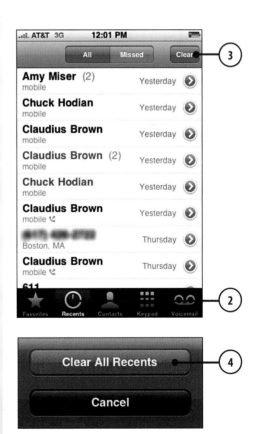

Adding Caller Information to Favorites

Earlier you learned how simple it is to place calls to someone on your favorites list. There are a number of ways to add people to this list, including adding someone who has called you.

1. Move to the Recents list.

2. Tap the Info button for the person you want to add to your favorites list. The Info screen appears. If the number is associated with a contact, you see that contact's information.

3. Scroll to the bottom of the screen.

4. Tap Add to Favorites. If the person has multiple numbers associated with his contact information, you see each available number. Numbers that are already set as favorites are marked with a blue star.

5. Tap the number you want to add as a favorite. You return to the Info screen, and the number is marked with a blue star to show that it is on your favorites list.

6. Repeat step 5 if you want to add the contact's other numbers to the favorites list. If all the numbers are assigned as favorites, the Add to Favorites button disappears.

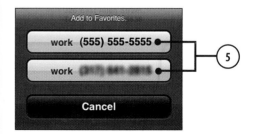

Using iPhone's Headset for Calls

Your iPhone includes earbud headset with a microphone on one of its cords. The mic includes a button in the center of the switch on the right side of the earbud's cable that you can use to do the following:

- **Answer**   Press the mic button once to answer a call.

- **End a call**   Press the mic button while you are on a call to end it.

- **Decline a call**   Press and hold the mic button for about two seconds. Two beeps sound when you release the button to let you know that your iPhone sent the call to voicemail.

- **Put a current call on hold and switch to an incoming call**   Press the mic button once and then tap again.

- **End a current call on hold and switch to an incoming call**   Press the mic button once and hold for about two seconds. Release the button and you hear two beeps to let you know that you ended the first call. The incoming call is ready for you.

- **Activate Voice Control (3GS only)**   Press and hold the mic button until you hear the Voice Control chime (see the next section).

Ringing

When you have headphones plugged into your iPhone and you receive a call, the ringtone plays on both the iPhone's speaker (unless the ringer is muted of course) and the headphones.

Using Voice Control (iPhone 3GS Only)

If you have an iPhone 3GS, you can speak commands to it to make phone calls. This is especially useful to keep your hands free, for such minor things as driving a car.

1. To activate Voice Control, press and hold the Home button or the mic button on the headset until you hear the Voice Control chime or see the Voice Control screen.

2. To call someone in your contacts, say, "Call *name*" or "Dial *name*," where *name* is the name of the person you want to call. If you have a specific number you want to call, include that as in "Call *name label*," where *label* is the label associated with the number, such as mobile or home.

3. If there is more than one contact with the name you spoke in step 2 (such as the same first name), the iPhone prompts you to say the full name of the contact you want to call; speak the contact's full name.

4. If the contact has more than one number and you didn't specify the one you want to use, you hear the audible message stating that there are multiple numbers and it starts speaking the labels of the numbers for the contact, such as mobile, work, home, and so on; speak the label of the number you want to call, such as mobile or work.

5. To dial a number not in your contacts, say "Dial *number*," where *number* is the number you want to dial.

6. Manage the call using the tools you learned about earlier. (After the call is underway, the iPhone exits Voice Control.)

Stop It!
If the iPhone starts to dial the wrong number, say "wrong," "no," "not that one," or even "nope" to stop the action.

Using Visual Voicemail

Visual voicemail just might be the best of your iPhone's many great features. No more wading through long, uninteresting voicemails to get to one in which you are interested. You simply jump to the message you want to hear. And because voicemails are stored on your iPhone, you don't need to log in to hear them. If that isn't enough for you, you can also jump to any point within a voicemail to hear just that part.

Recording a Greeting

The first time you access voicemail, you are prompted to record a voice-mail greeting. Follow the onscreen instructions to do so. You can also record a new greeting at any time.

1. Move to the Phone screen and tap Voicemail.

2. Tap Greeting.

3. To use a default greeting that provides only the iPhone's phone number, tap default.

4. To record a custom greeting, tap Custom.

5. Tap Record. The Recording Personal message appears, and recording begins.

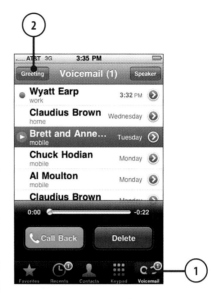

6. Speak your greeting. As you record your message, monitor the sound level using the gauge at the bottom of the screen. You should attempt to keep the volume level of your greeting at the mid-point of the gauge.

Missing Password

If something happens to the password stored on your iPhone for your voicemail, such as if you restore iPhone, you are prompted to enter your password before you can access your voicemail. Do so at the prompt and tap OK. The iPhone logs you in to voicemail, and you won't have to enter your password for a second time unless something happens to it again.

7. When you're done, tap Stop. The Play button becomes active.

8. Tap Play to hear your greeting.

9. If you aren't satisfied, repeat steps 5 through 8 to record a new message. You can only replace a recorded greeting; you can't change it.

10. When you are happy with your greeting, tap Save. The iPhone saves the greeting as the active greeting and returns you to the Voicemail screen.

Change Greeting

To switch between the default and the current custom greeting, move to the Greeting screen, tap the greeting you want to use (which is marked with a check mark), and tap Save.

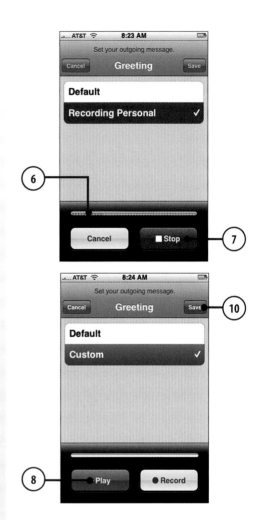

Listening to and Managing Voicemails

Unless you turned off the voicemail sound, you hear a tone each time a caller leaves a voicemail for you. In the Voicemail button on the Phone screen, you also see the number of new voicemails you have. (New is defined as those voicemails to which you haven't listened.)

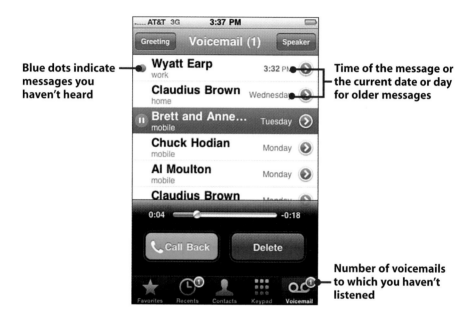

Blue dots indicate messages you haven't heard

Time of the message or the current date or day for older messages

Number of voicemails to which you haven't listened

If you receive a voicemail while your iPhone is locked, you see a message on the screen alerting you that your iPhone received a voicemail. (It also indicates a missed call, which is always the case when a call ends up in the voicemail.) Drag the slider to the right to jump to the Voicemail screen so you can work with the message.

Contacts or Numbers?

Like phone calls, if there is a contact associated with a number from which you've received a voicemail, you see the contact's name associated with the message. If there isn't a contact for the number, you see the number only.

New voicemail has been left

Finding and Listening to Voicemails

1. Move to the Phone screen and tap Voicemail. You see the Voicemail screen. The list contains each voicemail you've received.

2. Browse the list of voicemails.

3. To listen to a new voicemail, tap it. It becomes highlighted to let you know that it is the active voice-mail message and starts to play.

4. To listen to a message you have listened to before, tap the mes-sage and then tap the Play but-ton. It begins to play.

5. To hear the message on your iPhone's speaker, tap Speaker.

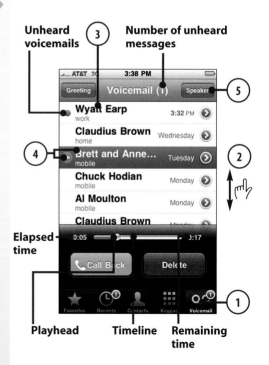

Unheard voicemails

Number of unheard messages

Elapsed time

Playhead

Timeline

Remaining time

6. To pause a message, tap its Pause button.

Moving Ahead or Behind

You can also drag the Playhead while a message is playing to rewind or fast-forward it. This is also helpful when you want to listen to specific information without hearing the whole message again.

7. To move to a specific point in a message, drag the Playhead to the point at which you want to listen.

8. Tap the Play button next to the voicemail you want to hear. The message plays from the Playhead's location.

9. To get more information about a message, tap its Info button. The Info screen appears. If the person who left the message is on your contacts list, you see her contact information. The number associated with the message is highlighted in blue.

10. To return to the Voicemail screen, tap Voicemail.

More than Just Information Only

Much of the information on the Info screen is active, meaning that you can tap it to do something. For example, to call a listed number, tap it. To send an email, tap an email address. To visit a website, tap its URL.

Deleting Voicemails

1. Move to the Voicemail screen.

2. Tap to select the message you want to delete.

3. Tap Delete. The iPhone deletes the message, the Deleted Messages option appears (the first time you delete a message), and the next unheard message is selected so it is ready for you to play (which enables you to quickly get through your new messages).

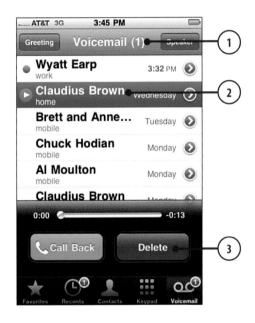

Listening to and Managing Deleted Voicemails

1. Move to the Voicemail screen.

2. Scroll down the screen until you see the Deleted Message options.

3. Tap Deleted Messages.

4. Listen to any deleted messages just as you do on the Voicemail screen.

5. To move a message back to the Voicemail screen, select it.

6. Tap Undelete. The iPhone restores the message to the Voicemail screen.

7. To remove all deleted messages permanently, tap Clear All.

8. Tap Clear All at the prompt. The iPhone erases the deleted messages and returns you to the Deleted screen.

9. To return to the Voicemail screen, tap Voicemail.

What's Missed

In case you're wondering, your iPhone considers any call you didn't answer as a missed call. So if someone calls and leaves a message, that call is included in the counts of both missed calls and new voicemails.

Returning Calls

1. Move to the Voicemail screen.

2. Tap the message for which you want to return a call.

3. Tap Call Back. The number associated with the message is called.

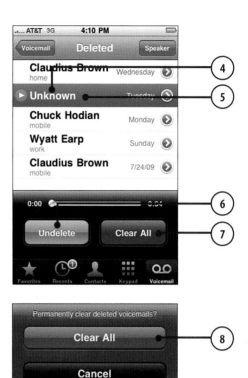

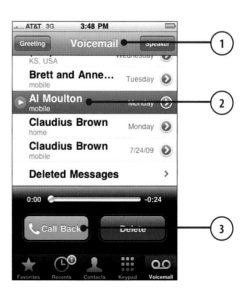

Changing Your Voicemail Password

1. Move to the Settings screen.

2. Tap Phone.

3. Tap Change Voicemail Password. The Password screen appears.

4. Enter your current password.

5. Tap Done.

6. Enter the new password.

7. Tap Done. The screen refreshes and prompts you to re-enter the new password.

8. Re-enter the new password.

9. Tap Done. The iPhone saves the new password and returns you to the Phone screen.

Lost/Forgot Your Password?

If you have to restore your iPhone or it loses your voicemail password for some reason and you can't remember the password, you need to get the password reset to access your voicemail on the iPhone. For most cell phone providers, this involves calling the customer support number and accessing an automated system that sends a new password to you via a text message. In the United States, the provider is AT&T and can be reached by calling 611 on the iPhone. Whatever provider you use, it's a good idea to know how to reset your voicemail password just in case.

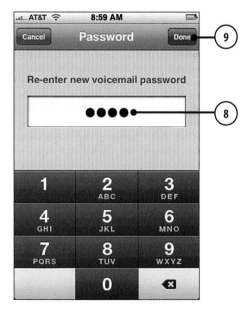

Tap to configure email accounts and settings.

Tap to use email.

In this chapter, you explore all the email functionality that an iPhone has to offer. Topics include the following:

→ Configuring email accounts on an iPhone
→ Configuring general email settings
→ Working with email

Emailing

For most of us, email is an important way we communicate with others, both in our professional and personal lives. Fortunately, the iPhone has great email tools so you can work with email no matter where you are. (Of course, you need to be connected to the Internet through a Wi-Fi connection to send or receive email.) You can read, send, reply, and do all the other email actions you might expect from the comfort and convenience of your iPhone.

You can configure multiple email accounts on an iPhone so you can access all of them from your iPhone. Even better, you can sync an iPhone's email accounts with your computers so you access the same email from multiple devices.

Configuring Email Accounts on an iPhone

Before you can start using an iPhone for email, you have to configure the email accounts you want to access with it. The iPhone supports a number of standard email services including MobileMe, Exchange (by far the most widely used email system in business), Gmail, Yahoo! Mail, and AOL. You can also configure any email account that uses POP (Post Office Protocol—and no, I'm not making that up) or IMAP (Internet Message Access Protocol); this is good because almost all email accounts provided through ISPs (Internet service providers) use one of these two formats.

There are many ways to configure email accounts on an iPhone, including the following:

- **Using MobileMe**   You can configure a MobileMe account on an iPhone with just a few simple steps. When you set up a MobileMe account on an iPhone, you also configure email access. See Chapter 4, "Configuring and Synchronizing Information on an iPhone," to learn how to set up a MobileMe account on an iPhone.

- **Syncing email accounts on computers**   You can configure email accounts on an iPhone by syncing it with your email accounts on both Windows PCs and Macs. This process is similar to moving other information onto an iPhone and is also covered in detail in Chapter 4.

- **Configuring Gmail, Yahoo! Mail, or AOL email accounts manually**   An iPhone is designed to work with these email accounts and has specific account configuration tools for them. In the next section, you learn how easy it is to set up one of these accounts on your iPhone.

- **Configuring an Exchange email account manually**   Microsoft's Exchange email system is the most widely used email in business. Fortunately (or unfortunately, depending on your point of view), you can configure an iPhone to work with your Exchange email account, so you have access to work-related email. (Hey, an iPhone can't be all fun and games!)

- **Configuring other email accounts manually**   If you have an account that isn't configured on a computer and isn't one of those listed in the previous bullets, you can add it to an iPhone manually with just a bit more work.

After you have created email accounts on an iPhone, you can do some advanced configuration to tweak the way they work.

>>>*step-by-step*

Configuring Gmail, Yahoo! Mail, or AOL Email Accounts on an iPhone Manually

An iPhone is designed to work easily with email accounts from these providers. Although the details vary slightly between these types of accounts, the following steps (which happen to show a Gmail account being configured) show you how to configure any of these accounts.

1. On the Home screen, tap Settings.

2. Scroll down the screen.

3. Tap Mail, Contacts, Calendars.

4. Tap Add Account.

5. Tap the kind of account you want to configure. The rest of the steps are for a Gmail account, but configuring Yahoo! Mail or AOL accounts is similar.

Gmail POPs Is for Me

If you don't have a Gmail account, you can sign up for a free one at mail.google.com. When you set up the account, make sure that you select the POP option. If you already have an account, log in to your Google account, choose Gmail settings, click the Forwarding and POP tab, choose the Enable POP for all mail option, and save your changes. If your Gmail account is not POP-enabled, it won't work on an iPhone.

6. Enter your name.

7. Enter your Gmail email address.

8. Enter your Gmail account password.

9. Change the default description, which is your email address, if you want to. This description appears on various lists of accounts.

10. Tap Save. Your account information is verified. When that process is complete, you see the Mail, Contacts, Calendars screen, which shows the account you configured on the Accounts list. The account is ready to use.

11. If you want to perform advanced configuration of the account, refer to "Performing Advanced Configuration of Email Accounts on an iPhone," later in this chapter.

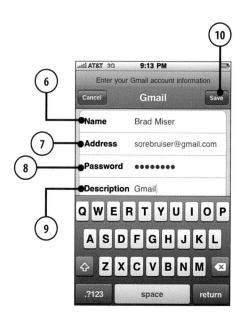

Bonus Task

Please go to this book's website at www.informit.com/title/9780789742315 and click the Downloads tab to find two additional tasks titled, "Managing Email Accounts," and "Deleting Email Accounts."

Email accounts configured on this iPhone

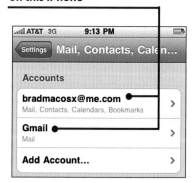

Configuring Exchange Email Accounts on an iPhone Manually

Microsoft Exchange is the most widely used system for corporate email. The iPhone's email application is compatible with Exchange, which is good news indeed.

There are two ways to connect an iPhone to an Exchange account (which can include email, calendar, and contacts). One is to go through an Outlook Web Access (OWA) service; this service enables you to access your Exchange account over the web. The good news about this is you don't need any support from your organization's IT department to configure an iPhone to access your Exchange account. The other option is for your organization's Exchange system to be configured to support iPhone email access directly; this does require support from the IT department. Some additional configuration work (and slight expense) is needed by the IT department to enable this.

If you already know you can access your Exchange account through OWA, you're ready to configure your Exchange account on an iPhone, and you can move ahead with these steps. If you aren't sure, check with your IT department to see if OWA is supported. If it is, use these steps to configure it on an iPhone. If OWA isn't supported, find out if the Exchange system has been configured to support iPhones and iPod touches. If it has, get the configuration information you need from your IT department and use that to configure the Exchange account on your iPhone. You do this similar to other types of accounts, mostly by providing the information related to your account in the appropriate locations.

>>>*step-by-step*

The following steps show you how to configure an Exchange account via OWA.

1. On the Home screen, tap Settings.

2. Scroll down the screen.

3. Tap Mail, Contacts, Calendars.

4. Tap Add Account.
5. Tap Microsoft Exchange.
6. Enter your email address.
7. Enter your domain.
8. Enter your username.

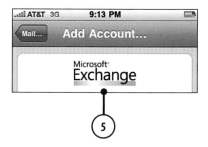

9. Scroll down the screen and enter your password.

10. Enter a description of the account. (The default is your email address.)

11. Tap Next. The account information is verified, and you see the Exchange screen with your information and some additional fields. (If the security certificate or other information can't be verified, just tap Accept anyway.)

12. Enter the server address. If you are using OWA, this might be something like owa.yourcompany.com. You don't enter the https:// before the address you use to move to the server via a web browser or the /exchange after that address. If you're not using OWA, enter the address provided by your IT department.

13. Tap Next. The account information is verified, and you see the controls that enable you to determine which information is synced on an iPhone.

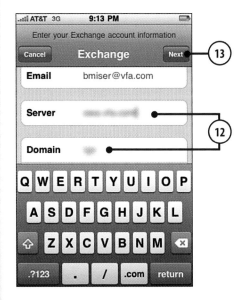

14. Tap ON for any of the information you don't want to be moved onto an iPhone; its status becomes OFF to show you it won't be moved onto the iPhone. If ON is shown, that information is moved onto the iPhone.

15. Tap Done. The sync is configured, and you move back to the Mail, Contacts, Calendars screen where you see your Exchange account. Under the account description, you see the information that is being synced with the account, such as Mail or Calendars.

16. Tap your Exchange account.

17. Tap Mail Days to Sync.

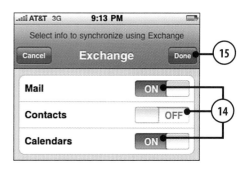

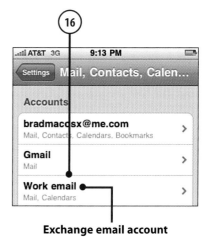

Exchange email account

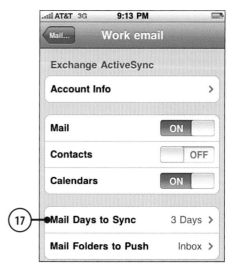

18. Tap the amount of time over which Exchange information should be synced. For example, to have one week of Exchange information on an iPhone, tap 1 Week.

19. Tap the Return button, which is labeled with your email account's description.

Problems Sending Mail?

You might have trouble sending email from some kinds of email accounts provided by an ISP when you are using a network that isn't provided by that ISP. For example, many email accounts provided by an ISP (such as a cable company) require that any mail being sent come from the IP address associated with that account, which means you can only send mail when you are accessing the Internet from a network with an IP address that the ISP's network recognizes (such as your home network). This won't be the case when you are out and about with an iPhone using a Wi-Fi network, so you can't send email from these accounts on an iPhone. You can still receive email for these accounts, but you can't send it.

There are several possible solutions. The easiest one is to select an account from which you can send email when you are outside of your network. (How to do this is explained later in this chapter.) In some cases, you can configure email to be sent by using a specific port. (You usually have to search the ISP's help information to find out what this is.) To do this, you need to use the Advanced configuration settings for the email account with which you are having trouble sending email; this is explained in the following section. The third option is to configure a different email account on an SMTP server (Simple Mail Transfer Protocol)—the server that sends email—that you can send email from for the account that you can't send mail from; use the information in the "Performing Advanced Configuration of Email Accounts on an iPhone" task to do this. Finally, you can enable the SMTP server that your iPhone provider includes if it does provide one; this is also covered in the next section.

Performing Advanced Configuration of Email Accounts on an iPhone

Different kinds of email accounts have different sets of advanced configuration options, but you access those options in a similar way for all accounts. The following steps show details for a MobileMe account. To do advanced configuration of other accounts, you use similar steps, but the details for the specific accounts you are configuring will differ.

1. Move to the Mail, Contacts, Calendars screen.

2. Tap the email account you want to configure.

3. Tap Account Info.

4. Tap Advanced.

5. Tap Drafts Mailbox.

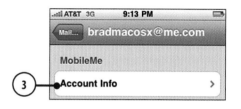

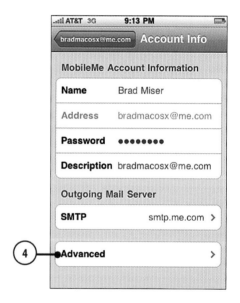

6. To have drafts of your emails stored on the iPhone, tap Drafts in the On My iPhone section, or to have them stored on the server, tap Inbox or one of the other folders in the On the Server section. The advantage of storing drafts on the server is you can work on them from any location that can access your MobileMe account, such as a computer. If you save them on an iPhone, you can only work on them using the iPhone.

7. Tap Advanced.

8. Using the information in steps 6 and 7, set the location where your sent email is stored and where deleted messages are stored. The options are the same as for draft messages.

9. Tap Remove.

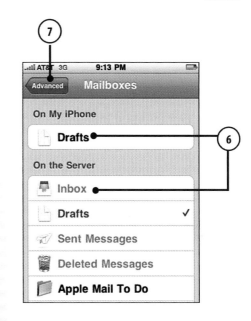

10. Choose when you want deleted email to be removed from the server. The longer the timeframe, the longer storage space on the server is used for deleted messages, but the longer you will be able to recover those messages. In most cases, the amount of space you have on the email server associated with the email account is limited, so it's better not to store messages you have deleted there for a long period of time.

11. Tap Advanced.

12. Scroll down so you see the Incoming Settings section.

13. If you should ever need to change any of the settings that enable you to retrieve email for the account, use the fields in the Incoming Settings section to do so. It is unlikely you will need to change these settings, assuming you synced the account with a computer or were careful when you first configured it. If you ever do change the settings, you need to make sure they match the incoming mail server information provided for the email account by the ISP.

14. Tap Account Info.

15. Tap SMTP. You move to the SMTP screen for the account. Here, you see all the SMTP servers for the various email accounts configured on your iPhone. At the top of the screen is the primary server, which is the one that iPhone always tries first when you send email from the account you are working with. The Other SMTP Servers list shows other servers that are configured. If a server's status is On, the iPhone will attempt to send email via that server if the primary fails. It's useful if you have at least two SMTP servers On for each email account.

16. If you need to enable or disable the primary server, tap it.

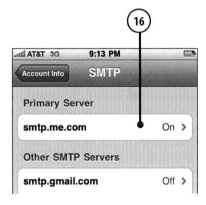

17. To turn the server off for the account, tap ON; the status becomes OFF, and that server will not be used to send email from the account.

18. Tap SMTP.

19. To configure another SMTP server for the account, tap it on the Other SMTP Servers list.

20. To disable the server for the account, tap ON so the status becomes OFF. That server won't be used when sending email through the primary account fails. To enable the server, tap OFF, so the status becomes ON. When sending messages through the primary server fails, the enabled server will be tried.

21. Tap SMTP.

22. Enable or disable other STMP servers.

23. To add a new SMTP server, tap Add Server.

24. Configure the server with the Add Server screen.

Changing SMTP Server Settings

If the fields for an SMTP server are disabled, it means the server is the primary for at least one of your email accounts, and so you can't change it from the current one. To make changes to that server, move to the Advanced screen for the email account for which it is the primary SMTP server and use its tools to make the changes to the server settings.

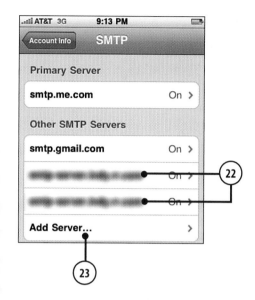

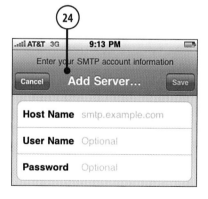

Configuring General Email Settings

There are several settings you use to configure how your iPhone handles your email.

Configuring How Email Is Retrieved

There are several ways email is retrieved on an iPhone. Using Push, email is automatically pushed from the email server onto an iPhone. Not all email accounts support push (MobileMe and Exchange accounts do), but its benefit is that email on an iPhone is always in sync with the email server, so you always have your most current email available to you. The downside is that pushing email to an iPhone consumes more battery power because of the near constant activity. An iPhone can also fetch email, which means that it contacts the server at defined intervals to get email. This approach doesn't retrieve email as fast as pushing, but it does use much less battery power. You can set an iPhone to fetch email at specific intervals, or you can fetch email manually.

>>>*step-by-step*

1. Move to the Mail, Contacts, Calendars screen.

2. Tap Fetch New Data.

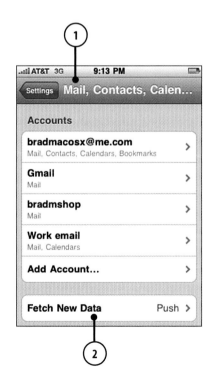

3. To enable email to be pushed to an iPhone, ensure the Push status is ON (if it isn't, tap OFF to turn it on); or to disable push to extend battery life, tap ON so the status becomes OFF.

4. Tap the amount of time when you want an iPhone to fetch email when Push is OFF and for those accounts that don't support pushing email to your iPhone; tap Manually if you want to only check for email manually for fetch accounts or when Push is OFF.

5. Scroll down the screen.

6. Tap Advanced. You see a list of all your active email accounts. Next to each account, you see if it is configured to use Push, Fetch, or Manual.

7. To change how an account gets email or other information, tap it. You see the account's screen. The options on this screen depends on the kind of account it is. You always have Fetch and Manual; you see Push only for email accounts that support it.

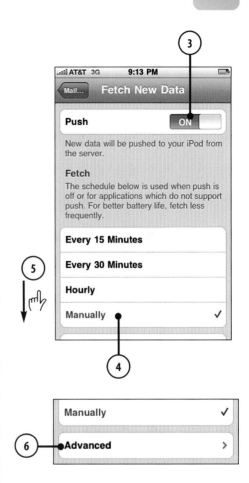

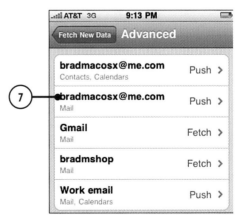

8. Tap the option you want to use for the account: Push, Fetch, or Manual. If you choose Manual, information is retrieved only when you manually start the process, regardless of the general Fetch schedule set on the Fetch New Data screen. If you selected Manually in step 4, you have to manually retrieve email even if you select Fetch on this screen.

9. Tap Advanced.

10. Repeat steps 7 through 9 for each account.

11. Tap Fetch New Data.

Dual Personality

MobileMe accounts are listed twice. One instance is for just email and is labeled Mail on the list. The other listing is for contacts and calendars. You can configure how new data is retrieved for each of these independently.

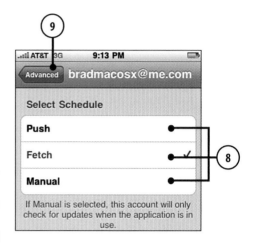

Configuring Global Email Settings

Your iPhone includes a number of settings that affect all your email accounts. You can also set preferences for specific email accounts, as you learn later in this chapter.

1. Move to the Mail, Contacts, Calendars screen.

2. Scroll down until you see the Mail section.

3. Tap Show.

4. Tap the number of recent messages you want an iPhone to display in the email application.

5. Tap Mail.

6. Tap Preview.

7. Tap the number of lines you want an iPhone to display for each email when you view the inbox.

8. Tap Mail.

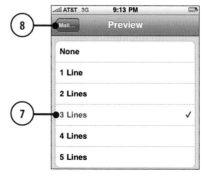

9. Tap Minimum Font Size.

10. Tap the smallest font size you want the iPhone to use for email. The larger the size, the easier to read, but the less information fits on a single screen.

11. Tap Mail.

12. Tap Show To/Cc Label to always see the To and Cc labels in email headers.

13. If you don't want to confirm your action when you delete messages, ensure that Ask Before Deleting is OFF. (If it shows ON, tap it so its status becomes OFF.)

14. If you always want images that are not part of the message to be loaded into a message when you read it, ensure Load Remote Images is ON. If you disable this, you can manually load images in a message. If you receive a lot of spam, you should disable this so you won't see images in which you might not be interested.

15. If you want to receive a blind copy of each email you send, tap Always Bcc Myself OFF. Its status becomes ON, and each time you send a message, you also receive a copy of it, but your address is not shown to the message's other recipients.

16. Tap Signature.

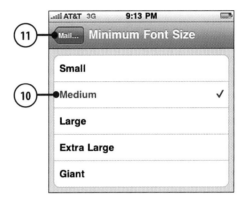

17. Enter the signature you want to append to each message you send. If you don't want an automatic signature, delete all the text on the screen.

18. Tap Mail.

19. Tap Default Account.

20. Tap the account you want to be your default. The default account appears at the top of list and is used as the From address for emails you send. (You can change it on messages when you send them.) It is also the one used when you send photos, YouTube videos, and so on.

21. Tap Mail. Now enable or disable email sounds.

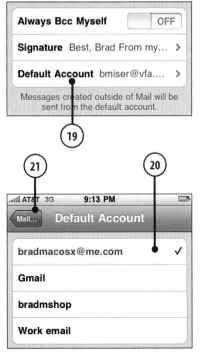

22. Tap Settings.

23. Tap Sounds.

24. To hear a sound when you receive new mail, make sure that the ON status for New Mail is shown; tap ON to turn the new mail sound off if you don't want to be notified when you receive messages.

25. To hear a sound when mail is sent, make sure that the ON status for Sent Mail is displayed; tap ON to turn the sent mail sound off if you don't want to hear this sound.

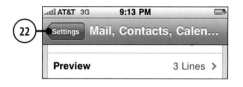

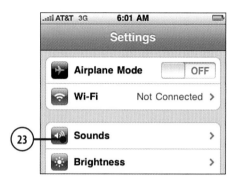

Working with Email

With your email accounts and settings configured, you're ready to start using your iPhone for email. When you move to the Home screen, you see the number of new email messages you have in the Mail button; tap the button to move to your email. Even if you don't have any new email, the Mail button still leads you to an iPhone's email application.

>>>step-by-step

Receiving and Reading Email

The iPhone's Mail application enables you to receive and read email for all the active email accounts configured on it.

1. On the Home screen, tap Mail. The Mail application opens, and you move to the last screen you used. If that isn't the Accounts screen, tap the return button in the upper-left corner of the screen until you reach the Accounts screen.

   You've got mail (email that is).

   Skip to step 3 if you have only one email account configured on an iPhone. You know this applies to you if you don't have an Accounts screen (that shows multiple email accounts) because you always move directly to your email account's screen when you tap the Mail button. Of course, if you only have or have configured only one email account on the iPhone, you won't see the Accounts screen.

   Next to each account on the Accounts screen, you see the number of new emails received in that account.

2. To read messages, tap the account that contains messages you want to read. You move to that account's screen; the name of the account is the account's description, which defaults to the email address. You see all the folders within that account. The number and type of folders you see depends on the type of account it is.

Loading More Messages

If more messages are available than are downloaded, tap the Load More Messages link. The additional messages download to the inbox you are viewing.

3. Tap Inbox. The inbox for that account opens, and you see all the messages it contains. Unread messages are marked with a blue dot. A paperclip icon indicates that a message includes an attachment. At the bottom of the screen, you see when the inbox was last updated, meaning the last time messages were retrieved.

4. Scroll up or down the screen to browse all the messages.

5. To read a message, tap it. The message screen appears. As soon as you open a message's screen, it's marked as read, and the email counter reduces by one. At the top of the screen, you see the number of the message and the total in the inbox (such as 2 of 10). Just below that is the address information, including who the message is from and who it was sent to. Under that, you see the message's subject along with time and date it was sent. Under that, you see the body of the message. If the message has an attachment, you see it at the bottom of the screen.

To

If you enabled the Show To/Cc Label setting, you see a small "To" or "Cc" next to each message's title where the email address in the message's To or Cc field is associated with one of the email addresses configured on your iPhone. When one of those isn't true, such as when you are part of distribution list, you won't see these labels.

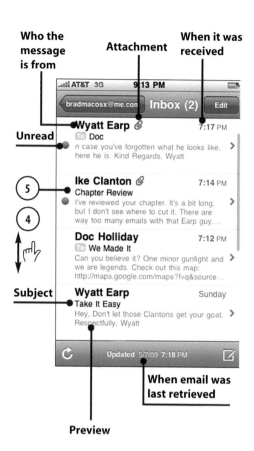

Who the message is from

Attachment

When it was received

Unread

5

4

Subject

Preview

When email was last retrieved

6. Unpinch your fingers on the message to zoom in. (If you double-tap on a email message, the iPhone assumes you want to copy some text and highlights the word on which you tapped.)

See More Address Info?

Tap the Details link located just under the down arrow at the top of the email screen to show more address information, such as the To and Cc sections. Tap Hide to hide that information again.

7. Drag the message around the screen to read it. To scroll up or down, left or right, just drag your finger around the screen.

8. Pinch your fingers or double-tap to zoom out.

Back in Time

To change the status of a message back to Unread, expand the header by clicking Details and tap Mark as Unread. The message is marked with blue dot again as if you'd never read it.

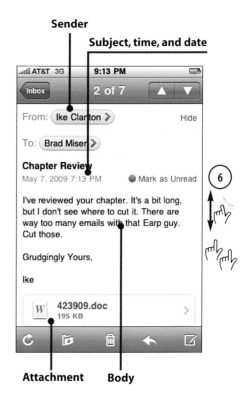

Sender
Subject, time, and date
Attachment   Body

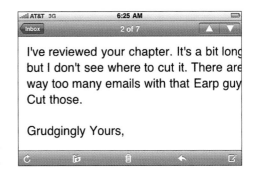

9. Rotate the iPhone 90 degrees to change its orientation.

Photos Attached

If the message includes a photo, an iPhone displays the photo in the body of the email message. You can zoom in (by unpinching) or out (by pinching or double-tapping) and scroll (by dragging) to view it just as you can with text.

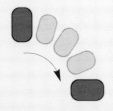

10. Rotate the iPhone again to return to the previous orientation.

11. To view a message's attachment, tap it. If the iPhone can display files of its type, the file downloads to the iPhone, and you see the file on a screen with the file's title as its name. If an iPhone can't display the attachment, you'll just see an icon for the attachment with no button to view it.

12. Scroll the document by dragging your finger up, down, left, or right on the screen.

13. Unpinch or double-tap to zoom in. (When you double-tap, the zoom causes the column of text to fill the screen.)

14. Pinch or double-tap to zoom out.

15. Tap Message. You move back to the message screen.

16. To view information for an email address, such as who sent the message, tap it. The Info screen appears; its title tells you how the person relates to the message. For example, if you tapped the email address in the From field, the screen title is From. If the person is on your Contacts list, you see his contact information. If not, you see as much information as the iPhone can determine based on the email address.

17. Tap Message. You move back to the email.

HTML Email

Mail can receive HTML email that behaves like a webpage. When you tap a link (usually blue text, but can also be photos and other graphics) in such an email, Safari opens and takes you to the link's source. You then use Safari to view the webpage. See Chapter 10, "Surfing the Web," for information about Safari.

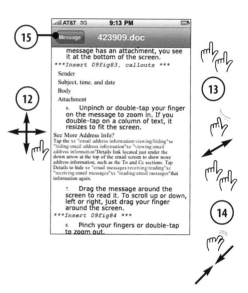

18. To read the next message in the inbox, tap the down arrow. The next message in the Inbox list replaces the current one.

19. To move to a previous message in the inbox, tap the up arrow.

20. To move back to the inbox, tap Inbox.

Large Messages

Some emails, especially HTML messages, are large and don't immediately download to the iPhone in their entirety. When you open a large message, you see that the entire message has not been downloaded. Tap the link to download the rest of it.

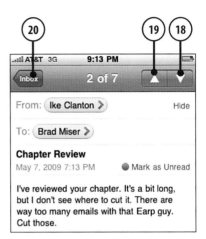

Sending Email

You can send email from any of your accounts.

1. Tap the New Mail button on any Mail screen. The New Message screen appears. If you tap the New Mail button while you are on the Accounts screen, the From address is the account from which you most recently sent or created a message; otherwise, the From address is the email account you are working with. Your signature is placed at the bottom of the message.

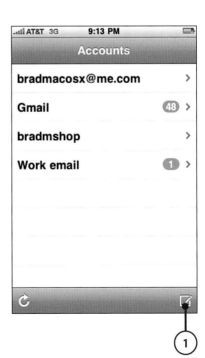

2. To type a recipient's email address, tap the To field and type in the address. As you type, an iPhone attempts to find matching addresses in your Contacts list or in emails you've sent or received and displays the matches it finds. To select one of those addresses, tap it, and the iPhone enters the rest of the address for you. Or just keep entering information until the address is complete.

3. To address the email using contacts, tap the Add button. The All Contacts screen appears.

4. Use the All Contacts screen to find and select the contact to which you want to address the message. (See Chapter 5, "Managing Contacts," for the details about working with contacts.) When you tap a contact with one email address, that address is pasted into the To field, and you return to the New Message window. When you tap a contact with more than one email address, you move to the Info screen; tap the address to which you want to send the message.

5. Repeat steps 2 through 4 to add all the recipients to the message.

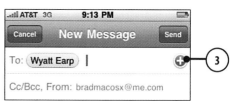

6. Tap the Cc/Bcc, From line. The Cc and Bcc lines expand.

Removing Addresses
To remove an address, tap it so it is highlighted in a darker shade of blue and then tap the Delete button on the iPhone's keyboard.

7. Use steps 2 though 4 to add recipients to the Cc field.

8. Use steps 2 though 4 to add recipients to the Bcc field.

9. To change the account from which the email is sent, tap the From field.

10. Drag up or down the wheel to spin it to see all the addresses available to you.

11. Tap the account you want to use to send the message. It is marked with a check mark, and the address is placed in the From field.

12. Tap in the Subject line.

13. Type the subject of the message.

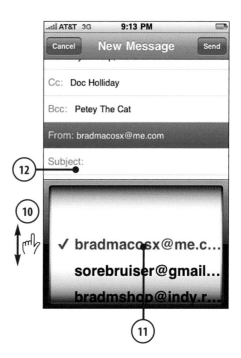

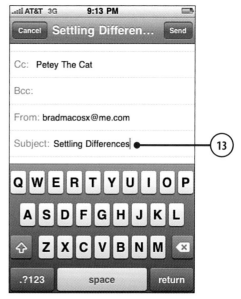

14. Scroll down the screen until you see the body area.

15. Tap in the body and type the body of the message above your signature. Remember that as you type, the iPhone attempts to correct spelling and makes suggestions to complete words. (See Chapter 1, "Getting Started with Your iPhone," for the details of working with text.)

16. To make the keyboard larger, rotate the iPhone clockwise or counterclockwise.

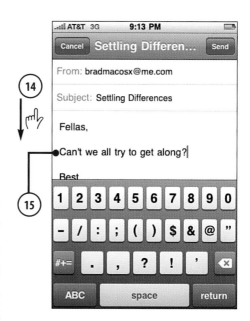

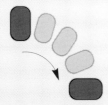

17. When you finish the message, tap Send. The iPhone sends it. You see the progress of the send process at the bottom of the screen. If you've enabled the send mail sound, when the message has been sent, the sound plays.

Saving Your Work in Progress

If you want to save a message without sending it, tap Cancel. A prompt appears; choose Save to save the message. When you want to work on the message again, move to the account's screen and open the Drafts folder. Tap the message, and you move back to the New Message screen as it was when you saved the message. You can make more changes to the message and then send it or save it again.

Replying to Email

Email is all about communication, so Mail makes it simple to reply to messages.

1. Open the message you want to reply to.

2. Tap the Action button.

3. Tap Reply to reply to only the sender or tap Reply All to reply to everyone who received the original message. The Re: screen appears showing a new message addressed to just the sender or to everyone who received the message, depending on the action you selected.

4. Use the message tools to write your reply, to add more To or Cc recipients, or to make any other changes you want.

5. Tap Send. The iPhone sends your reply.

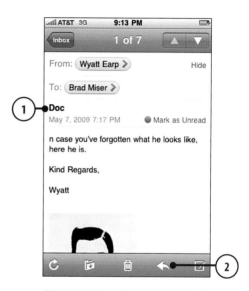

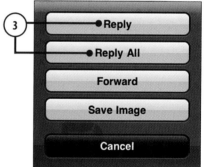

Sending Email from All the Right Places

You can send email from a number of different places on an iPhone. For example, you can share a photo with someone by tapping the Email button. Or you can tap a contact's email address to send an email from your contacts list. In all cases, the iPhone creates a new message that includes the appropriate content, such as a photo or link, and you use Mail's tools to complete and send the email.

Forwarding Email

When you receive an email that you think others should see, you can forward it to them.

1. Read the message you want to forward.

2. Tap the Action button.

3. Tap Forward. The Forward screen appears. The iPhone pastes the contents of the message you are forwarding at the bottom of the message below your signature.

4. Address the forwarded message using the same tools that you use when you create a new message.

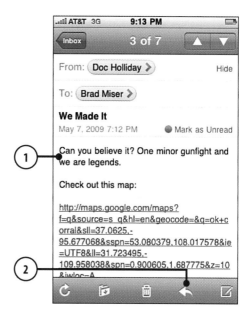

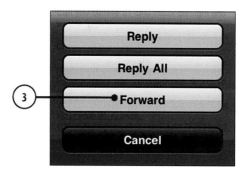

5. Type your commentary about the message above your signature.

6. Scroll down to see the forwarded content. Forwarded content is in blue and is marked with a vertical line along the left side of the screen.

7. Edit the forwarded content as needed.

8. Tap Send. The iPhone forwards the message.

Large Messages

Some emails, especially HTML messages, are so large that they don't immediately download to the iPhone in their entirety. When you forward such messages before they finish downloading, your iPhone prompts you to wait until the download finishes before forwarding. If you choose not to wait, the iPhone forwards only the downloaded part of the message.

Managing Email

Following are some ways you can manage your email.

Checking for New Messages

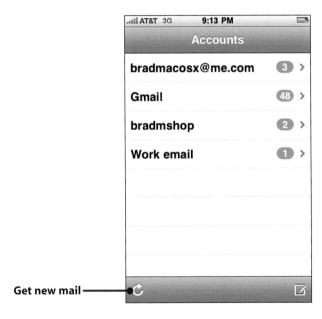

Get new mail

You can check for new mail from any Inbox or message screen by tapping the Get New Mail button. The iPhone retrieves and downloads all the email for that account since the iPhone last checked it. If you get new mail from the Accounts screen, messages in all your accounts are retrieved. The iPhone also retrieves messages whenever you move into the Inbox of any account.

The bottom of the Mail screens always shows the status of the most recent check.

Determining the Status of Messages

Unread message

Message to which you've replied

Read message

Message you've forwarded

When you view an Inbox, you see icons next to each message to indicate its status (except for messages that you've read but not done anything else with).

Dumpster Diving

As long as an account's trash hasn't been emptied (you learned how to set that earlier in the chapter by configuring the Remove setting for an account), you can work with a message you've deleted by moving to the account's screen and opening its Trash folder.

Working with the Email

>>>step-by-step

Deleting Email from the Inbox

1. Move to the inbox for the account from which you want to delete email.

2. Tap Edit. A selection circle appears next to each message. The Delete and Move buttons appear at the bottom of the screen.

3. Select the messages you want to delete by tapping their selection circles. As you select each message, the counter in the Delete button increases by one, and the message's selection circle is marked with a check mark.

4. Tap Delete. The iPhone deletes the selected messages and exits Edit mode. (If you enabled the warning prompt, you have to confirm the deletion.)

Yet Another Way to Delete

While you are on the Inbox screen, drag your finger to the left or right across a message. The Delete button appears. Tap the button to delete the message.

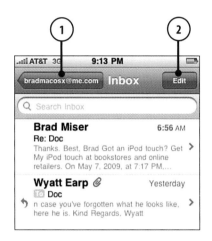

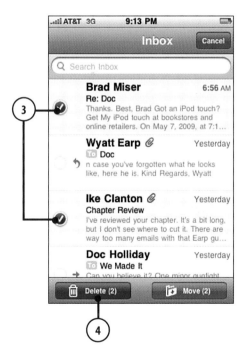

Organizing Email from the Message Screen

1. Open a message that you want to move to a folder.

2. Tap the Mailboxes button. The Mailboxes screen appears. At the top of this screen, you see the current message. Under that, you see the mailboxes available under the current account.

3. Tap the folder to which you want to move the message. The message moves to that folder, and you move to the next message in the Inbox.

Organizing Email from the Inbox

1. Move to the inbox for the account from which you want to organize email.

2. Tap Edit. A selection circle appears next to each message. The Delete and Move buttons appear at the bottom of the screen.

3. Select the messages you want to move by tapping their selection circles. As you select each message, the counter in the Move button increases by one, and the message's selection circle is marked with a check mark.

4. Tap Move.

5. Tap the folder into which you want to place the messages. They are moved into that folder, and you return to the Inbox, which is no longer in Edit mode.

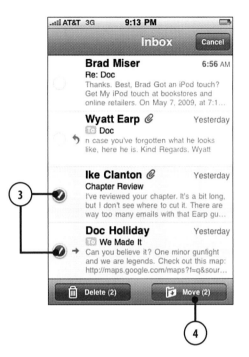

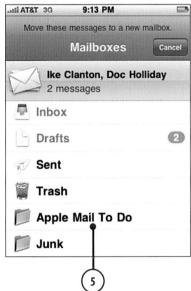

It's Not All Good

You can't create new mail folders on an iPhone. To create a new folder for an account, use another tool, such as an email application on your computer or the account's website. New folders become available on the account's screen on the iPhone after you sync the associated email account.

Viewing Messages in a Folder

1. Move to the account screen for the account containing the folders and messages you want to view. You see all the folders for the account.

2. Tap the folder containing the items you want to view. That folder's screen appears on which you see the messages it contains. In some cases, this can take a few moments if that folder's messages haven't been downloaded to your iPhone.

3. Tap a message to view it.

Saving an Image Attached to a Message

1. Move to the message screen of an email that contains images.

2. Tap the Action button.

3. Tap Save *X* Images, where *X* is the number of images attached to the message. (If there is only one image, the command is just Save Image.) The images are saved in the Saved Photos album in the Photos application (see Chapter 13, "Working with Photos and Video," for help working with the Photos application). The next time you sync an iPhone, the images are moved onto the computer.

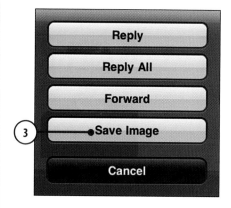

Searching Email

1. Move to the screen you want to search, such as an account's Inbox or a folder's screen.

2. Scroll to the top of the screen until you see the Search tool.

3. Tap in the Search tool.

4. Tap the message field you want to search: From, To, Subject, or All.

5. Enter the text for which you want to search. As you type, the iPhone searches the field you selected in step 4 or the entire message if you select All. Messages that meet your search are shown above the keyboard.

6. When you've completed your search term, tap Search. The keyboard closes and you see the messages that met your search.

7. Work with the messages you found.

8. To clear a search and exit Search mode, tap Cancel; to clear a search but remain in Search mode, tap the Clear button.

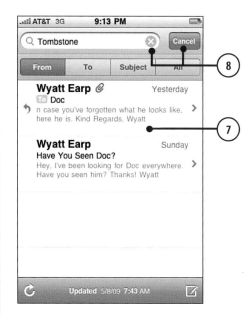

It's Not All Good

The iPhone's Mail application doesn't include any spam tools. If you put an already-spammed address on an iPhone, all the spam is going to come right to your iPhone, which can be a nuisance.

The best thing to do is to keep your important addresses from being spammed. Consider using a "sacrificial" email account when you shop, post messages, and in the other places where you're likely to get spammed. If you do get spammed, you can stop using the sacrificial account and create another one to take its place. (MobileMe's email aliases are perfect for this.) Or you can delete the sacrificial account from an iPhone and continue to use it on your computer where you likely have spam tools in place.

A more complicated way to avoid spam on an iPhone is by filtering all email through an account that does have spam filtering. For example, you can create a Gmail account and route all your email through it. Use the Gmail account's spam tool to manage the spam and then add only that Gmail account to your iPhone.

Communicate while on the move.

Configure the sound you hear when new messages arrive.

In this chapter, you'll explore the text messaging functionality that your iPhone has to offer. The topics include the following:

→ Configuring the New Text Message sound
→ Configuring messaging preferences
→ Sending text messages
→ Receiving and replying to text messages
→ Working with text messages

Texting

Text messaging enables you to have conversations with other people and to communicate information quickly and easily. You can use the iPhone's Messages application to send, receive, and converse via text messages. You can maintain any number of conversations with other people at the same time, and your iPhone lets you know whenever you receive a new message. Additionally, many organizations use text messaging to send important updates to you, such as airlines communicating flight status changes.

iPhone's text messages are sent via your cell network based on telephone numbers. You can send text messages to and receive messages from anyone who has a cell phone capable of text messaging (and most are these days); you can also text with anyone who uses a text messaging application, as long as their messages can be received via a phone number. You can also include images in the messages you send to others and view images sent to you.

It's Not All Good

There is one definite and another potential problem with the iPhone's text messaging. The definite problem is that it is a lot more expensive than it should be on many networks. For example, under the current AT&T plan in the United States, you must pay $5 per month for 200 text messages (if you are heavy user of text messaging, that isn't very many messages), while for a FamilyTalk plan, unlimited text messaging is $30 per month, which is outrageous based on how little data is required to be communicated for text messages. If you don't have any text messaging in your plan, it's even worse at a cost of $.20 per message. (All these figures are for the AT&T network in the United States; if you use iPhone on a different network, you might have other text messaging options.)

The potential problem depends on how much you use text messaging and the kind of features you need. Since iPhone was originally released, I've read and heard from iPhone users who tell me the text messaging capabilities provided by the iPhone's application are a bit limited, and with the iPhone 3.0 software, these capabilities are not much improved (though the ability to include images in text messages is a welcome improvement). I think it does a reasonable job for short, brief messages that are meant to be temporary; anything more complicated should be moved elsewhere, such as to email or a phone call.

If you rely on text messaging as an important form of communication, I recommend that you explore an Internet-based text messaging application instead of iPhone's cell phone-based application. For example, at press time, you can download and use the AOL AIM instant messaging application for free. Because this uses the Internet for text chatting, there is no limit or cost to the number of messages you can send, and the AIM application has more features than iPhone's Messages application. Even better, you aren't limited to chatting through cell phone applications; you can communicate with anyone who uses an AIM-compatible chat application on computers or other devices. For more information about finding, installing, and using iPhone applications, see Chapter 15, "Installing and Maintaining iPhone Applications."

>>>*step-by-step*

Configuring the New Text Message Sound

When you receive a new text message, iPhone plays an alert tone so you know a message has arrived. You can choose the alert sound you want to hear or disable this sound if you don't want to hear it.

1. Move to Settings and tap Sounds.

2. Tap New Text Message. The New Text Message screen appears.

3. Tap the sound you want to hear when a new message arrives. You hear the sound you selected; if you don't want any sound to play, tap None.

   Whenever a new text message arrives, you'll hear the sound you selected (unless you selected None or if you have muted your iPhone, in which case new messages will arrive with no audio fanfare).

Configuring Messaging Preferences

There are a number of preferences you can configure for your messages.

1. Move to Settings and tap Messages.

2. If you don't want to see a preview of messages when you receive them, tap ON next to Show Preview. Its status becomes OFF, and you don't see previews of messages. Instead, you see the name of the sender and the generic "Text Message" text.

3. By default, you are alerted three times for each text message you receive if you ignore the alerts; if you want to be alerted only once, tap ON next to Repeat Alert. You only see one alert for each message.

4. If you don't want to allow photos and videos to be included in your messages, tap ON next to MMS Messaging. Its status becomes OFF and you won't be able to include images or videos with your messages.

5. If you want to include a subject line with your messages, tap OFF next to Show Subject field. Its status becomes ON, and you are able to include a subject with your messages.

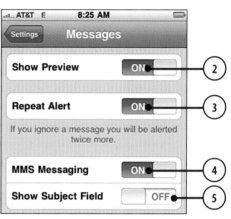

MMS Messages

The iPhone's Messages application supports Multimedia Messaging Service (MMS) that enables you to include photos and videos in your text messages. However, not all providers support this; in which case, you won't have the option to show the Subject field nor will you see the Photo button when you send messages. If you don't see these options, contact your provider to see if MMS is supported.

Sending Text Messages

You can send text messages by entering a number manually or by choosing a contact from your contacts list. (For help configuring your contacts, see Chapter 5, "Managing Contacts.")

1. On the Home screen, tap Messages.

2. Tap New Message.

3. If the person to whom you are sending the message is not in your contacts, skip to step 7; if the person is in your contacts, tap Add.

4. Scroll on the screen to find the contact to whom you want to send a message. (Remember that you can tap a letter on the index to quickly jump to a section of the contacts list.)

5. Tap the contact to whom you want to send the message. If the person you select has more than one phone number, the contact's Info screen opens so you can tap the number to which you are going to send the message. If there is only one number for the contact, that number is used for the new message automatically; you return to the New Message screen where you see the contact's name in the To field; the cursor is placed in the Send box; and you can skip to step 9.

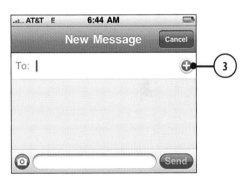

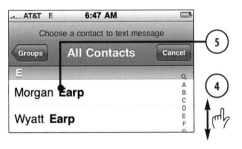

6. If the contact has more than one number, tap the number to which you want to send the text message. You return to the New Message screen; the name of the contact you selected is shown in the To field, and the cursor moves into the Send box. Skip to step 9.

Change Your Mind?

To remove a contact from the To box, tap it once so it becomes highlighted in blue and then tap the Delete key on the keyboard.

7. Type the name or number to which you want to send the text message. As you type a name, iPhone tries to match the number you type to someone on your contacts list; it presents a list of numbers and contacts that it thinks matches; tap one of these to select it. If you type a number, keep entering it until it's complete.

8. Tap the Send bar. The cursor moves into it and if the number you entered matches a number in your contacts, the contact's name replaces the number in the To field. If not, the number remains as you entered it.

Subject

If you've enabled the Subject Field preference, you can include a subject line with your messages. That is not typical for most text messages so I haven't shown it here. This is only allowed when your cell provider has enabled MMS messaging.

9. If you want to send the message to more than one recipient, tap to the right of the current recipient and use steps 3 through 8 to enter the other recipients' information, either by selecting contacts or entering phone numbers. As you add recipients, they appear in the To field.

10. Type the message you want to send in the Send bar. (If the cursor isn't there already, tap in the Send bar to move it there before you type.)

11. Tap Send. The Send status bar appears as the message is sent.

When it's complete, you see a new conversation screen if the message was not sent to someone you were previously text messaging with, or you move back to the existing conversation screen if you already have a text message conversation going with the recipient.

Multiple Recipients

When you address a message to more than one person, it is sent to each person, but becomes a separate conversation from that point on. If one or more of the recipients reply to the message, only you see the responses. In other words, replies to your messages are sent only to you; not to all the people to whom you sent your message.

Larger Keyboard

Like other areas where you type, you can rotate the iPhone to move into landscape mode, in which the keyboard orientation is larger as is each key. This can make texting easier, faster, and more accurate.

Who you sent it to   When you sent it

The message you sent

Receiving and Replying to Text Messages

When you receive a new text message (be it a new conversation or a new message in an ongoing conversation), you hear the new message sound (unless you've turned it off or muted iPhone). If you are working with the Messages application, the new message is appended to an ongoing conversation or a new conversation is started. If you are working on another screen, you see the new message window on iPhone's screen.

1. Read the message.

2. Tap Close if you want to ignore the message for now; you can always read it later. (See the section "Working with Text Messages," in this chapter for details.) Skip the rest of these steps.

3. To reply to the message, tap Reply. You move to the conversation screen and see the previous messages in the conversation if there are any, and the Send bar appears.

Who message is from   Message content

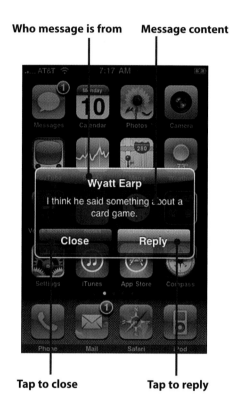

Tap to close   Tap to reply

Messages While iPhone Sleeps

If you receive a text message while iPhone is sleeping, you hear the new text message alert sound, and iPhone wakes up temporarily. The message text, without any controls, appears on the Locked iPhone screen. If you don't do anything about it, the message stays on the screen for a few seconds and then disappears while iPhone returns to its slumber. If you unlock the iPhone, you move into the Messages application and can work with the new message.

4. Tap the Send bar.

5. Type your reply.

6. Tap Send. The message is sent, and you see your message added to the conversation.

7. When the person replies to you, read the reply on the left side of the screen under your message.

8. Repeat steps 5 through 7 to reply and read replies to you.

9. Tap Messages. You move to the Text Message screen on which you see all the text message conversations in progress.

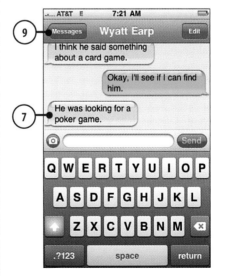

Working with Text Messages

As you send and receive messages, the interaction you have with each person becomes a separate text conversation, consisting of all the messages that have gone back and forth. You manage these conversations from the Messages screen.

How Many Messages Do I Have?

As you receive new text messages, a red circle on the Messages button on the Home screen indicates the number of new messages you have received. When you read a new message, this number is reduced so that it always indicates how many messages you've received but not read.

>>>*step-by-step*

Conversing in Text

Use the Messages application to manage your text messages.

1. On the Home screen, tap Messages. The Messages screen appears. On this screen, you see each conversation you have going. The name of the conversation is the name of the person associated with it. If a person can't be associated with it, you see the number you are conversing with. If the message is such that you can't reply to it (for example, when you request information about your AT&T account), you see a number of some sort.

2. Scroll the list to see all the conversations you have on-going.

3. Tap a conversation you want to read or reply to. The conversation screen appears; the name of the screen is the person with whom you are conversing—or her number if she isn't in your contacts list.

Person with whom you're conversing

When the last message was received

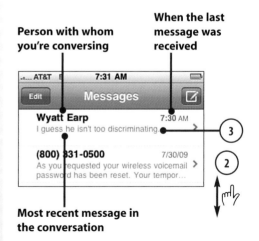

Most recent message in the conversation

4. Read the messages in the conversation. Your messages are on the right side of the screen in green, whereas the other person's are on the left in gray. Messages are organized so the newest message is at the bottom of the screen.

5. Scroll the conversation screen to see all the messages it contains.

6. If you don't want to add to the conversation, skip to step 10. To add a new message to the conversation, tap in the Send bar. The keyboard appears.

7. Type your message.

8. Tap Send. The message is sent, and you see your message added to the conversation.

9. Repeat steps 7 and 8 as long as you want to keep conversing.

10. Scroll to the top of the screen.

11. To call the person with whom you're conversing, tap Call.

12. To see the person's contact information, tap Contact Info.

13. When you're done, tap Messages. You return to the Text Messages screen and see the most recent message in the conversation shown with the date and time it was sent.

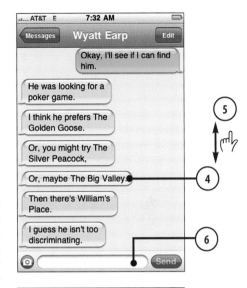

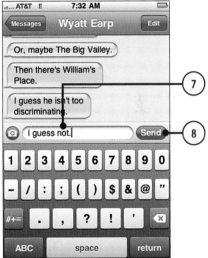

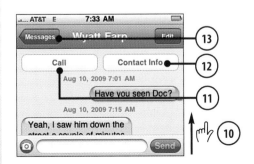

Including Images in Text Conversations

You can include any image or photo stored on your iPhone in a text conversation. Suppose you've taken a photo that you would like to share with someone. You can easily do that by texting the photo to the person.

Limitations, Limitations

Not all carriers support MMS messages (that can contain images and video) and the size of messages can also be limited. Check with your carrier for more information about what is supported and if there are additional charges for using MMS messages.

1. Move into the conversation with the person to whom you want to send a photo or start a new conversation with that person.

2. Tap the Photo button.

3. To capture a new photo or video to send, tap Take Photo or Video and move to step 7; to send a photo or video already stored on your iPhone, tap Choose Existing.

4. Use the Photos application to find the photo you want to send. (For more information about working with photos and videos, see Chapter 13, "Working with Photos and Video.")

5. Tap the photo you want to send.

6. Tap Choose. You move back to the conversation and see the image in the Send box; move to step 9.

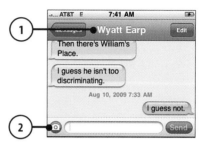

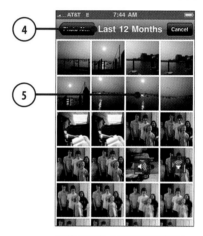

7. Take the photo or video you want to send. (For more information about taking photos or videos, see Chapter 13.)

8. Tap Use.

9. Type the message you want to send with the photo.

10. Tap Send. The message and photo are sent.

Problems?

If a message you try to send is undeliverable or has some other problem, it is marked with an exclamation point inside a red circle. Tap that icon and tap Try Again to attempt to resend the message.

Deleting Messages

Old text conversations never die, nor do they fade away. All the messages you receive from a person stay in the same conversation. Over time, you can build up a lot of messages in one conversation. When a conversation gets too long, you can clear it, like so.

1. Move to a conversation containing an abundance of messages.

2. Tap Edit.

3. Tap messages you want to remove. They are marked with a checkmark inside a red circle and the buttons at the bottom of the screen show the number of messages you have selected.

4. To remove the messages, tap Delete. The messages are removed and you return to the conversation.

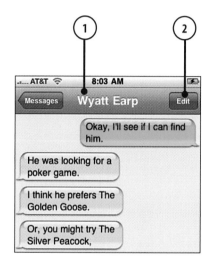

Clear All Messages

To clear all the messages in a conversation, tap Clear All and then Clear Conversation at the prompt. The conversation remains, but all the messages it contains are deleted.

Pass It On

If you want to send one or more messages to someone else, select them and tap the Forward button. A new messages is created and the messages you selected are pasted into it. Select the person to whom you want to send the messages and tap Send.

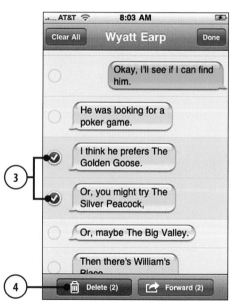

Deleting a Conversation

If a conversation's time has come, you can delete it.

1. Move to the Messages screen.

2. Tap Edit. Unlock buttons appear next to each conversation.

3. Tap the Unlock button next to the conversation you want to delete. The Delete button appears.

4. Tap Delete. The conversation is removed.

5. When you've deleted all you want, tap Done. You return to the Text Messages screen.

A Faster Way

Another way to delete a conversation is to drag your finger over it to the left or right. The Delete button appears. Tap the Delete button to delete the conversation.

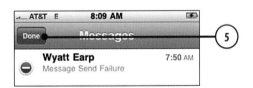

Tap here to see when and where you're supposed to be.

Go here to get all the time you need.

Tap here to configure time, date, and calendar settings.

In this chapter, you explore all the time and calendar functionality that an iPhone has to offer. Topics include the following:

→ Configuring an iPhone's calendar, date, and time settings
→ Working with calendars
→ Using an iPhone as a clock

Managing Calendars and Time

When it comes to time management, an iPhone is definitely your friend. Using the iPhone's Calendar application, you can view calendars that have been synchronized with your computer's calendars. Of course, you can also make changes on your iPhone, and they sync with calendars on your computers so you have consistent information no matter what device you use. The iPhone's handy Clock application provides multiple clocks and alarms.

Configuring an iPhone's Calendar, Date, and Time Settings

You should configure a few time, date, and calendar settings before you start using an iPhone to manage your calendars and time.

>>>*step-by-step*

1. On the Home screen, tap Settings.

2. Tap General.

3. Scroll down the screen.

4. Tap Date & Time.

5. To have your iPhone display time on a 24-hour clock, tap the 24-Hour Time OFF button, which becomes ON to show you the iPhone is now showing time on a 24-hour scale. To have the iPhone use a 12-hour clock, tap ON to turn off 24-hour time again.

6. If you don't want iPhone to set its time automatically using its cellular network time (in other words, you want to manage your iPhone's time manually), tap ON next to Set Automatically. The status becomes OFF, and two additional options appear; follow steps 7 through 19 to set those options or skip to step 20 if you leave the setting for time to be set automatically.

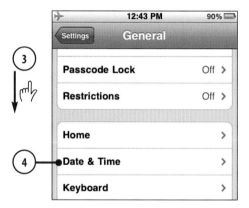

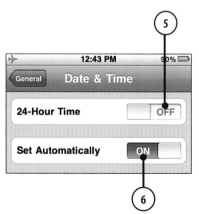

7. Tap Time Zone.

8. Type the name of the city that you want to use to set an iPhone's time zone. As you type, an iPhone lists the cities that match your search.

9. When the city you want to use appears on the list, tap it. You move back to the Date & Time screen, which shows the city you selected in the Time Zone field.

10. Tap Set Date & Time.

Bonus Task

Please go to this book's website at www.informit.com/title/ 9780789742315 and click the Downloads tab to find an additional task titled, "Using an iPhone as a Stopwatch."

11. Tap the date button. The date selection wheel appears.

12. Drag up and down on the month wheel until the center bar shows the month you want to set.

13. Drag up and down on the date wheel until the correct day of the month is shown in the center bar.

14. Scroll and select the year in the same way.

15. Tap the time button. The time selection wheel appears.

16. Scroll the hour wheel until the center bar shows the hour you want to set.

17. Use the minutes wheel to select the minutes you want to set, as shown in the center bar.

18. Tap AM or PM.

19. Tap Date & Time.

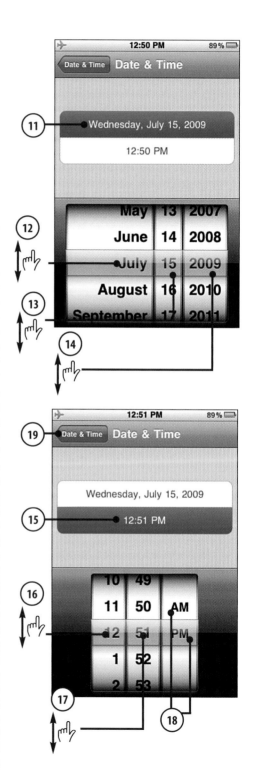

20. Tap General.

21. Tap Settings.

22. Tap Mail, Contacts, Calendars.

23. Scroll down until you see the Calendars section.

24. If you don't want to be alerted when you receive invitations to an event, tap ON next to New Invitation Alerts. Its status becomes OFF to show that you won't see these alerts. To be alerted again, tap OFF so the status becomes ON.

25. To set the period of time over which past events are synced, tap Sync.

26. Tap the amount of time you want events to be synced; tap All Events to have all events synced, regardless of their age.

27. Tap Mail.

28. Tap Time Zone Support.

29. To have the iPhone display meeting and event times on its calendars based on the iPhone's current time zone (either set automatically through the cellular network or set in steps 10 through 19), tap Time Zone Support ON; it becomes OFF to show you time zone support is disabled. Skip to step 33.

30. If you leave Time Zone Support ON, tap Time Zone.

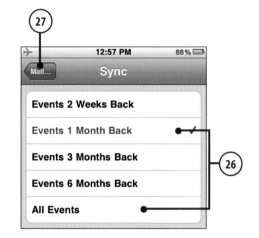

31. Type the name of the city that you want to use to set the time zone. As you type, the iPhone lists the cities that match your search.

32. When the city you want to use appears on the list, tap it. You move back to the Time Zone Support screen, and the city you selected is shown.

It's Not All Good

The Time Zone Support feature is a bit confusing. If Time Zone is ON, the iPhone displays event times according to the time zone associated with the time zone you select on the Time Zone Support screen. When Time Zone Support is OFF, the time zone used for the calendars is the iPhone's current time zone that is set automatically based on your cellular network or your manual setting.

For example, suppose you set Indianapolis (which is in the Eastern time zone) as the iPhone's time zone. If you enable Time Zone Support and then set San Francisco as the time zone, the events on your calendars will be shown according to the Pacific time zone because that is San Francisco's time zone rather than Eastern time (Indianapolis' time zone).

In other words, when Time Zone Support is ON, the dates and times for events become fixed based on the time zone you select for Time Zone support. If you change the iPhone's time zone, there is no change to the dates and times for events shown on the calendar because they remain set according to the time zone you selected in the Time Zone support.

In any case, you need to be aware of the time zone you are using on your calendars (the one you select if Time Zone Support is on or the time zone of your current location if it is off) and the time zone with which events are associated. With some calendar applications (such as iCal on a Mac), you can associate an event with a specific time zone when you schedule it. This is helpful because the event should be shown at the proper time regardless of the Time Zone Support setting on the iPhone.

33. Tap Mail.

34. Tap Default Calendar. You see the list of all calendars configured on your iPhone based on its sync settings and any calendars you have created there.

35. Tap the calendar that you want to be the default, meaning the one that is selected unless you specifically choose a different one.

36. Tap Mail.

37. Scroll up the screen. To keep your calendar information current, you can configure information to be pushed from where it is managed, such as an Exchange server or MobileMe, onto your iPhone whenever changes are made.

38. Tap Fetch New Data.

Saving Power

Push syncing causes an iPhone to use more power, which means your battery life is shorter. If your calendar or other information doesn't change that fast, use the Fetch option instead and set a relatively long time between fetches. To do this, move to the Fetch New Data screen and turn Push to OFF. Then tap the amount of time between fetches on the list of times, such as Hourly. Your iPhone will fetch the information only at the appointed times, which saves battery power compared to Push. Choose Manually if you want to only fetch information at your command.

39. If the status of Push isn't ON, tap OFF so it becomes ON.

40. Scroll down until you see the Advanced command.

41. Tap Advanced. You see the list of all your accounts. Under each account, you see the information that is currently being synced to the iPhone. Along the right edge of the list, you see how the information is being moved, either Push or Manual.

42. Tap an account from which you are getting calendar information.

43. Tap Push to have the account's information pushed onto an iPhone or Manual to update your calendar information manually.

44. Tap Advanced.

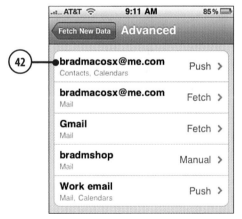

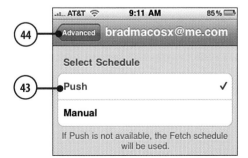

45. Repeat steps 42 through 44 for each account providing calendar information.

46. Tap Fetch New Data. Your time, date, and calendar configuration is complete.

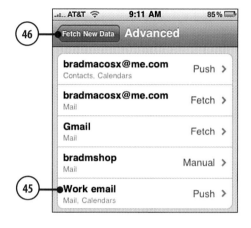

Small Events

The events browser at the bottom of the Month view is small and requires a lot of scrolling. It's usually better to use the Month view to select a date and then switch to the Day view to browse the events on that day.

Working with Calendars

An iPhone can manage your work, personal, and other calendars. In most cases, you'll be moving calendar information from a computer onto your iPhone, but you can add events directly to an iPhone's calendar too. (And when you do, they move to your computer's calendar the next time you sync.)

There are a number of ways to sync an iPhone's calendar to calendars on your computers. You can use iTunes, MobileMe, or Exchange (Windows Outlook only) to sync calendar information with Outlook (Window PCs) or iCal (Macs). Syncing calendars is covered along with the other information syncing options in Chapter 4, "Configuring and Synchronizing Information on an iPhone." Before working with your iPhone's calendars, use Chapter 4 to set up calendar syncing and then come back here.

Viewing Calendars ▶

You use the Calendar application to view time, and you can choose how you view it, such as by month, week, or day.

1. On the Home screen, tap Calendar. You return to the most recent calendar screen you were viewing. If that was a specific calendar, you see that calendar. If you were most recently viewing the Calendars screen, you move directly to that Calendars screen. On the Calendars screen, you see a list of all your calendars, grouped by the account with which they are associated. If you see the Calendars button in the upper-left corner of the screen, tap it to move to that screen. If you have only one calendar on your iPhone, the Calendars screen is hidden, and you always move directly to your sole calendar; in that case, skip to step 3.

2. Tap the specific calendar you want to view; tap the All *accountname* (where *accountname* is the name of the account from which the calendars come) or tap All Calendars at the top of the screen to see all your calendars at the same time.

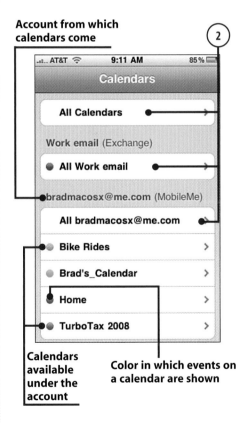

Account from which calendars come

Calendars available under the account

Color in which events on a calendar are shown

3. Tap Month. The Month view appears.

4. Tap a date in which you are interested. It moves into focus and is highlighted in blue, and the event list at the bottom of the screen shows the events associated with that date.

5. Scroll the list of events.

6. To see detailed information for an event, tap it. The Event screen appears.

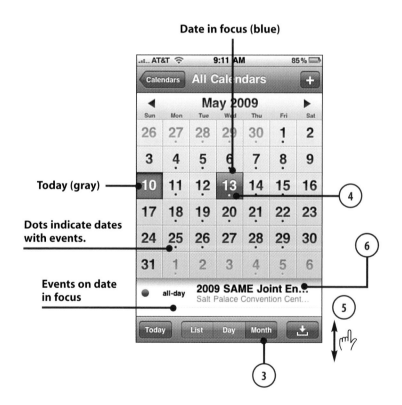

Date in focus (blue)

Today (gray)

Dots indicate dates with events.

Events on date in focus

7. Read information about the event; scroll down to see all of it, if needed.

8. To change the event, tap Edit.

9. Use the Edit screen to make changes to the event's information. The edit tools work just like when you create a new event; see "Adding Events to a Calendar Manually," later in this chapter for the details.

Clear My Calendar!

To delete an event from the calendar, open its Edit screen, scroll to the bottom, and tap Delete Event. Tap Delete Event again, and the event is removed from the calendar.

10. When you finish making changes, tap Done.

11. Tap the Return button, now labeled with the event's month. You move back to the Calendar window.

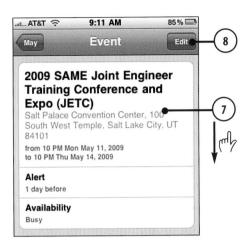

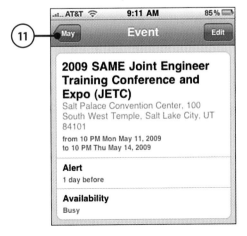

12. To move ahead to the next month, tap Next.

13. To move back to the previous month, tap Back.

14. To move the focus to today, tap Today.

15. Tap List. The view changes to the List view showing each day in a heading with the events for that day immediately underneath the day and date heading. At the top of the calendar, you see the calendar with which the events are associated (All Calendars, if you are viewing all the calendars on the iPhone).

16. Scroll the list of dates.

17. To view or change an event's details, tap it. The Event screen appears; this screen works just as it does when you access it from the Month view.

18. Tap Day. The Calendar changes to Day view.

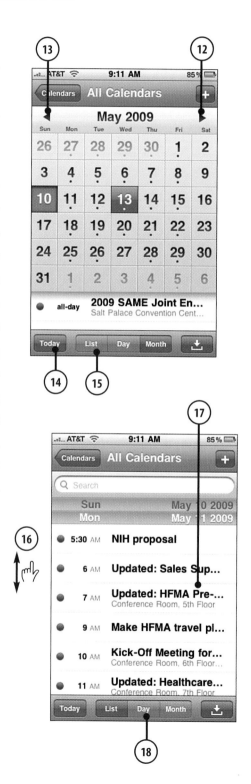

19. Scroll up and down to see the entire day.

20. Tap Back to move to the previous day.

21. Tap Forward to move to the next day.

22. To view or change an event's details, tap it. The Event screen appears; this screen works just as it does when you access it from the Month view.

Color indicates the calendar with which an event is associated.

Adding Events to a Calendar Manually

When you are on the move, you can manually add events to an iPhone calendar.

1. View the calendar to which you want to add an event or view All Calendars; you can add events to any calendar in any view.

2. Tap the Add button. The Add Event screen appears.

3. Tap Title Location.

4. With the cursor in the Title bar, type the title of the event.

5. Tap the Location bar and type the location of the event.

6. Tap Done. You move back to the Add Event screen.

7. Tap Starts Ends.

8. Tap Starts. It is highlighted in blue.

9. To make the event an all day event , tap All-day OFF; its status becomes ON, and the date selection wheels appear. Follow steps 10 through 16. To set a time for the event, leave the All-day status as OFF and complete steps 17 through 23.

10. Drag the month wheel until the event's month is shown in the center bar.

11. Drag the date wheel to set the event's date.

12. Drag the year wheel to set the year in which the event occurs.

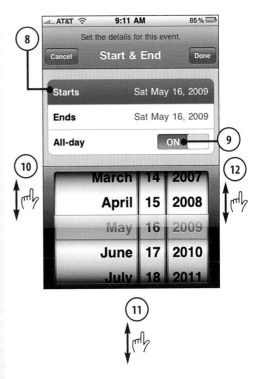

13. Tap Ends.

14. Use the month, date, and year wheels to set the end date for the event.

15. Tap Done. You return to the Add Event screen, and the event's dates are set.

16. Skip to step 24.

17. Scroll the date wheel until the center bar shows the date of the event.

18. Scroll the hour wheel until the center bar shows the hour the event starts.

19. Scroll the minute wheel until the center bar shows the minute the event starts.

20. Tap AM or PM.

21. Tap Ends. It is highlighted in blue.

22. Use the date, hour, and minute wheels and tap AM/PM button to set the end date and time.

23. Tap Done. You move back to the Add Event screen.

24. To make the event repeat, tap Repeat and follow steps 25 through 30. The Repeat Event screen appears. For a nonrepeating event, skip to step 31.

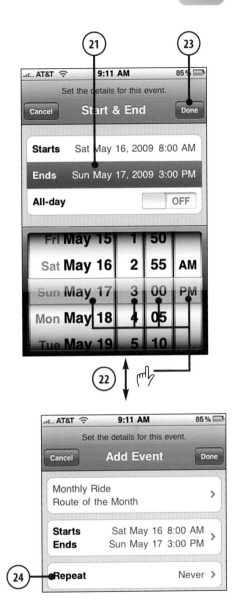

25. Tap the frequency with which you want the event repeated, such as Every Day, Every Week, or so on.

26. Tap Done. You move back to the Add Event screen.

27. Tap End Repeat to set a time at which the event stops repeating. If you want the event to be repeated forever, skip to step 31.

28. To have the event repeat ad infinitum, tap Repeat Forever and skip to step 30.

29. To set an end to the repetition, use the month, date, and year wheels.

30. Tap Done. You move back to the Add Event screen.

31. To set an alert for the event, tap Alert. The Event Alert screen appears. If you don't want to set an alert, skip to step 37.

32. Select when you want to see an alert for the event.

33. Tap Done. You move back to the Add Event screen.

Alert, Alert!

To hear a sound when an event alert occurs, open the Sounds screen (choose Home, Settings, Sounds), and ensure that ON appears next to Calendar Alerts. If OFF appears, tap it to make event alarms audible as well as visual.

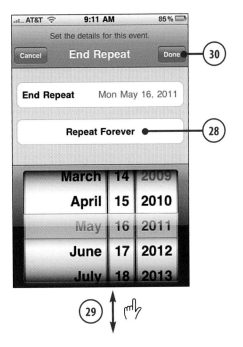

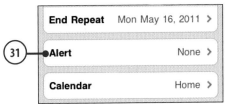

34. To set a second alert, tap Second Alert. The Event Alert screen appears.

    Not all calendars, including Outlook calendars you are syncing through Exchange, support second alerts; if you don't see the Second Alert command or if you don't want to set a second alert, skip to step 37.

35. Select when you want to see a second alert for the event.

36. Tap Done. You move back to the Add Event screen.

37. To change the calendar with which the event is associated, tap Calendar; to leave the current calendar selected, skip to step 40.

38. Tap the calendar with which the event should be associated.

39. Tap Done.

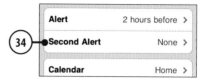

40. Tap Notes. The Notes screen appears.

41. Type information you want to associate with the event.

42. Tap Done. You return to the Add Event screen.

43. Tap Done. The event is added to the calendar you selected. Any alarms trigger according to your settings.

Keeping in Sync

When you sync an iPhone, information moves both ways. When you add or make a change to a calendar from the computer, the changes move to the iPhone the next time you sync. Likewise, when you add or change events on an iPhone, those changes move to the calendar on the computer during the next sync.

New event

It's Not All Good

Unfortunately, you can't choose the alert sound for an event. All event alarms use the standard calendar event alarm sound.

Adding Events to the Calendar by Accepting Invitations

When someone invites you to an event from Outlook via an Exchange account, you receive an invitation notification in the Calendar. You can accept these invitations, at which point the event is added to your calendar, or you can decline the event if you don't want it added to your calendar.

>>>step-by-step

1. When you receive an invitation, you see an alert on the screen; tap View to see the details. You move to the Invitations screen.

2. Tap the invitation. You see its Info screen.

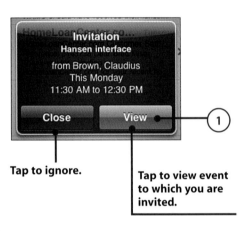

Tap to ignore.

Tap to view event to which you are invited.

Managing Invitations

If you tap the Close button on an invitation or at any other time, you can always move back to the Invitations screen by tapping the Invitations button in the lower-right corner of the Calendar window. This button also shows the number of invitations you've received but not yet made a decision about.

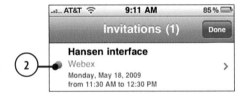

Availability

Exchange events support the Availability field, which indicates the status of your time during an event on your calendar. For example, if your time is marked as Busy and someone tries to invite you to an event using Outlook, the calendar shows you being unavailable and so the person knows you are already committed for that time. Your Availability can be set by tapping the Availability command on the Info screen, but in most cases, you can just let your availability be set by your response. For example, if you accept an invitation, that event's time is marked as Busy on your calendar automatically.

3. Scroll the event to see all of its details.

4. View details about whom the invitation is from and attendees by tapping their areas. You move to detail screens for each.

5. To configure an alarm for the event, tap Alert and use the resulting Alert screen to choose an alert.

It's Not All Good

The current version of the Mail application can't do anything with attachments that are event invitations (.ics files). That means when you receive an email invitation to an event, you can't add it to a calendar on your iPhone by opening the attachment (which is what should happen and what does happen when you use an email application on a computer). If you can see the event's information in the subject line or body of the email message, you can create an event on your calendar manually, but invitations from some email applications don't have this information, so they are useless to you on your iPhone. You need to work with iCal or other calendar applications on a computer to accept or reject these invitations.

The only kind of events that come as invitations are meeting requests from Outlook that come in through an Exchange account, and you see only the Invitation button when you are using an Exchange account.

Also you can't invite other people to events that you set up on an iPhone; you have to use a calendar application on a computer to do that.

Hopefully, these issues will be resolved with a future iPhone software update, and all invitations will work like those sent via Exchange. In the current version, working with invitations and with meetings that involve other people is very limited, so you'll have to rely on your calendar application on a computer to manage them properly.

6. To choose the calendar on which the event should be shown, tap Show in Calendar, and on the resulting screen, tap the appropriate calendar.

7. To add comments to the event, tap Add Comments and use the Comments screen to enter text about the event.

8. Indicate what you want to do with the event by tapping Accept, Maybe, or Decline. If you accept the event or tap Maybe, the event is added to the calendar with the status you indicated. (For example, Accepted and your time is set to Busy if you tap Accept.) If you decline, the event is not placed on a calendar, and the recipient receives a notice that you have declined.

After you make a decision, you move to the Invitations screen, where you see the status of all the invitations you've received. Events you've accepted or declined appear briefly and then disappear as the appropriate action is taken (such as adding an event you've accepted to the calendar).

9. Tap Done. You move to the calendar; if you accepted or indicated maybe, the event is added to your calendar.

Working with Event Alarms

When an event's alarm goes off, you see an onscreen alert and hear the calendar event sound (if it is enabled). Tap View Event to view details on the Event screen or tap Close to dismiss the alarm.

If the event has a second alarm, it also goes off according to the schedule you set. Handle it the same way as you did the first alarm.

Tap to dismiss the alarm.

Tap to see the event's info.

Using an iPhone as a Clock

An iPhone is also useful as an alarm clock, timer, and stop watch. In addition to the primary time you learned to set earlier in the chapter, you can set clocks for a variety of locations.

Telling Time with an iPhone

Current time

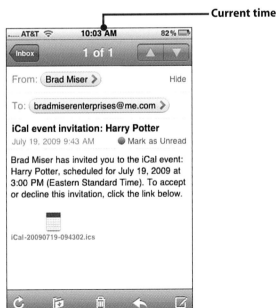

Your iPhone displays the current time at the top of most of its screens for easy viewing.

Current time and date

When your iPhone is locked/asleep and you press the Sleep/Wake button or the Home button, the current time and date appears on the screen. If you don't unlock the iPhone, it goes to sleep again in a few seconds, making this an easy way to check the current time without using much battery power.

Using the Clock Application

You can set an iPhone to display a number of clocks with each clock having a specific time zone associated with it. This makes it possible to know the time in several locations at once. Even better, you can configure multiple alarms to remind you of important events, such as getting out of bed. The Clock also provides a basic but serviceable stopwatch and timer.

Creating, Configuring, and Using Clocks

You can create multiple clocks, with each showing the time in a different time zone. If you travel a lot or if you know people in different time zones, this is an easy way to see the time in multiple locations.

1. On the Home screen, tap Clock. The Clock screen appears.

Like Night and Day

Based on the associated time zone, a clock's face is black if the current time is between sunset and sunrise (in other words, it's dark there) or white if the time there is in daylight hours.

2. Tap World Clock. The World Clock screen appears. You see a clock for each location you have config- ured.

3. To add a clock, tap the Add but- ton. The Select City screen appears.

City associated with a clock

Time and date in that city

4. Type the name of the city with which the new clock is associated; this determines the clock's time zone. As you type, the iPhone tries to match cities to what you are typing and presents a list of matching cities to you.

Missing City

If an iPhone can't find the specific city you want, just choose a city in the same time zone. The city you select determines the time zone of the clock. However, there is an issue with the clock's name, which is addressed in the "It's Not All Good" section in this task.

5. Tap the city you want to associate with the clock. You return to the World Clock screen, and the clock is created, showing the current time in that city.

6. To remove a clock or to change the order in which clocks appear on the screen, tap Edit. Unlock buttons appear next to each clock.

7. Tap the clock's Unlock button next to the one you want to delete. The Delete button appears.

8. Tap Delete. The clock is deleted.

9. Repeat steps 7 and 8 until you've deleted all the clocks you no longer want to see.

10. Drag clocks up and down the screen by their list icons to change the order in which they appear.

11. Tap Done.

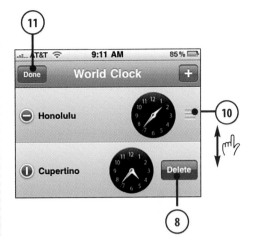

It's Not All Good

Unfortunately, you can't rename clocks to reflect the actual city in which you are interested. So if you can't find the specific city you want when you set the time zone, make sure you select one that you easily recognize as being in the same time zone as the city where you really want to know the time.

Setting and Using Alarms

Your iPhone is a very handy alarm clock on which you can set and manage multiple alarms.

1. On the Home screen, tap Clock. The Clock screen appears.

2. Tap Alarm. The Alarm screen appears. You see the currently set alarms, listed by their times, with the earlier alarms toward the top of the screen.

3. To add an alarm, tap Add. The Add Alarm screen appears.

4. To configure the alarm to repeat, tap Repeat; to set a one-time alarm, skip to step 8.

Alarm label

Alarm days

3

Status

Alarm time

2

5. Tap the day of the week on which you want the alarm to repeat. It is marked with a check mark.

6. Repeat step 5 as many times as you need. The most frequently an alarm can repeat is once per day.

7. Tap Back. The Repeat option shows you the days you selected for the alarm to repeat.

8. To choose the alarm sound, tap Sound. The Sound screen appears.

Silent Alarm

If you select the None sound, you won't hear anything when the alarm goes off, but a visual alarm displays.

9. Browse the list of available sounds.

10. Tap the sound you want to use for the alarm. You hear the sound, and it is marked with a check mark.

11. After you have selected the sound you want to use, tap Back. You move back to the Add Alarm screen, which now shows the sound that will play when the alarm goes off.

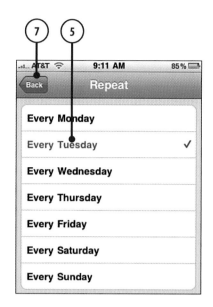

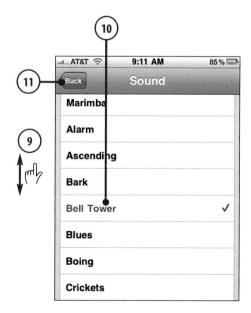

12. To disable the Snooze function, tap ON. The status becomes OFF. When an alarm sounds and you dismiss it, it won't appear again. With Snooze set to ON, you can tap Snooze to dismiss the alarm, and it returns at 10-minute increments until you dismiss it.

13. To name the alarm, tap Label. (To leave the default label, which is "Alarm," skip to step 17.) The Label screen appears. The label is what appears on the screen when the alarm activates, so you might want to give it a meaningful label.

14. To remove the current label, tap the Clear button.

15. Type the label for the alarm.

16. Tap Back. You return to the Add Alarm screen, which shows the label you created.

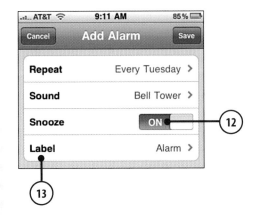

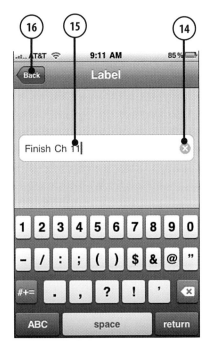

17. Scroll the hour wheel until you see the hour you want to set in the center bar.

18. Scroll the minute wheel until you see the minute you want to set in the center bar.

How iPhone Alarms Are Like Those on Bedside Clocks

You can't set an alarm for a specific date; they are set only by day of the week, just like a bedside alarm clock. To set an alarm for a specific date, configure an event on the calendar and associate an alarm with that event.

19. Tap AM or PM.

20. Tap Save. You return to the Alarm screen, which now shows the new alarm you set. When the appointed time arrives, the alarm sounds and displays on the screen (or just displays on the screen if it is a silent alarm).

Changing Alarms

You can change existing alarms in several ways.

1. Move to the Alarm screen.

2. Tap Edit. Unlock buttons appear next to each alarm.

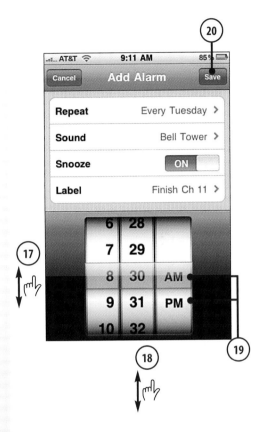

3. To delete an alarm, tap its Unlock button. The Delete button appears.

4. Tap Delete. The alarm is deleted.

5. To change an alarm, tap it. The Edit Alarm screen appears.

6. Use the controls on the Edit Alarm screen to make changes to the alarm. These work just as they do when you create an alarm. (See the preceding task, "Setting and Using Alarms," for details.)

7. Tap Save. The alarm is changed, and you return to the Alarms screen.

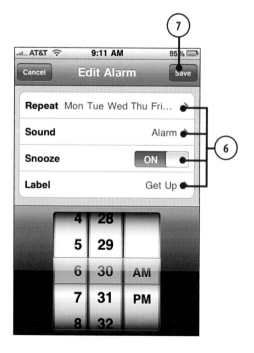

8. To disable an alarm, tap ON. Its status becomes OFF, and it is no longer active.

9. To enable an alarm, tap OFF. Its status becomes ON, and it sounds and appears at the appropriate times.

Managing Alarms

At least one alarm is active.

When at least one alarm is active, you see the Alarm Clock icon in the upper-right corner of the screen next to the Battery icon.

Alarm label

Tap to snooze. ___ **Tap to dismiss.**

When an alarm triggers, you see an onscreen message and hear the sound associated with it. If the alarm is snooze-enabled, tap Snooze to dismiss it; it returns in 10 minutes. To dismiss the alarm, tap OK. You can also dismiss an alarm by pressing the Sleep/Awake button.

Not Dismissed So Easily

When you dismiss an alarm, it isn't deleted, but its status is set to OFF. To re-enable the alarm, move to the Alarm screen and tap its OFF button. The status becomes ON, and the alarm activates at the next appropriate time.

Tap to configure Safari.

Tap to have the World Wide Web
in the palm of your hand.

In this chapter, you explore the amazing web browsing functionality that your iPhone has to offer. The topics include the following:

→ Configuring Safari settings
→ Browsing the web

Surfing the Web

Wouldn't it be nice to browse the web wherever you are using a real web browser instead of the modified browsers available on most cell phones or other small, mobile devices? And wouldn't it be nice not to have to be concerned with pages being formatted for proper display on a mobile device? Obviously, considering you have an iPhone, you know you have all these niceties because iPhone has a full-featured web browser: Safari. You can browse the web from any location that has a Wi-Fi network that offers an Internet connection and anytime you are connected to a cellular data network. So virtually anywhere you are, the web is with you.

Configuring Safari Settings

Before you surf, take a couple of minutes to configure iPhone's Safari settings.

1. On the Home screen, tap Settings.

2. Scroll down the page until you see Safari.

3. Tap Safari.

4. To leave Google as the default search engine, skip to step 7. To change the default search engine from Google to Yahoo!, tap Search Engine.

5. Tap Yahoo!. It is now checked to show you it is the selected search engine.

6. Tap Safari.

7. Tap AutoFill. This is a great feature that enables you to quickly complete forms on the web by automatically filling in key information for you.

8. To use contact information stored on your iPhone to complete forms, tap OFF next to Use Contact Info. Its status becomes ON.

Contact!

To learn how to configure and use contacts, see Chapter 5, "Managing Contacts."

9. Tap My Info.

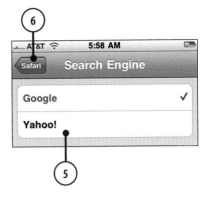

10. Find and tap your contact information. This tells Safari what information to fill in for you on forms, such as your name, address, and so on. You move back to the AutoFill screen and see your name in the My Info section.

11. To enable Safari to remember user names and passwords for websites you log in to, tap OFF next to Names & Passwords. Its status becomes ON.

12. Tap Safari.

It's Not All Good

Be careful about allowing Safari to remember user names and passwords if you access websites with sensitive information, such as a banking website. If Safari remembers this information for you, anyone who uses your iPhone can log in to your account on these sites because Safari automatically fills in the required information to log in. If you lose control of your iPhone, your sensitive information might be compromised. To remove the user names and passwords stored on your iPhone, tap Clear All on the AutoFill screen. When you confirm by tapping Clear AutoFill Data, all the information stored is deleted.

13. To disable the fraud warning function, tap ON next to Fraud Warning. Unless you have some particularly good reason to disable this, I recommend you leave it enabled.

14. To disable JavaScript functionality, tap JavaScript ON. Its status becomes OFF to show you it is no longer active. Some webpages might not work properly with JavaScript turned off, but it is more secure.

15. To disable plug-ins, tap Plug-Ins ON. Its status becomes OFF, and plug-ins no longer work with Safari.

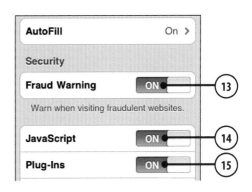

Keep Plug-Ins Enabled

Unless you have a specific reason not to allow plug-ins, leave that option enabled so you can get the most functionality possible. On the iPhone, you can only enable or disable plug-ins; you can't choose specific plug-ins to install or manage as you can with a web browser on a computer.

16. To disable pop-up blocking, tap Block Pop-Ups ON. Its status becomes OFF, and pop-ups are no longer blocked. Some websites won't work properly with pop-ups blocked, so you can use this setting to temporarily enable pop-ups while you use a specific website that requires them.

17. To configure how cookies are handled, tap Accept Cookies. The Accept Cookies screen appears.

18. Tap the kind of cookies you want to accept. The Never option blocks all cookies. The From visited option accepts cookies only from sites you visit. This is the setting I recommend you choose as it enables websites you visit to store necessary information on your iPhone. The Always option accepts all cookies; I don't recommend this option because if you get directed to a site by another site that you didn't intend to visit, its cookies can be stored on your iPhone.

19. Tap Safari.

20. Scroll to the bottom of the screen.

21. To clear the history of websites you have visited, tap Clear History.

22. Tap Clear History at the prompt. This removes the websites you have visited from your history list. The list starts over, so the next site you visit is added to your history list again.

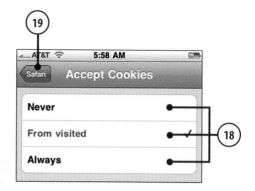

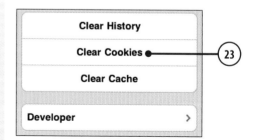

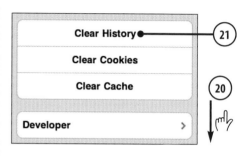

It Never Happened

To remove the information associated with your web browsing, perform steps 21 through 26 and also clear the AutoFill data as described in the previous "It's Not All Good" sidebar.

---

23. To remove all cookies from iPhone, tap Clear Cookies.

24. Tap Clear Cookies at the prompt. Any sites that require cookies to function re-create the cookies they need the next time you visit them, assuming that you allow cookies.

25. To clear the web browser's cache, tap Clear Cache. The cache stores information from websites so you can return to that information without downloading it from the web again.

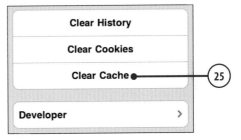

26. When prompted, tap Clear Cache to confirm the action. The next time you visit a site, its content is downloaded to the iPhone again.

Developer?

The Developer setting enables the Debug Console to be turned ON or OFF. The Debug Console enables website developers to check their websites on an iPhone for errors so that those sites can be updated to work properly with an iPhone. If you aren't a website developer, you probably won't need to use this tool. If you are a website developer, enable the tool when you are evaluating your website using Safari on an iPhone.

Got Internet Connection?

An iPhone can get to the web via a Wi-Fi network that offers an Internet connection. It can also access the Internet via a cellular data network. The performance of cellular data networks ranges from high-speed, offering very nice performance, to very low speed, making the web crawl. In some cases, such as with AT&T's EDGE network in the United States, you might find the speed of a low-speed cellular data network to make browsing almost unbearable. However, sites that are specifically formatted for mobile devices can be useful even when a low-speed connection is all that is available to you. To learn how to connect an iPhone to Wi-Fi and cellular data networks, see Chapter 2, "Connecting to the Internet, Bluetooth Devices, and iPhones/iPods."

Browsing the Web on an iPhone

If you've used a web browser on a computer before, using Safari on an iPhone will be a familiar experience. If you've not used a web browser before, don't worry because using Safari on an iPhone is simple and intuitive.

Syncing Bookmarks

You can synchronize your Internet Explorer favorites or Safari bookmarks on a Windows PC or Safari bookmarks on a Mac to your iPhone so you have the same set of bookmarks available on your iPhone that you do on your computer and vice versa. You can do this via the sync process or wirelessly using MobileMe. See Chapter 4, "Configuring and Synchronizing Information on an iPhone," for details. If you use Internet Explorer or Safari, it's a good idea to synchronize before you start browsing on your iPhone so you avoid typing URLs or re-creating bookmarks.

>>>*step-by-step*

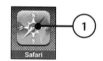

Moving to Websites via Bookmarks

Using bookmarks that you've moved from a computer onto iPhone makes it easy to get to websites that are of interest to you. You can also create bookmarks on iPhone (you learn how later in this section) and use them just like bookmarks you've imported from a computer.

1. On the iPhone Home screen, tap Safari.

2. Tap the Bookmarks button.

3. Scroll up or down the list of book-marks.

4. To move to a bookmark, skip to step 9. To open a folder of book-marks, tap it.

___

Change Your Mind?

If you decide not to visit a book-mark, tap Done. You return to the page you were previously viewing.

___

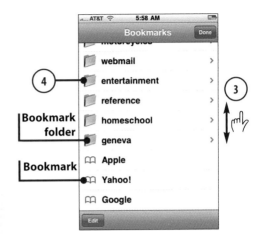

5. Browse the folder's screen.

6. You can keep drilling down into folders by tapping the folder whose bookmarks you want to see.

7. To return to a previous screen, tap the return button, which is labeled with the name of the cur-rent folder you are viewing, the folder you most recently visited, or with Bookmarks if you are viewing a folder on the "top" level of the Bookmarks folder.

8. Repeat steps 5 through 7 until you see a bookmark you want to visit.

9. Tap the bookmark you want to visit. Safari moves to that website.

10. Use the information in the section titled "Viewing Websites" later in this chapter to view the webpage.

iPhone Webpages

Some websites have been specially formatted for iPhones and iPod touches. These typically have less complex information on each page so they load more quickly. When you move to a site like this, you might be redirected to the iPhone version automatically. There is typically a link that takes you to the "regular" version too. (It's often called the classic version.) Sometimes the version formatted for handheld devices offers less information or fewer tools than the regular version. Because Safari is a full-featured browser, you can use whichever version you prefer and that is supported by your current connection speed.

Moving to Websites by Typing a URL

Although it might not be fun to type URLs, sometimes that's the only way you have to get to a website.

1. On the iPhone Home screen, tap Safari.

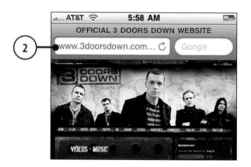

2. Tap in the Address bar. The keyboard appears along with the Search bar. If you've visited a site recently, the URL of the current webpage appears in the Address bar, and the page you last visited appears on the screen.

3. If an address appears in the Address bar, tap the Clear button to remove it.

4. Type the URL you want to visit. If it starts with "www," you don't have to type "www." As you type, Safari attempts to match what you are typing to a site you have visited previously or to one of your bookmarks and presents a list of those sites to you.

.com for All

Because so many URLs end in "com," there's a handy .com key on the keyboard. You can quickly enter a URL by typing the text before ".com" and then tapping the .com button to complete it.

5. If one of the sites shown is the one you want to visit, tap it. You move to that webpage; skip to step 8.

6. If Safari doesn't find a match, continue typing until you enter the entire URL.

7. Tap Go. You move to the webpage.

8. Use the information in the section that follows to view the webpage.

Viewing Websites

Even though your iPhone is a small device, you'll be amazed at how well it displays webpages designed for larger screens. Unlike most smart phones or other small mobile devices, you can view and work with standard webpages about as well as you can with a computer.

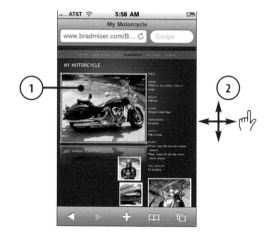

1. Use Safari to move to a webpage as described in the previous two sections.

2. To scroll a webpage, drag your finger right or left or up or down.

3. To zoom in manually, unpinch your fingers.

4. To zoom in automatically, tap your finger on the screen twice.

5. To zoom out manually, pinch your fingers.

6. To zoom on a column or a figure, tap it twice.

7. To move to a link, tap it once. The webpage to which the link points opens.

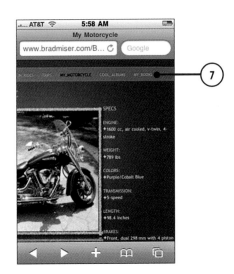

Do More with Links

To see options for a link or graphic, tap your finger on it and hold your finger down for a second or so. A prompt appears. Tap Open to open the page at which the link points. Tap Open in New Page to open the page in a new Safari window. Tap Copy to copy the link's URL so you can paste it elsewhere, such as in an email message. Tap Save Image to save the associated image in the Photo application (see Chapter 13, "Working with Photos and Video," for information about working with photos.) Tap Cancel to return to the current page and take no action.

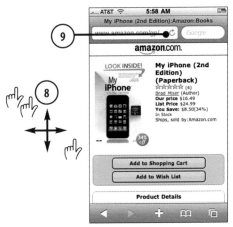

8. Scroll and zoom on the page to read it.

9. To refresh a page, tap Refresh. (Note: While a page is loading, this is the Stop page button (X); tap it to stop the rest of the page from loading.)

10. To view the web in landscape mode, rotate the iPhone 90 degrees.

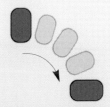

11. To move to a previous page you've visited, tap Back.

12. To move to a subsequent page, tap Forward.

Where Art Thou, Address Bar?

If you lose sight of the Address bar when you're scrolling pages, tap the status bar once where the time displays. You scroll to the top of the screen and can see the Address bar again.

Searching the Web

Earlier you learned that you can set Safari to search the web using Google or Yahoo! by default. Whichever search engine you choose, you search the web in the same way.

1. Move to a webpage.

2. Tap in the Search bar, which before you start typing has Google or Yahoo! in the background to show you which engine you are using.

3. Type your search word(s). As you type, Safari attempts to find a previous search that matches what you type.

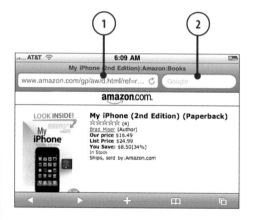

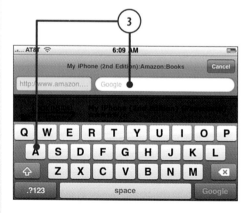

4. To move to a previous search, tap it, or when you've entered your search term, tap Google or Yahoo! (The button name depends on the search engine you are using.) The website performs the search, and you see the results on the search results page.

5. Use the search results page to view the results of your search. These pages work just like other webpages. You can zoom, scroll, and tap links to explore results.

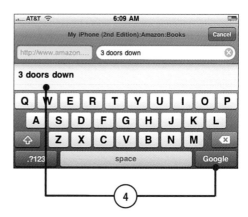

Safari Has a Good Memory

Safari remembers the last search you performed. To clear a search, click the Clear button located at the right end of the Search bar.

Returning to Previous Websites

As you move about the web, Safari tracks the sites you visit and builds a history list. You can use this list to return to sites you've visited.

1. Open a webpage and tap the Bookmarks button.

2. Tap the Return button until you move to the Bookmarks screen. (You might go directly there; Safari remembers your last location.)

3. If necessary, scroll to the top of the page so you see the History folder.

4. Tap History.

5. Scroll the page to browse all the sites you've visited. The most recent sites appear at the top of the screen. Earlier sites are collected in folders for each day, starting with Earlier Today and moving back one day at a time.

6. To return to a site, skip to step 7; to view sites in one of the folders, tap the folder containing the site you want to visit. That date's screen appears.

7. Tap the site you want to visit. The site opens.

8. Use the techniques you learned earlier in this chapter to view the content of the page.

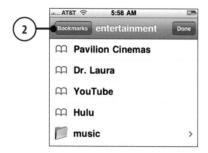

Erasing the Past

To clear your browsing history, tap the Clear button at the bottom of any of the History screens. Tap Clear History at the prompt, and it will be as if you've never been on the web.

It's Not All Good

Unfortunately, bookmarks that you create on the iPhone are only useful on the computer to which they are copied if you use Internet Explorer (Windows PCs) or Safari (Mac). If you use Firefox or other web browsers, the bookmarks moved onto the computer from the iPhone are of no value (without going through extra gyrations at least).

>>>step-by-step

Saving and Organizing Bookmarks

In addition to moving bookmarks from a computer onto your iPhone, you can add new bookmarks to the iPhone, and they'll move onto the computer the next time you sync. You can organize bookmarks on your iPhone, too.

Saving Bookmarks

1. Move to a webpage that you want to save as a bookmark.

2. Tap the Action button.

3. Tap Add Bookmark. The Add Bookmark screen appears. The top field is the name of the bookmark. The middle field shows its URL. The lowest field shows where the bookmark will be stored.

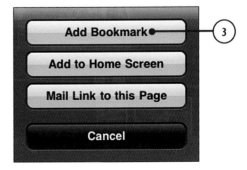

4. Edit the bookmark's name as needed, or to erase the current name (which is the webpage's title) and start over, tap the Clear button; then type the new name.

5. Tap Bookmarks. The Bookmarks screen appears. Starting at the top level, Bookmarks, you see all the folders on the iPhone in which you can place the bookmark you are saving. The folder that is currently selected is marked with a check mark.

6. Scroll the screen to find the folder in which you want to place the new bookmark. You can choose any folder on the screen.

7. To choose a location for the new bookmark, tap it. You return to the Add Bookmark screen, which shows the location you selected.

8. Tap Save. The bookmark is created and saved in the location you specified. You can use the Bookmarks tool to move to it at any time.

Location, Location

The location shown in the third bar is the last one in which you stored a bookmark. The first time you add a bookmark, this bar is called Bookmarks because that's the default location. After you choose a different location, the bar is relabeled with that location's name, which the iPhone remembers the next time you add a new bookmark.

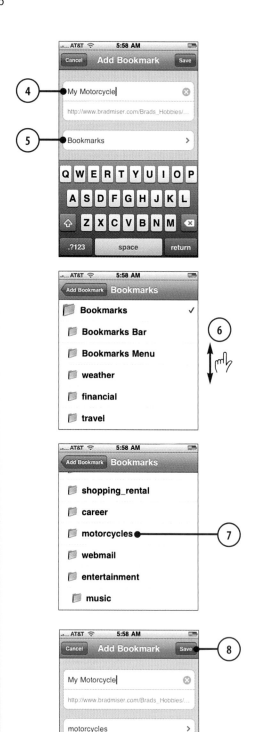

Organizing Bookmarks

1. Move to the Bookmarks screen.

2. Tap Edit. The unlock buttons appear next to the folders and bookmarks you can change; some folders, such as the History folder, can't be changed. The Order buttons also appear on the right side of the screen.

3. Drag the Order button next to the bookmark or folder you want to move up or down the screen. As you move between existing items, they slide apart to make room for the folder or bookmark you are dragging. The order of the items on the list is the order in which they appear on the Bookmarks screen.

4. To change the name and location of a folder, tap it.

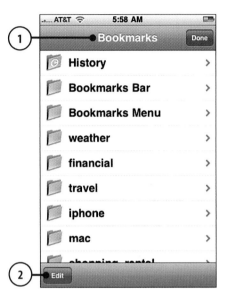

5. Change the name in the name bar.

6. To change the location of the folder, tap the Location bar, which is labeled with the bookmark's current location and is always the lowest bar on the screen.

7. Scroll the list of bookmarks until you see the folder in which you want to place the folder.

8. Tap the folder into which you want to move the folder you are editing.

9. Tap Done. You move back to the Bookmarks screen, which reflects any changes you made.

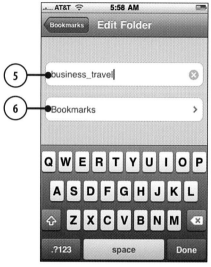

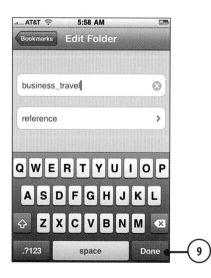

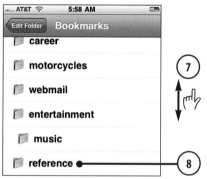

10. Tap a bookmark you want to change.

Editing a Bookmark

If the bookmark you want to change isn't on the screen you are editing, tap Done to exit Edit mode. Then open the folder containing the bookmark you want to edit and tap Edit.

11. Change the bookmark's name in the name bar.

12. If you want to change a bookmark's URL, tap the URL bar and make changes to the current URL.

13. To change the location of the folder or bookmark, tap the Location bar and follow steps 7 and 8.

14. Tap Done. You move back to the previous screen, and any changes you made, such as changing the name or location of a bookmark, are reflected.

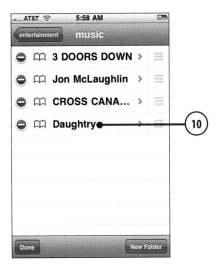

15. To create a new folder, tap New Folder.

16. Enter the name of the folder.

17. Follow steps 6 though 8 to choose the location in which you want to save the new folder.

18. Tap Done. The new folder is created in the location you selected. You can place folders and bookmarks into it by using the Location bar to navigate to it.

19. Tap Done. Your changes are saved, and you exit Edit Bookmarks mode.

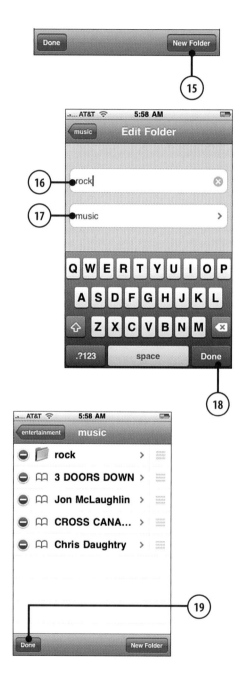

Deleting Bookmarks or Folders

1. Move to the Bookmarks screen containing the folder or bookmark you want to delete.

2. Tap Edit. The unlock buttons appear next to the folders and bookmarks you can change; some folders, such as the History folder, can't be changed. The Order buttons also appear.

3. Scroll up and down the screen to find the bookmark or folder you want to delete.

4. Tap its unlock button.

5. Tap Delete. The folder or bookmark is deleted. Deleting a folder also deletes all the bookmarks it contains.

6. Repeat steps 4 and 5 to delete other folders or bookmarks.

7. Tap Done. You move out of Edit mode.

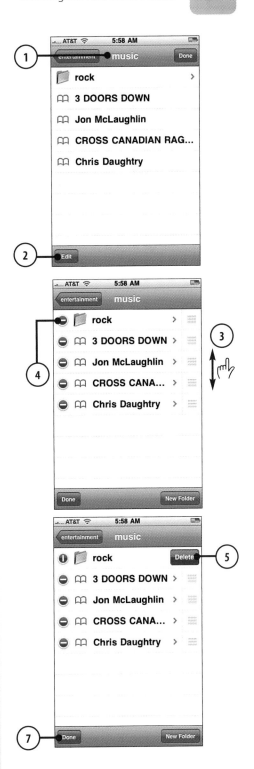

Creating a Bookmark on the Home Screen

You can add a bookmark icon to the Home screen so you can visit a webpage from there; this handy trick saves you several navigation moves to get into Safari and then you can move to the page you want via typing the URL or using a bookmark.

1. Use Safari to move to a webpage to which you want to have easy access from the Home screen.

2. Tap the Action button.

3. Tap Add to Home Screen.

4. If needed, edit the name of the icon on the Home Screen. The default name is the name of the webpage, but you will want to keep the name short because it has a small amount of room on the button on the Home Screen.

5. Tap Add. You move to the Home Screen and see the icon you added. You can return to the site at any time by tapping this icon.

Location Is Everything

You can organize the buttons on the pages of the Home Screen so you can place your webpage buttons in convenient locations. See Chapter 16, "Customizing an iPhone," for details.

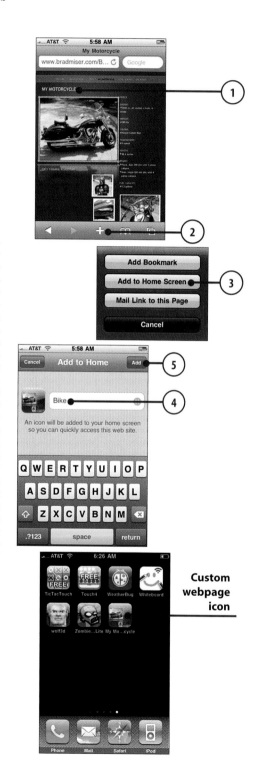

Custom webpage icon

Emailing a Link to a Webpage

Sometimes when you visit a webpage, you want to share it with others. Using Safari, you can quickly email links to webpages you visit.

1. Use Safari to navigate to a webpage whose link you want to email to someone.

2. Tap the Action button.

3. Tap Mail Link to This Page. A new email message is created, and the link to the webpage is inserted into the body. The subject of the message is the title of the webpage.

4. Complete and send the email message. (See Chapter 7, "Emailing," for all you need to know about using iPhone email.) When the recipient receives your message, he can visit the website by clicking the link.

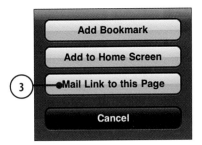

Completing Web Forms

Just like web browsers on a computer, you can provide information through webpages in Safari by completing forms, such as to log in to your account on a website or request information about something. You can manually enter information or use AutoFill to have Safari add the information for you. (This must be enabled using Safari settings as explained at the beginning of this chapter.)

>>>*step-by-step*

Completing Forms Manually

1. Open Safari and move to a website containing a form.

2. Zoom in on the fields you need to complete.

3. Tap in a field. The keyboard pops up.

4. Enter information in the first field.

5. Tap Next. If there isn't another field on the form, this button is disabled, so skip this step. If it is enabled, you move to the next field on the form.

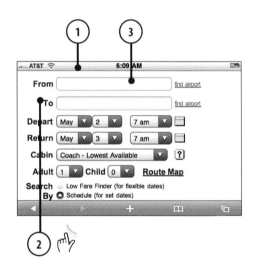

Those Wheels Keep on Spinnin'

When you have to make a selection on a form, such as a date, a selection wheel appears on the iPhone's screen. You can drag up or down to spin the wheel and then tap on what you want to select to enter the appropriate information into the field.

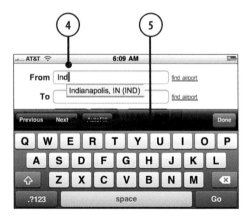

6. Repeat steps 4 and 5 to complete all the fields on the form.

7. Tap Done. The keyboard closes, and you move back to the web-page.

8. Tap Search, Submit, Go, Login, or another button to provide the form's information to the website.

Completing Forms with AutoFill

1. Open Safari and move to a web-site containing a form. Zoom in on the fields you need to complete, and tap in a field. The keyboard pops up.

2. Tap AutoFill. Safari fills any fields it can, based on the information in Contacts. Any fields that Safari tries to complete are highlighted in yellow.

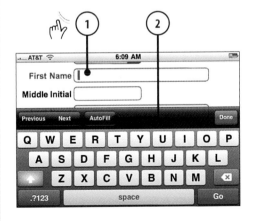

3. Use the steps in the previous section to review all the fields and to edit any that AutoFill wasn't able to complete or that need to be changed.

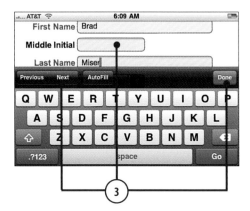

Signing In Automatically

If you enable Safari to remember user names and passwords, you can log in to some websites automatically. When Safari encounters a site for which it recognizes and is able to save login information, you are prompted to allow Safari to save that information. Once saved, this information is entered for you automatically.

1. Move to a webpage that requires you to log into an account.

2. Enter your account's user name and password.

3. Tap the button to log in to your account, such as Submit, Login, and such. You are prompted to save the login information.

4. To save the information, tap Yes. The next time you move to the login page, your user name and password are entered for you automatically. (Tap Never for this website if you don't want the information to be saved and you don't want to be prompted again. Tap Not Now if you don't want the information saved now but do want to be prompted to save it again later.)

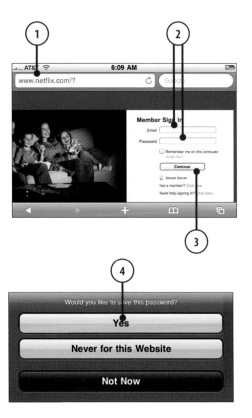

Opening and Managing Multiple Webpages at the Same Time

Using Safari, you can open and work with multiple webpages at the same time. Some links on webpages open a new page, or you can open a new page manually at any time.

1. Using Safari, open a webpage.

2. Tap the Page Manager button.

Safari Keeps Working

As you move to webpages, you can immediately tap the Page Manager button to open more pages. Pages continue to load in the background as you move between the Page Manager and individual pages.

---

3. Tap New Page. A new webpage opens. The counter on the Page Manager button increases by one to show you how many pages are open.

4. Use Safari's tools to move to another webpage. You can enter a URL, use a bookmark, perform a search, and so on.

5. View and work with the webpage.

6. Repeat steps 2 through 5 to open as many webpages as you want to see.

7. Tap the Page Manager button again. You see a thumbnail representation of each open webpage.

8. To move between pages, drag your finger to the left or to the right until the page you want to view is in focus.

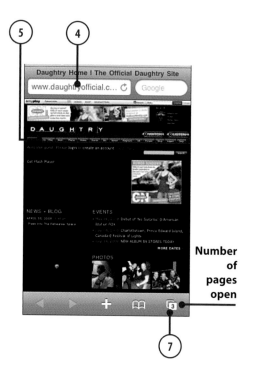

Number of pages open

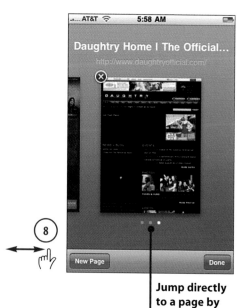

Jump directly to a page by tapping its dot.

9. To move to the page in focus, tap it or tap Done. You move to the webpage and can view it.

10. Tap the Page Manager button. You move back to the Page Manager.

11. To close an open page, tap its Close button. The page closes and disappears from the Page Manager screen, and the counter is reduced by one.

Tap here to configure an iPhone for audio.

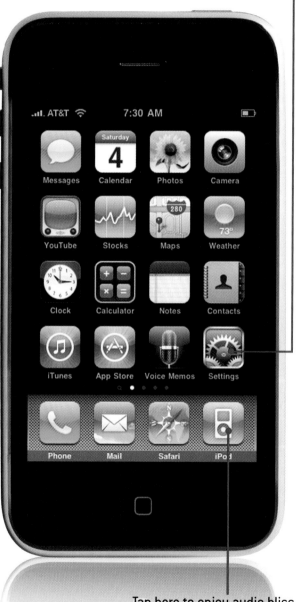

Tap here to enjoy audio bliss.

In this chapter, you'll explore all the audio functionality the iPhone offers. The topics include the following:

→ Finding and listening to music
→ Controlling audio content with the iPod control bar
→ Finding and listing to podcasts
→ Customizing your iPhone for music

11

Listening to Music, Podcasts, and Other Audio

The primary reason iPods have become such a phenomenon is that they are amazingly powerful devices for listening to all kinds of audio, including music, podcasts (which came into existence because of iPods), audiobooks, and others. After you move audio content onto your iPhone (learn how to stock your iPhone with great audio in Chapter 3," Moving Audio, Video, and Photos onto Your iPhone"), you can use the iPhone's fantastic and fun iPod application to enjoy that content in many ways.

Finding and Listening to Music

There are two fundamental steps to listening to music and other audio content. First, find the content you want to listen to by using one of the many search options your iPhone offers. Second, after you find and select what you want to hear, use the iPhone's playback controls to listen to your heart's content.

Turn It Up! (Or Down!)

No matter which technique you use to find and play music, you can control the volume using the Volume keys on the left side of iPhone. Press the upper part of the rocker switch to increase volume or the lower part to decrease it. While you are pressing the switch, a volume indicator appears on the screen to show you the relative volume level as you press a key.

>>>*step-by-step*

Using the Cover Flow Browser to Find and Play Music

The Cover Flow Browser simulates what it's like to flip through a stack of CDs; you can quickly peruse your entire music collection to get to the right music for your current mood.

1. On the Home screen, tap the iPod button.

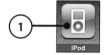

2. Tap one of the category buttons, such as Playlists or Artists.

3. Rotate your iPhone 90 degrees in either direction, and the Cover Flow Browser appears; the Browser shows all the music stored on your iPhone no matter which category you chose in step 2. Each cover represents an album from which you have at least one song stored on your iPhone.

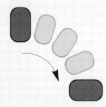

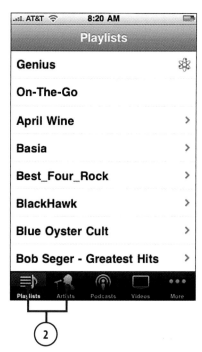

4. To browse your tunes, drag a finger to the right to move ahead in the albums or to the left to move back; the faster you drag, the faster you "flip" through the albums. The album cover that is directly facing you, front and center on the screen, is the album in focus, meaning that it's the one you can explore.

Jump to an Album

Tap any album cover you see on the screen to quickly bring that album into focus.

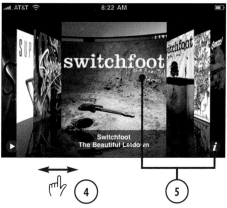

5. To see the songs on an album, move it into focus and tap its cover or tap the Info button. The Contents screen appears, showing you a list of all the songs on that album.

Text Labels for Album Covers

When you first view the Cover Flow Browser, you see only album covers. After you select and play music and then move back to the Browser, you see text labels under the album cover. These labels are artist (top line of the text) and album name (bottom line of text) for any album you aren't playing; when an album containing a song that is currently playing is in focus, you also see the title of the song that is playing on the middle row of text.

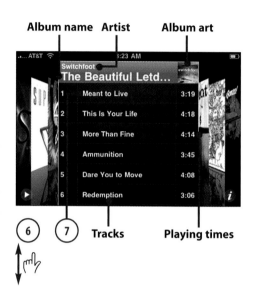

6. To browse the list of songs, drag your finger up or down the screen.

7. To play a song, tap it. The song plays and is marked with a blue Play button arrow on the list of songs. The Play icon appears near the battery icon in the upper right corner of the screen. The Pause button appears in the lower left corner of the screen.

8. To pause a song, tap the Pause button. The music pauses, and the Play button replaces the Pause button.

9. To play a different song, tap it.

10. To return to the album's cover, tap its title information, tap the Info button, or just tap outside of the album cover.

11. While you're listening, you can continue browsing to find more music you want to listen to. (When the iPhone starts playing the next song in the album you are currently playing, the cover for that album jumps back into focus.)

12. Rotate the iPhone 90 degrees to see the Now Playing screen.

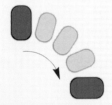

13. Use the Now Playing screen to control the music (covered in detail in the "Playing Music" task later in this section).

Missing Album Artwork

When an iPhone doesn't have artwork for an album, you see a generic musical note icon as the album cover in the Cover Flow Browser. You can use iTunes to associate artwork with albums that don't currently have it. The next time you sync your iPhone, the new album artwork appears in the Browser.

Using Playlists to Find Music

Finding and listening to music in your iTunes playlists that you moved onto your iPhone is simple.

1. On the Home screen, tap the iPod button.

2. Tap the Playlists button. The list of all playlists on your iPhone appears.

3. Slide your finger up and down the list to browse your playlists.

4. Tap the playlist that you'd like to explore. The list of songs in that playlist appears with the title of the playlist at the top of the screen.

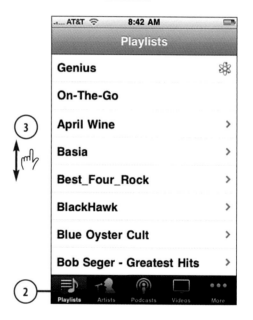

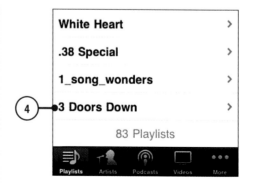

5. Drag your finger up and down to browse the songs the playlist contains. (You can also search a playlist by browsing up until you see the Search bar at the top of the screen; learn how in the section "Searching for Music" later in this chapter.)

6. When you find a song you want to listen to, tap it. The song begins to play, and the Now Playing screen appears.

7. Use the Now Playing screen to control the music (covered in detail in the "Playing Music" section later in this chapter).

8. Tap the Return button to move back to the playlist's screen. (When you are viewing a playlist's screen, the song currently playing is marked with the speaker icon.)

Back to the Browser

No matter how you end up there, you can always move between the Now Playing screen and the Cover Flow Browser by rotating the iPhone 90 degrees. Whenever the iPhone is oriented horizontally, the Browser appears.

Song title —
Album —
Artist —

Music video —

Using Artists to Find Music

You can find music on iPhone by artist.

1. On the Home screen, tap the iPod button.

2. Tap Artists. The list of all artists whose content is on iPhone appears. Artists are grouped by the first letter of their first name or by the first letter of the group's name.

3. Drag your finger up and down the list to browse all available artists. (At the top of the screen, you see the Search tool by which you can search for specific artists. See "Searching for Music" later in this chapter for more information.)

4. To jump to a specific artist, tap the letter along the right side of the screen for the artist's or group's first name; to jump to an artist or group whose name starts with a number, tap # at the bottom of the screen.

5. Tap an artist whose music you'd like to explore. A list of songs by that artist appears. If you have more than one album by that artist, the songs are organized by album; otherwise, you'll simply see a list of the songs on the one album from which you have music, and you can skip to step 8.

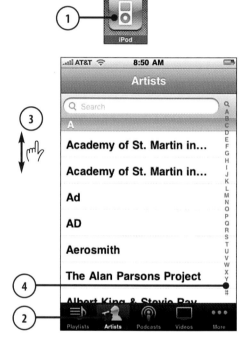

6. Drag your finger up and down the screen to browse the artist's albums.

7. To see the contents of an album, tap it, and the list of contents screen appears with the album's title at the top of the screen. Or to view all the songs by the artist, skip to step 13.

8. Drag your finger up and down the screen to browse all the songs on the selected album.

9. When you find the song you want to listen to, tap it. The song begins to play, and the Now Playing screen appears.

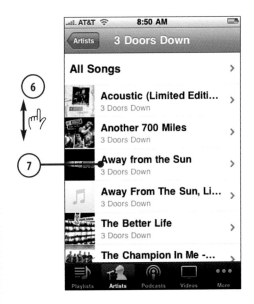

10. Use the Now Playing screen to control the music (covered in detail in the "Playing Music" task later in this section).

11. To move back to the previous screen, tap Return. If you only have one album by the artist, you move back to that album's screen and can skip to step 17 to return to the Artists screen. If you have more than one album, you move back to the artist's screen.

12. To move back to the artist's screen, tap Return (which is labeled with the artist's name).

13. To see all the songs by the artist, tap All Songs. You see the list of all songs by the artist, organized alphabetically.

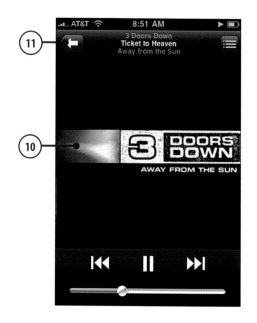

14. Browse the list or tap a letter to move to a song you want to hear.

15. Tap the song you want to hear. The song begins to play, and the Now Playing screen appears.

16. Use the Now Playing screen to control playback of the music (covered in detail in the "Playing Music" task later in this section).

17. Tap Return to move back to any of the previous screens to find and play more music.

To Now Playing and Back

Whenever music is playing or paused, the Now Playing screen is active even when it isn't visible. You can move to the Now Playing screen by tapping the Now Playing button located in the upper right corner of the screen. You can return from the Now Playing screen back to where you were by tapping the Return button located in the upper left corner of the Now Playing screen.

Using the Songs Tool to Find Music

You can use the Songs tool to easily find specific songs.

1. On the Home screen, tap the iPod button.

2. Tap Songs. You see a screen show-ing all the songs on the iPhone, organized alphabetically. Under each song, you see the artist and album from which the song comes.

No Songs Button on the Toolbar?

If you don't see the Songs button on the toolbar at the bottom of the screen, tap More and then tap Songs on the More screen. You learn more about More later in this chapter.

---

3. Drag your finger up and down the list to browse all available songs. (If you browse to the top of the screen, you see the Search tool with which you can search for specific songs. See "Searching for Music" later in this chapter.)

4. To jump to a specific song, tap the letter along the right side of the screen for the song's name; to jump to a song whose name starts with a number, tap the # sign at the bottom of the alpha-betical index.

5. Tap the song you want to play. The song begins to play, and the Now Playing screen appears.

6. Use the Now Playing screen to control the music (covered in detail in the "Playing Music" task later in this section).

Using Albums to Find Music

Like the other categories, you can use Albums to find music quickly and easily.

1. On the Home screen, tap the iPod button.

2. Tap Albums. You see a screen showing all the albums on the iPhone, organized alphabetically by album title (the iPhone ignores "the" in titles). Under each album, you see the artist for that album.

No Albums Button on the Toolbar Either?

If you don't see the Albums button on the toolbar at the bottom of the screen, tap More and then tap Albums on the More screen.

---

3. Browse all available albums. (If you browse to the top of the screen, you see the Search tool with which you can search for specific albums. See "Searching for Music" later in this chapter.)

4. To jump to a specific album, tap the letter along the right side of the screen for the album's name; to jump to an album whose name starts with a number, tap the # symbol at the bottom of the alphabetical index.

5. Tap the album you want to explore. You move to the album's screen on which you see all the songs it contains.

6. Browse the songs on the album.

7. Tap the song you want to play. The song begins to play, and the Now Playing screen appears.

8. Use the Now Playing screen to control the music (covered in detail in the "Playing Music" task later in this section).

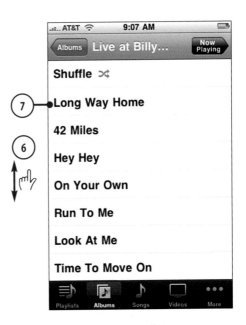

Using the More Menu to Find Music

The More menu shows you all the content categories on iPhone. You can use this menu to access content when it can't be found by one of the category buttons at the bottom of the screen.

1. On the Home screen, tap the iPod button.

2. Tap More. The More screen appears, showing you the content categories on your iPhone that aren't shown on the toolbar at the bottom of the screen.

3. Tap the category in which you are interested, such as Genres. That category's screen appears.

4. Browse the category and drill down into its detail to get to songs you want to hear. Browsing categories is similar to browsing playlists, artists, songs, and albums. (If you browse to the top of the screen, you see the Search tool with which you can search in most categories. See "Searching for Music" later in this chapter.)

Your Faves

As you learn a little later in this chapter, you can configure the toolbar to contain the buttons you use most frequently.

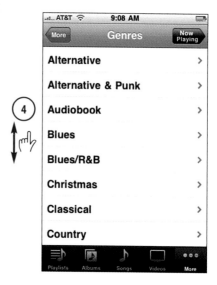

Searching for Music

Browsing is a useful way to find music, but it can be faster to search for specific music in which you are interested. You can search most of the screens that you browse, and when a category has a lot of options, such as Songs, searching can get you where you want to go more quickly than browsing. Here's how.

1. Move to a screen you can browse; this example uses the Songs screen, but you can search most screens similarly.

2. Browse to the top of the screen so you see the Search tool.

3. Tap in the Search tool. The keyboard appears.

4. Type the text or numbers for which you want to search. As you type, the items that meet your search criterion are shown; the more you type, the more specific your search becomes. Below the Search tool, you see the results organized into categories, such as Albums and Songs.

5. When you think you've typed enough to find what you're looking for, tap Search. The keyboard disappears.

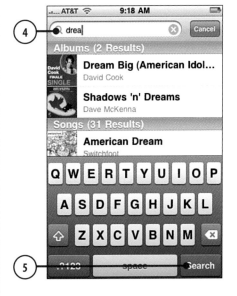

6. Browse the results.

7. Tap songs or albums to get to the music you want to play.

Clearing or Editing a Search

You can clear a search by tapping the "x" that appears on the right end of the Search tool after you have entered text or numbers. You can edit the search text just like you edit any other text (see Chapter 1, "Getting Started with Your iPhone" to learn about entering and editing text).

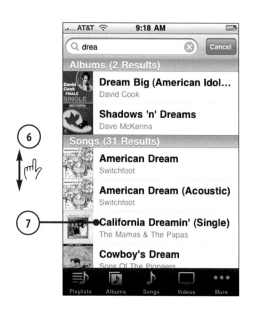

Using the Genius to Find Music

The Genius feature finds music and builds a playlist based on songs that "go with" a specific song. How the Genius selects songs that "sound good" with other songs is a bit of a secret, but it works amazingly well. You can have the Genius build a playlist for you in a couple of ways and then work with the Genius playlist similar to other kinds of playlists.

Creating a Genius Playlist Based on the Current Song

1. Find and play a song using any of the techniques you learned earlier in this chapter.

2. If the Timeline bar doesn't appear on the Now Playing screen, tap the screen so the Timeline and controls appear.

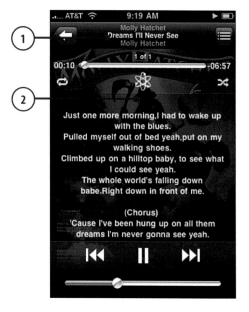

3. Tap the Genius button. While the music plays, the Genius playlist is created, and you move to the Genius screen where you see the songs that the Genius selected; the song that is currently playing is at the top of the list and is marked with the Genius icon.

4. Tap any song on the playlist to start playing it.

5. Tap the New button to start a new Genius playlist (see the "Creating a Genius Playlist By Selecting a Song" section in this chapter).

6. To have the Genius change the playlist, tap Refresh. Songs might be added, and the order in which they are listed might be changed.

7. To save the playlist, tap Save. The name of the playlist changes from Genius to the name of the song on which the playlist was based. The New button disappears, and the Delete button appears.

They Really Are Genius

Genius playlists appear on the Playlists screen like other playlists you have created, except they are marked with the Genius icon, and they appear at the top of the Playlists screen (instead of being listed alphabetically). You can play Genius playlists just like others on the Playlists screen, and you can edit them (covered in the "Refreshing a Genius Playlist" section). Genius playlists are also moved into your iTunes Library on your computer the next time you sync your iPhone.

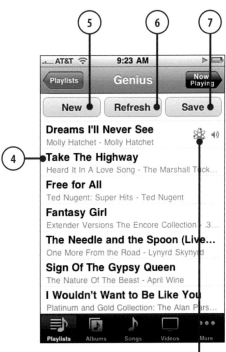

Song the Genius used to create the playlist

Creating a Genius Playlist By Selecting a Song

1. Move to the Playlists screen.

2. Tap Genius. The Songs screen appears.

3. Browse or search for the song on which you want the playlist to be based.

4. Tap the song on which you want the playlist to be based. The Genius creates the playlist, and it appears briefly on the Genius screen. It starts to play automatically, and you move to the Now Playing screen.

5. Tap the Return button. You move back to the Genius screen.

6. Use steps 4 through 7 in the previous task to work with the playlist.

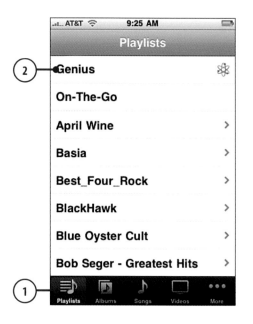

Refreshing a Genius Playlist

1. Move to the Playlists screen.

2. Tap the Genius playlist you want to manage; Genius playlists are named with the name of the song on which they are based, and they have the Genius icon. The Genius playlist's screen appears.

3. Tap Refresh. The Genius builds a new playlist based on the same song. The resulting playlist might have the same or different songs, and they might be in a different order. The refreshed playlist replaces the previous version.

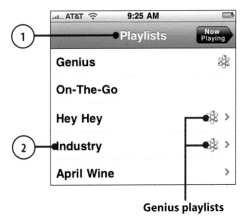

Genius playlists

Deleting a Genius Playlist

To delete a Genius playlist, move to its screen and tap the Delete button. The playlist is deleted (of course, the songs on your iPhone are not affected). If you have synced your iPhone since you saved the playlist, you won't see the Delete button because the playlist has been saved to your iTunes Library. To delete a playlist after you've synced your iPhone, delete it from your iTunes Library and then resync your iPhone.

Finding Music by Shuffling

This section is a bit of a contrivance because when you shuffle music, you don't really find it, but rather you rely on your iPhone to select music "randomly." There are two ways to shuffle music: You can use the Shuffle option, or you can shake your iPhone.

Shuffling with the Shuffle Option

1. Move to a source of songs. There are many ways to do this, such as selecting a playlist, browsing an artist, and so on.

2. Browse to the top of the screen if you aren't there already.

3. Tap Shuffle. Your iPhone selects a song from the group you were browsing and plays it; you move to the Now Playing screen. After that song plays; the iPhone selects another one and plays it. This continues until all the songs in the source have played.

Shuffling by Shaking

1. Move to a source of songs that you want to shuffle through. There are many ways to do this, such as selecting a playlist, browsing an artist, and so on.

2. Tap a song. It starts to play, and you move to the Now Playing screen.

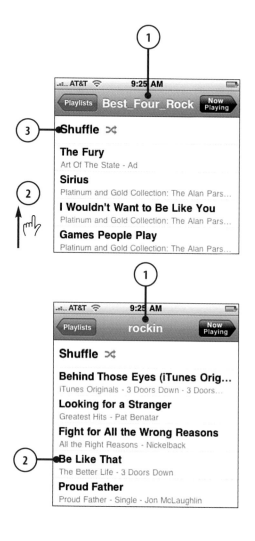

3. Gently shake your iPhone. You hear the shuffle sound and a song is selected at random and begins to play. You can shake your iPhone at any time to move to the next randomly selected song. After the first time you shake it, the Shuffle button is activated so the music plays in Shuffle mode from then on.

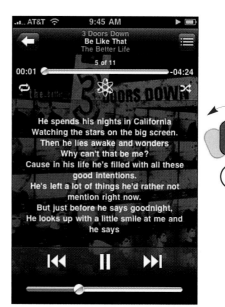

Finding Music by Speaking (iPhone 3GS only)

If you have an iPhone 3GS, you can speak voice commands to find and play music (see Chapter 1 for more information about working with voice commands). You can speak the name of a playlist, album, or artist to find and play the associated music.

1. Activate voice command mode by pressing and holding the Home button or the button on the earbud headset until you hear the voice command chime or see the Voice Control screen.

2. Speak the voice command. For example, to find and play a playlist, say, "play *playlistname*," where *playlistname* is the name of the playlist you want to find and play. You'll hear the iPhone repeat the command it thinks it heard and then perform it.

More Spoken Commands for Music

There are a number of commands you can speak to find, play, and control music (and other audio). "Play *artist*" plays music by the artist you speak. "Play *album*" plays the album you name. In both cases, if the name includes the word "the," you need to include "the" when you speak the command. "Shuffle" plays a random song. "Play more like this" uses the Genius to find songs similar to the one playing and plays them. "Previous track" or "next track" does exactly what they sound like they do. To hear the name of the artist for the song currently playing, say "Who sings this song?"

It's Not All Good

Voice commands work pretty well, but they aren't perfect. Make sure you confirm the command by listening to the feedback the phone provides when it repeats your command. Sometimes, a spoken command can have unexpected results, which can include making a phone call to someone on your Contacts list. If you don't catch such a mistake before the call is started, you might be surprised to hear someone answering your call instead of hearing music you intended to play.

Playing Music

As you have seen, the Now Playing screen appears whenever you play music. This screen provides many controls and options for playing music.

Lyrics and the Timeline Bar

You can add lyrics to songs in iTunes. Tap the Now Playing screen once to show the lyrics. Tap it again to hide them. Lyrics and the Timeline bar are in the state they last were each time you were on the Now Playing screen. If you display lyrics and the Timeline bar and move away from the Now Playing screen, they will be displayed the next time you move back. Likewise, if they are hidden when you move away, they remain hidden when you return.

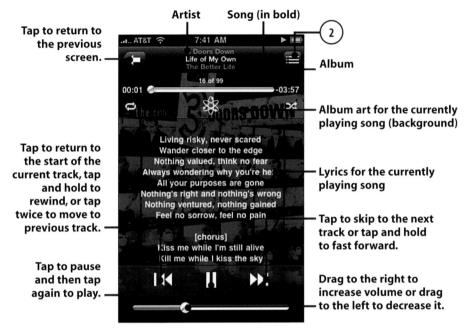

Tap to return to the previous screen.

Artist   Song (in bold)

2

Album

Album art for the currently playing song (background)

Tap to return to the start of the current track, tap and hold to rewind, or tap twice to move to previous track.

Lyrics for the currently playing song

Tap to skip to the next track or tap and hold to fast forward.

Tap to pause and then tap again to play.

Drag to the right to increase volume or drag to the left to decrease it.

Activate voice commands and say "next," "previous," "pause, or "play" to perform those actions (3GS only).

1. Find and play a song or album. The Now Playing screen appears, and you can use its controls.

2. Tap the Track List view button. The Album Cover view is replaced by the Track List view. Here you see the list of all tracks on the album from which the current song comes, even if you aren't listening to the album itself (such as when you are listening to a playlist). You see the order of tracks on the album along with their names and playing times.

3. Drag your finger up and down to browse through the tracks in the album.

4. Tap a song to play it.

5. Rate the song currently playing by tapping one of the dots. Stars replace the dot you tapped to give the song a star rating between one and five stars.

6. Tap the Album Cover button. You return to the Album Cover view.

7. If you don't see the Timeline bar, tap the album cover once. The Timeline bar appears. (If a song has lyrics associated with it, they appear along with the Timeline bar.)

8. To repeat the current album until you stop playing it, tap the Repeat button. When the album is set to repeat indefinitely, the Repeat button turns blue. To repeat the album one time, tap the Repeat button again. When the album is set to repeat once, the button turns blue and contains a small "1." To turn off repeat, tap the button again so it is white.

9. To move ahead or back in the song, drag the Playhead to the right or left.

10. To play the songs on the album randomly, tap the Shuffle button.

11. If the song has lyrics, browse up and down the screen to read all the lyrics.

12. Tap the album cover again. The Timeline bar and lyrics (if there are any) disappear.

Song currently playing

Timeline bar

Tap to create a Genius playlist.

13. Tap the Return button. You move back to the screen from which you selected music to play. Tap the Now Playing button. You return to the Now Playing screen.

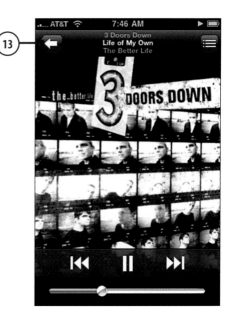

Viewing Albums

As soon as you play a song from the Track List view screen, you jump to Album mode. From that point on, you are working only with the album from which the current song came. For example, if you play a playlist, switch to Track List view and play a different song on the same album; you change the content to only that album, so the next song that plays is the next one on the album, not the next one in the playlist. When you tap the Return button, you move to the album's screen instead of the playlist's screen. If you view only the song's information or give it a rating in Track List view, when you move back to the Cover view, you are still working with the original source, such as a playlist.

Controlling Audio Content with the iPod Control Bar

Because you can do so much more on iPhone than just listen to music, you'll often be doing something else, such as browsing the web while music is playing. It would be a nuisance to have to move back into the iPod functions to perform basic actions, such as pausing music. Fortunately, with the iPod control bar, you don't have to.

>>>*step-by-step*

Configure the iPod Control Bar

First, configure how you want to activate the control bar.

1. On the Home screen, tap Settings.

2. Tap General.

3. Scroll down until you see the Home option.

4. Tap Home.

5. If you want to see and use the playback controls when you press the Home button twice, tap iPod.

6. To make the iPod control bar active when music is playing, ensure ON shows next to iPod Controls; if not, tap OFF, which turns the function off.

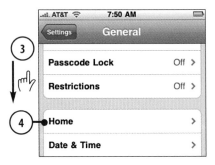

Use the iPod Control Bar

Use the control bar to do the following tasks.

1. Play music.

2. Move away from the Music
   screens, such as by moving back
   to the Home screen and then
   opening the web browser.

3. Tap the Home button twice. The
   screen you were using fades into
   the background, and the iPod
   control bar appears.

4. Use the controls on the bar to
   control music.

5. When you're done, tap Close. The
   control bar closes, and you move
   back to whatever you were doing.

**Tap to return to the start
of the current track, tap
and hold to rewind, or
tap twice to move to the
previous track.**

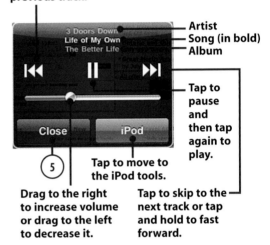

Artist
Song (in bold)
Album

**Tap to
pause
and
then tap
again to
play.**

**Tap to move to
the iPod tools.**

**Drag to the right
to increase volume
or drag to the left
to decrease it.**

**Tap to skip to the
next track or tap
and hold to fast
forward.**

Finding and Listening to Podcasts

An iPhone is a great way to listen to your podcasts. Like all other audio functions, you first find the podcast you want to listen to and then use iPhone's
audio playback controls to hear it.

>>>step-by-step

1. On the Home screen, tap the iPod button.

2. Tap the More button. The More screen appears, showing you all the content categories on the iPhone.

3. Tap Podcasts. The Podcasts screen appears, showing you the podcasts to which you are subscribed and that have been moved onto the iPhone.

4. Browse or search for a podcast to which you want to listen.

5. Select a podcast by tapping it. The list of episodes for that podcast is shown; the name of the list screen is the name of the podcast. Podcasts to which you haven't listened are marked with a blue dot.

More Episodes

If you tap Get More Episodes, you move into the iTunes Store application where you can find and download more episodes of the podcast or add different podcasts to your iPhone. This is covered in Chapter 3.

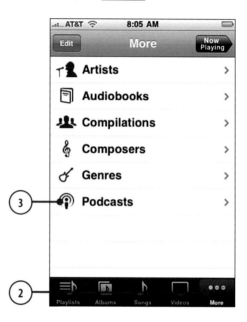

6. Tap the episode you want to hear. The podcast begins to play, and the Now Playing screen appears.

7. If the Timeline bar isn't showing, tap the screen. The Timeline bar appears. Some of the controls are the same as for music, while there are some that are unique to podcasts.

8. To repeat the last 30 seconds, tap the Repeat button.

Video Podcasts

When a podcast is a video podcast, the video plays on the Now Playing screen. You can also play video podcasts using the iPhone's video playback tools, which you learn about in the next chapter.

9. To change the speed at which the podcast plays, tap the 1x button; the podcast plays at twice the normal speed, and the button shows 2x. Tap it again to play the podcast at one-half speed, and the button shows 1/2x. Tap the button again to return to normal speed.

10. Tap the email button to share the episode you are listening to with someone else. When you tap this, a new email message is created. This message contains a link to the podcast that the recipient can click to access it. You address and complete the message and then send it (see Chapter 7, "Emailing," for the steps to send email). The recipient clicks the link to move to the iTunes Store to try out the podcast.

11. Use the other controls on the Now Playing screen, which work just as they do when you are playing music.

Audiobooks

Another excellent iPod function is the capability to listen to audiobooks. You can get these from the iTunes Store, Audible.com, and many other locations. After you add audiobooks to your iTunes Library, you determine whether they are moved to iPhone by using the music-syncing tools. The tools and techniques for listening to audiobooks are similar to listening to podcasts.

Customizing Your iPhone for Music

You can use your iPhone as an iPod just fine without performing any of the steps in this section. However, because this book is named *My iPhone*, you should explore these options to make iPhone your own.

>>>*step-by-step*

Building and Editing an On-The-Go Playlist

You can build a special playlist on iPhone by selecting songs to include in your custom playlist. This is called the On-The-Go playlist because, well, you build it while you are on the go.

Creating and Listening to an On-The-Go Playlist

1. Move to the Playlists screen.

2. Tap On-The-Go. The Songs screen appears.

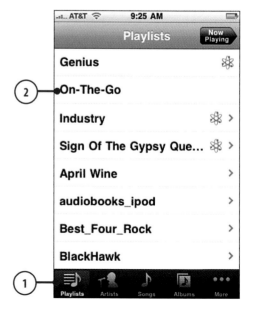

Add from Anywhere

While you're in Playlist-building mode, you can add content from any iPod screen. For example, to add content by artist instead of by song, tap the Artists button. The Artists screen appears. Tap the artist whose music you want to add to the playlist and add the songs by that artist by tapping those songs or clicking the Add buttons. You can add content by genre, composer, and so on in the same way.

3. Browse all the songs on iPhone or scroll to the top of the screen and search for songs.

4. To add a song to the playlist, tap the song or the Add button. After you add a song, it is grayed out to show it's already part of the playlist. You can add the same song to the playlist only one time.

5. Repeat steps 3 and 4 until you've added all the songs you want the playlist to contain.

6. Tap Done. You move to the On-The-Go playlist screen and see the songs it contains.

7. Play the On-The-Go playlist just like playlists you've moved from the iTunes Library.

All at Once

You can add all the songs shown on any screen by tapping Add All Songs.

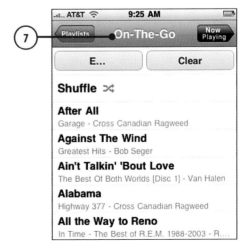

Changing an On-The-Go Playlist

1. Move to the Playlists screen as described in the previous task and tap the On-The-Go playlist option. You see the On-The-Go playlist screen.

2. Tap Edit. The screen changes to Edit mode.

Clear It

To remove all songs from a playlist, tap Clear and then tap Clear Playlist again. The playlist is returned to an empty state.

3. To add songs, tap the Add button; this works just like when you added songs to the playlist originally. (See the previous section for details.)

4. To change the order in which songs play, tap the List button and drag a song to its new position on the playlist.

5. To remove songs, tap the Unlock button. The Delete button appears.

6. Tap Delete. The song is removed from the playlist.

7. When you're finished making changes, tap Done. You move back to the On-The-Go playlist screen.

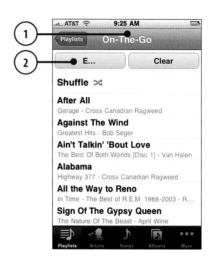

>>> Go Further

SAVING THE ON-THE-GO PLAYLIST

When you sync your iPhone, the On-The-Go playlist moves into your iTunes Library where you can work with it just like playlists you create in iTunes. For example, you can change its name, its content, and so on.

Each time you change the On-The-Go playlist on the iPhone, a new version is created. When you sync, that version moves into iTunes, and its name is updated with a sequential number, as in On-The-Go1, On-The-Go2, and so on. Each version becomes a new playlist in your iTunes Library.

>>>step-by-step

Configuring the iPhone's Music Toolbar

The five buttons at the bottom of the iPod screen enable you to get to specific content quickly. You can choose four of the buttons that appear on the screen to make accessing content by the categories that are most useful to you even easier and faster.

1. Move to the More screen.

2. Tap Edit. The Configure screen appears.

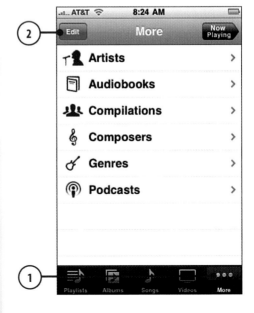

3. Drag the button you want to add to the toolbar to the location of one of the buttons currently there. As you hover over the current button, it lights up to show you that it will be the one replaced when you lift your finger. The button you dragged replaces the button over which you placed it. The original button is moved onto the Configure screen.

4. Repeat step 3 until the four buttons you want to be on the toolbar are there. (The fifth button is always the More button.)

5. Drag the buttons on the toolbar around until they are in the order you want them to be.

6. Tap the Done button. The iPod toolbar contains the buttons you placed on it along with the More button.

Configuring the iPhone's Music Settings

There are a few Music settings you use to configure various aspects of iPhone's audio functionality.

1. Tap the Home button to move back to iPhone's Home.

2. Tap Settings.

3. Scroll down and tap iPod.

4. Tap ON next to Shake to Shuffle if you don't want your iPhone to shuffle to the next song when you shake it. The status becomes OFF, which means if you shake your iPhone, songs play in the order they are listed in the source you are playing. Press OFF to enable shuffling by shaking again.

5. Tap Sound Check if you want the iPhone to attempt to even the volume of the music you play so that all the songs play at about the same relative volume level. Sound Check's status is indicated by OFF or ON. When you tap the Sound Check button, its status toggles from one to the other.

6. To set an equalizer, tap the EQ bar. The EQ screen appears.

7. Scroll the screen to see all the equalizers available to you.

8. Tap the equalizer you want the iPhone to use when you play music; the current equalizer is indicated by the check mark. To turn the equalizer off, select Off.

9. Tap iPod.

10. To set a limit to the volume level on iPhone, tap Volume Limit. The Volume Limit screen appears.

11. Drag the volume slider to the point that you want the maximum volume level to be.

12. To lock this control so that it can't be changed without a passcode, tap Lock Volume Limit. The Set Code screen appears.

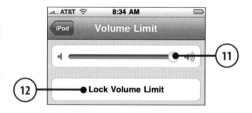

13. Tap a four-digit code.

14. Re-enter the code to confirm it. If the code matches, you return to the Volume Limit screen, and the code is set.

15. To make changes to a locked volume limit, tap Unlock Volume Limit.

16. Enter the code. The volume limit is unlocked, and you can change it again.

Forgot the Code?

If you forget the passcode, you can reset or restore iPhone to clear it. See Chapter 17, "Maintaining an iPhone and Solving Problems," to learn how.

---

17. Tap iPod to move back to the iPod Settings screen.

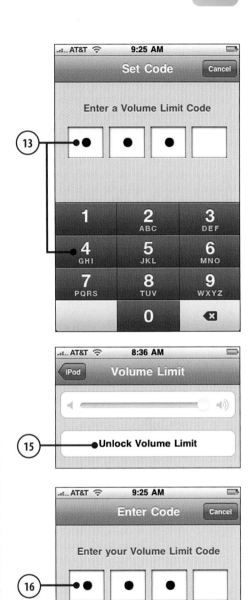

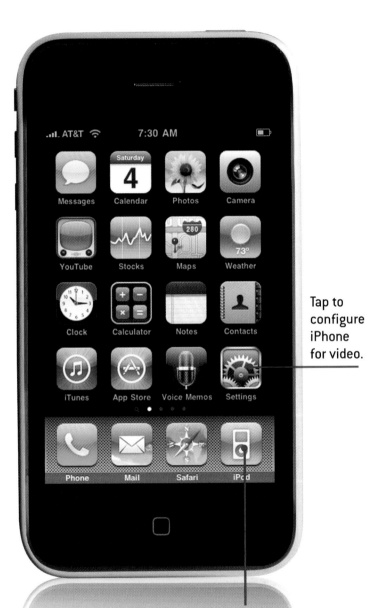

Tap to configure iPhone for video.

Tap to enjoy movies, TV shows, and other video right in the palm of your hand.

In this chapter, you explore all the video functionality the iPhone offers. The topics include the following:

→ Finding and watching video content, including movies, TV shows, and video podcasts
→ Configuring iPhone video settings

Watching Movies, TV Shows, and Other Video

Your iPhone is a great way to enjoy different types of video, including movies, episodes of your favorite TV series, and video podcasts. Be prepared to be amazed; the high quality and portability more than make up for the relatively small screen size (well, relatively small in today's world of 50-inch+ TVs that is!). Like music and other content, the first step is to find the video you want to watch. Then you use iPhone's video tools to watch that video. You can also configure some aspects of how your iPhone plays video content.

Finding and Watching Video

Like listening to audio, watching video is a two-step process. First, find the content you want to watch. Second, select, play, and control playback.

>>>step-by-step

Finding Video

If you read Chapter 11, "Listening to Music, Podcasts, and Other Audio," you pretty much already know how to find video content on your iPhone because this is quite similar to finding audio content.

1. On the Home screen, tap the iPod button.

2. Tap Videos. The Videos screen appears, showing you the video content on your iPhone.

3. Scroll the screen to see all the video content, which is organized by type, such as Rented Movies, Movies, TV Shows, and Music Videos. Content you haven't watched yet is marked with a blue dot; as you watch video content, the blue dot empties to indicate how much of the video you have watched. If you've just started the video, the dot might still be full, but the more you watch, the more empty it becomes. If you have multiple episodes of a TV series, you see the name of the series and the number of episodes.

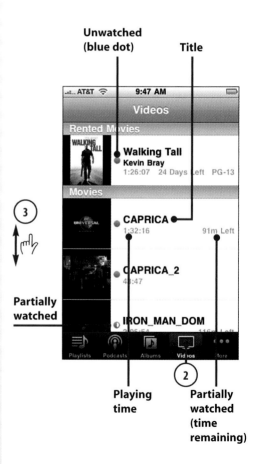

Unwatched (blue dot)   Title

Partially watched

Playing time   Partially watched (time remaining)

4. To watch one of the episodes of a TV series of which more than one is stored on your iPhone, tap the series. You see the episodes of the series that are available.

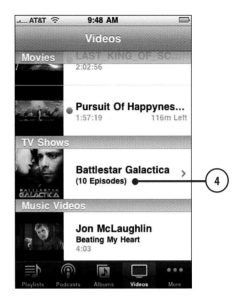

5. To watch a movie, an episode of a TV series, or a music video, tap it.

6. Rotate the iPhone 90 degrees. The screen rotates, and the content begins to play.

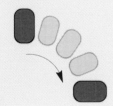

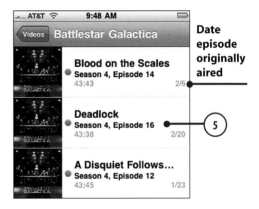

Date episode originally aired

7. Watch and control the video; see the next section for details of controlling video.

Are You Searching for Something to Watch?

If you scroll to the top of the Videos screen, you see the Search tool you can use to search for specific video.

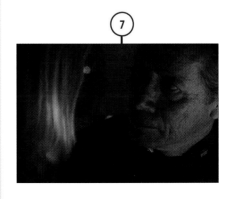

>>>*step-by-step*

Watching Video

When you play video, it is always oriented in landscape mode so that it can fill the screen.

1. Tap the video you are watching. The video controls appear.

2. Drag the playhead to the right to move ahead or to the left to move backward.

3. Tap the Scale button to scale the video to fit the screen or to show it in its native scale. After a few seconds, the video controls disappear.

4. To change the language for a movie or TV show, tap the Language button. (Not all video content supports this feature; the button appears only when you are watching content that does support it.)

Scale This

If native scale of the video is not the same proportion as the iPhone screen and you play it in its original scale, the video might not fill the screen. When you scale the video, it fills the screen, but some content might be cut off.

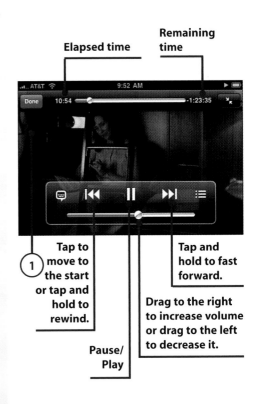

Elapsed time | Remaining time

Tap to move to the start or tap and hold to rewind.

Pause/ Play

Tap and hold to fast forward.

Drag to the right to increase volume or drag to the left to decrease it.

5. Tap the language you want to use.

6. Tap Done.

Remember Where You Were

For most kinds of video, iPhone remembers where you left off. So if you stop a movie and restart it, iPhone will pick up where you left off even if you've done a lot of other things since.

7. To move to a specific chapter in the video, tap the Chapter button. (Not all video content supports this feature; the button appears only when video content has chapters.) You move to the movie's Chapter Guide.

8. Tap the chapter you want to watch or tap Done to return to the video at the same location. You move back to the viewing screen, and the video plays.

9. When you're done watching, tap Done (if the controls aren't visible, tap the screen, then tap Done). You move back to the Videos screen.

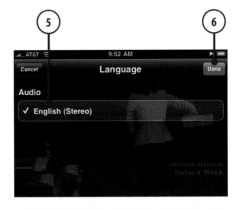

>>>*step-by-step*

Watching Rented Movies

As you learned in Chapter 3, "Moving Audio, Video, and Photos onto Your iPhone," you can rent movies from the iTunes Store and move them onto an iPhone. The steps to watch a rented movie are the same as watching other kinds of video.

When you move to a rented movie, you see important time information about its viewing status and can play it.

1. Move to the Videos screen.

2. Scroll to the top of the screen, where you see the Rented Movies section. Under each rented movie, you see the time remaining in the rental period (days if you haven't watched the movie yet).

3. Tap the rented movie you want to watch. You're prompted with a message that after you start the movie, you have 24 hours to watch it.

4. Tap OK. The movie starts to play.

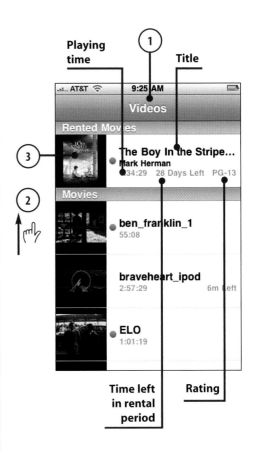

Playing time

Title

The Boy In the Stripe...
Mark Herman
34:29   28 Days Left   PG-13

Rented Movies

Movies

ben_franklin_1
55:08

braveheart_ipod
2:57:29   6m Left

ELO
1:01:19

Time left in rental period

Rating

Do you want to play this rented movie?

It will expire 24 hours after you start watching it.

Cancel   OK

5. Use the video controls to play the movie.

6. To stop the movie, tap Done. You move back to the Videos screen.

7. Note how much time you have left to watch the movie, shown in hours. When this period expires, the movie disappears from your iPhone.

Rental Caveats

You need to be aware that rented movies have two time limitations. One is that you can keep rented movies on your iPhone for 30 calendar days, starting from the time you downloaded the rented movies to your computer (not from the time when you synced the rented content from your computer to your iPhone). The second limitation is that after you start playing a rented movie, you have 24 hours to finish watching it. (Though you can watch it as many times as you want within that 24-hour period.) When either of these time periods expires, the rented content disappears from whatever device it is on.

Another difference between rented content and other kinds of content is that rented content can exist on only one device. When you move rented content from your computer to your iPhone, it disappears from the computer (unlike music or movies you own that remain in your iTunes Library where you can listen to or view that content). This also means that rented content can be on only one iPhone, iPod touch, or other kind of iPod at the same time. However, you can move rented movies back and forth among devices as much as you want. So you can start watching a movie on your iPhone and move it back to your computer to finish watching it (within the 24-hour viewing period, of course).

Watching Video Podcasts

Like the audio podcasts you learned about in the previous chapter, video podcasts are episodic content, though as you can tell by their name these episodes contain both audio and video content. Another difference is that there are quite a number of video podcasts that have only one episode. Watching a video podcast is similar to watching other kinds of video content.

1. Move to the Videos screen.

2. Scroll down until you see the Podcasts section.

3. Tap the video podcast you want to watch. You move to the episode list for that podcast.

4. Scroll or search to find the episode you want to view.

5. Tap the episode you want to watch. You move to the viewing screen, and the episode begins to play.

6. Use the video controls to watch the episode.

Deleting Video

If you want to free up some of the iPhone's memory for other things, you can delete video directly from the iPhone.

1. Move to the Videos screen.

2. Drag left or right on the video you want to delete. The Delete button appears.

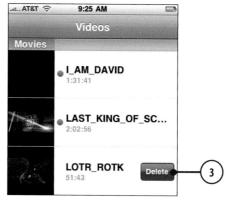

Gone but Not Forgotten

Deleting video from iPhone removes it only from the iPhone (except for rented content, which exists only on the iPhone). The video content remains in your iTunes Library, even after the next sync. You can add video back to iPhone again by including it in a sync. In fact, unless you remove the video content from the sync settings for the iPhone, it will be moved back onto your iPhone the next time you sync.

3. Tap Delete. The content is deleted from the iPhone.

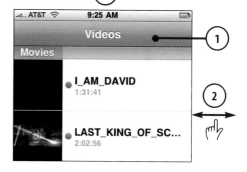

Music Videos

You can access music videos from the Music Videos section of the Videos screen or from the music screens, such as playlists, artists, and so on. When you play a music video from the Videos screen, it plays in the normal movie player. When you play a music video from music screens, it plays on the Now Playing screen; instead of seeing album art on the screen, you see the music video.

Configuring iPhone's Video Settings

There are a few settings you use to configure various aspects of iPhone's video functionality.

>>>*step-by-step*

1. Tap the Home button to move to iPhone's Home screen.

2. Tap Settings.

3. Scroll down the screen and tap iPod.

4. Tap Start Playing.

5. Tap Where Left Off to have iPhone remember where you last were watching in a video so it resumes at the same location when you play it again or From Beginning to have iPhone always start video content playback from the beginning.

6. Tap iPod to move back to the iPod screen.

7. To enable or disable Closed Captioning on video, tap the Closed Captioning button. Its status is indicated by ON or OFF. When you tap the button, it toggles between the two states.

8. To enable or disable widescreen playback when you play the output of the iPhone on a television, tap the Widescreen button. Its status is indicated by ON or OFF. When you tap the button, it also toggles between the two states.

9. To select a specific output format when you play iPhone content on a TV, tap TV Signal.

10. To choose the NTSC format (for U.S. televisions for example), tap NTSC, or to choose the PAL format (European televisions are some that use this format), tap PAL.

11. Tap iPod to return to the iPod screen.

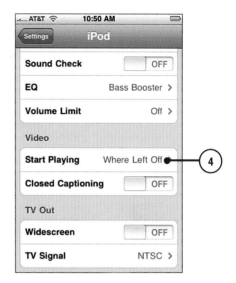

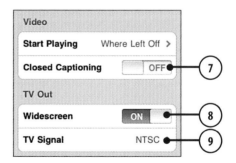

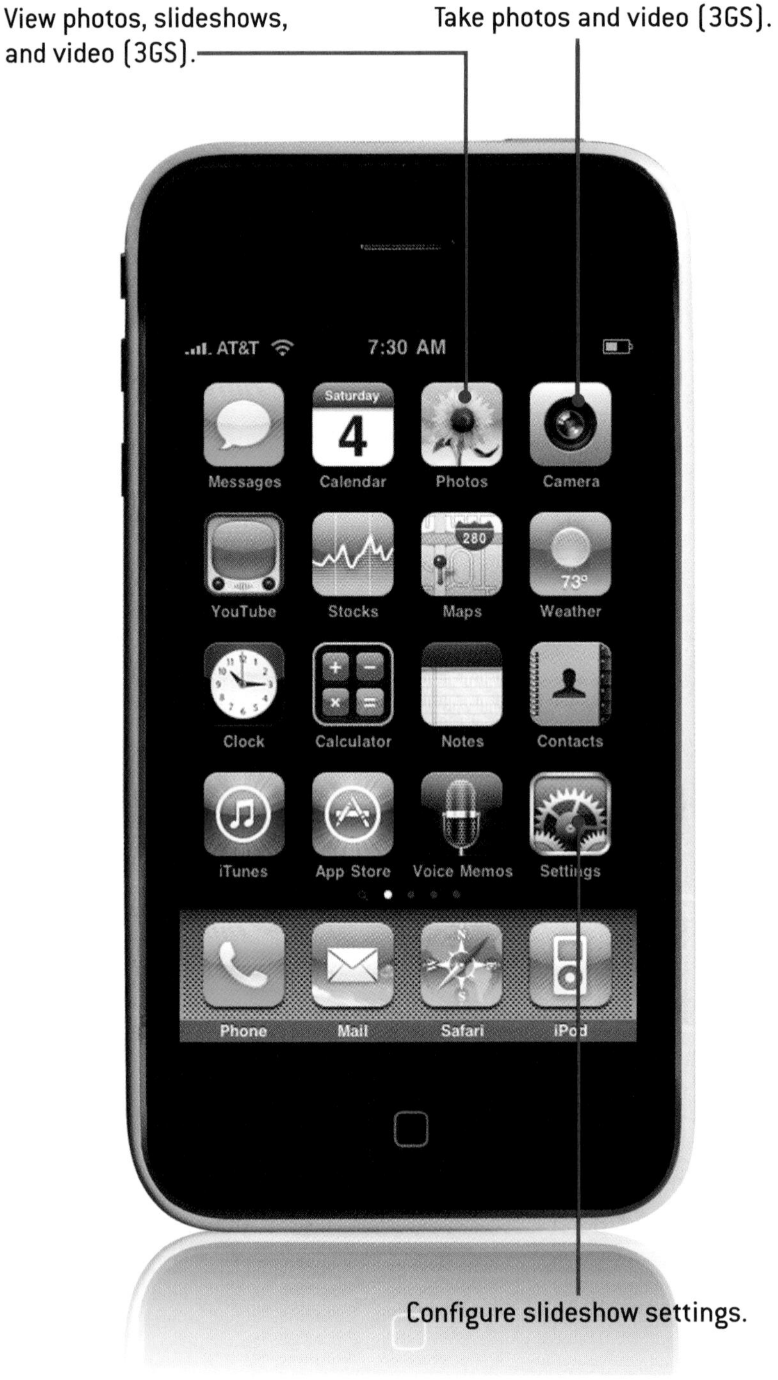

View photos, slideshows, and video (3GS).

Take photos and video (3GS).

.ıll. AT&T 🗢   7:30 AM

Messages   Calendar   Photos   Camera

YouTube   Stocks   Maps   Weather

Clock   Calculator   Notes   Contacts

iTunes   App Store   Voice Memos   Settings

Phone   Mail   Safari   iPod

Configure slideshow settings.

In this chapter, you'll explore all the photo and video functionality that iPhone has to offer. Topics include the following:

→ Taking photos with your iPhone
→ Taking video on an iPhone 3GS
→ Viewing and working with photos on an iPhone
→ Viewing, editing, and working with video on an iPhone 3GS
→ Moving photos and video from an iPhone onto a computer

Working with Photos and Video

Although it might not replace your primary digital camera, the iPhone's built-in camera takes reasonable photos, especially given how easy the camera function is to use and the fact that you'll likely have iPhone with you at all times. If you have an iPhone 3GS, you can capture video just as easily.

Whether you've taken them on iPhone or moved them from a computer onto iPhone, you can view your photos individually and as slideshows. If you decide some of the photos you've taken on iPhone are worthy of adding to your photo collection, you can move them from the iPhone onto your computer. If you have an iPhoto 3GS, you can edit video and move it to your computer just like you move photos.

>>>*step-by-step*

Taking Photos with Your iPhone

The iPhone's camera (and video camera on a 3GS) lens is located on the backside of iPhone in the upper-left corner. Using iPhone's camera is just about easy as it could be.

1. On the Home screen, tap Camera. The Camera screen appears; initially it has a shutter, but after a few moments the window opens, and you start seeing through iPhone's lens.

2. To capture a photo in landscape mode, rotate iPhone so that it's horizontal; of course, you can use either orientation to take photos just as you can with any other camera.

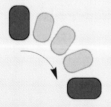

Sensitive, Isn't It!

The iPhone's camera is pretty sensitive to movement, so if your hand moves while you are taking a photo, it's likely to be blurry. Sometimes, part of the image will be in focus while part of it isn't, so be sure to check the view before you capture a photo. If you are getting blurry photos, the problem is probably your hand moving while you are taking them.

3. If you have an iPhone 3GS, ensure the Photo/Video switch is set to Photo.

4. Frame the subject on the iPhone's screen.

5. If you are using an iPhone 3GS, tap where you want the camera to focus. (If you aren't using a 3GS, skip this step.) The spot where you tapped is enclosed in a blue box, and the iPhone's camera focuses on that spot and sets the exposure.

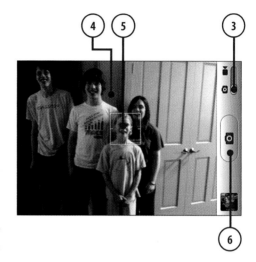

6. When the photo is properly framed, tap the Camera button. The iPhone captures the photo, and the shutter closes while the photo is recorded in iPhone's memory. When the shutter opens again, you're ready to take the next photo.

7. To see the photo you most recently captured, tap the Thumbnail button. The photo appears on the screen with iPhone's photo-viewing controls.

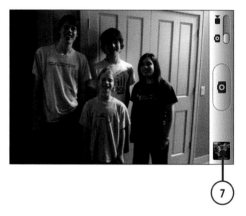

Bonus Task

Please go to this book's website at www.informit.com/title/ 9780789742315 and click the Downloads tab to find an additional task titled, "Using a Photo as Wallpaper."

8. Use the photo-viewing tools to view the photo (see "Viewing and Working with Photos on an iPhone" later in this chapter for the details).

9. To delete a photo, tap the Trashcan and then tap Delete Photo. The iPhone deletes the photo, and you see the next photo in the Photo Roll album.

10. Tap Done. The iPhone moves back to the camera, and you can take more photos.

No Flash

The iPhone doesn't have a flash so taking photos in low-light conditions can be a challenge. Don't expect to get great results if your subject isn't well lit.

Shutter Sounds

When you capture a photo, you hear the iPhone's shutter sound, unless you have muted it.

Location, Location!

If you allow it, the iPhone uses its GPS to tag the location where photos and video were captured. (Of course, you have to be in a location where the iPhone can receive the GPS signal.) Some applications can use this information, such as iPhoto (where you can use this data to locate your photos on maps, find photos by their locations, and so on).

Taking Video with an iPhone 3GS

With an iPhone 3GS, you can capture video. Here's how.

1. On the Home screen, tap Camera.

2. To capture video in landscape mode, rotate iPhone so that it's horizontal; of course, you can use either orientation to take video just as you can with any other videocamera.

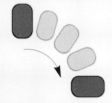

3. Set the Photo/Video switch to Video. The Record button appears.

4. Frame the subject on the iPhone's screen.

You Are Recording

When you tap the Record button, you hear the start/stop recording tone. When you stop recording, you hear the same tone. That's assuming you don't have the iPhone muted of course.

5. To start recording, tap the Record button. The iPhone starts capturing video; you see a counter on the screen showing how long you've been recording.

6. To stop recording, tap the Record button again.

7. To preview the video clip, tap the Thumbnail button.

8. Use the video-viewing tools to view or edit the clip (see "Viewing, Editing, and Working with Video on an iPhone 3GS" later in this chapter for the details).

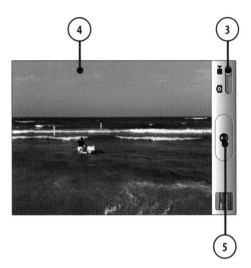

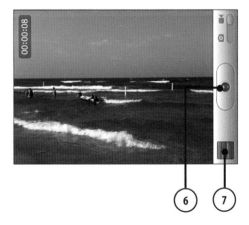

TAKING IPHONE SCREENSHOTS

There are times when it is useful to capture screen images off the iPhone's screen (such as when you are writing a book about your iPhone). The iPhone includes a screen capture utility you can use to take a picture of whatever is on iPhone's screen at any point in time.

When the screen you want to capture appears, hold the Home button down and press the Wake/Sleep button. The screen flashes white and the shutter sound plays to indicate the capture has been taken. The resulting image is stored in the Camera Roll album. You can view the captures you take, email them, or move them onto a computer as you can with other kinds of photos.

Viewing and Working with Photos on an iPhone

After you've loaded iPhone with great (and maybe a few not-so-great) photos, you can use the Photos application to view them individually and as slideshows. You can also use the photos on iPhone for a number of tasks, such as setting iPhone's wallpaper or emailing them.

>>>step-by-step

Viewing Photos Individually

Any photo on iPhone, whether you've taken it with iPhone's camera or moved it onto iPhone via a sync, can be viewed at any time.

1. On the Home screen, tap Photos. The Photo Albums screen appears. On this screen, you see various collections of photos. The Camera Roll contains all the photos you've taken on the iPhone or only those you've taken since the last time you moved all its photos

onto a computer and then deleted them from the iPhone. The rest of the items are photo albums or other collections that you've moved from a computer onto iPhone.

2. Browse the screen until you see an album containing photos you want to view.

3. Tap the album you want to view. You see the preview screen for that album with a thumbnail for each photo it contains.

4. To view a photo, tap it. The photo display screen appears. When the photo first appears, the photo viewing controls appear on the screen. After a moment, they disappear.

5. To view the photo in landscape orientation, rotate your iPhone.

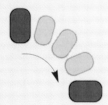

6. Unpinch or double-tap on the photo to zoom in.

7. Pinch or double-tap on the photo to zoom out if you are zoomed in.

8. Drag on the photo to scroll in it if you are zoomed in.

9. Tap once to view the photo tools. The toolbars appear on the screen.

10. Tap Back or drag quickly to the right to view the previous photo in the album.

11. Tap Forward or drag quickly to the left to view the next photo in the album.

12. Tap the Action button. Choose the action you want to take; these are explained in the sections "Emailing a Photo," "Texting a Photo," "Sending a Photo to MobileMe," "Assigning a Photo to a Contact," and "Using a Photo as Wallpaper" later in this chapter.

13. Tap the Return button, which is labeled with the current photo album's name. You move back to the photo album's screen.

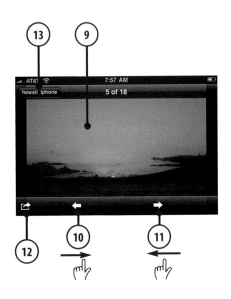

Viewing Photos as a Slideshow

You can view photos in slideshows. Before you start watching your own slideshows, take a few moments to configure iPhone's slideshow settings to set your slideshow preferences.

>>>step-by-step

Configure Slideshow Settings

1. On the Home screen, tap Settings.

2. Scroll down until you see Photos.

3. Tap Photos.

4. Tap Play Each Slide For.

5. Tap the amount of time you want each slide in a slideshow to appear on the screen.

6. Tap Photos.

7. Tap Transition.

8. Tap the transition you want to use when slides change.

9. Tap Photos.

10. To make slideshows repeat until you stop them, tap Repeat OFF. Its status becomes ON to indicate you have to stop slideshows manually. When the status is OFF, slideshows play through once and then stop.

11. To view photos in a random order in a slideshow, tap Shuffle OFF. Its status becomes ON so you know photos will appear in random order during slideshows. To have photos appear in the order they are in the selected album, tap ON so the status becomes OFF.

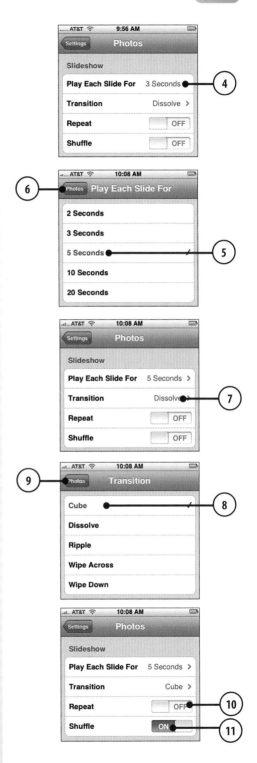

Watching Slideshows

1. On the Home screen, tap Photos.

2. Browse the screen until you see an album containing photos you want to view in a slideshow.

3. Tap the album you want to view in a slideshow.

4. Tap Play. The slideshow begins to play.

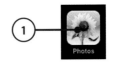

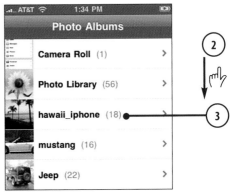

It's Not All Good

Unfortunately, you can't associate music with a slideshow so that the music plays automatically when you watch the slideshow. If you want to hear music while a slideshow plays, use the iPod functions to start the music and then move to and start the slideshow.

5. To view the slideshow in landscape mode, rotate the iPhone. The slideshow plays, each slide appearing on the screen for the length of time you set. The transition you selected is used to move between photos. If you set slideshows to repeat, the slideshow plays until you stop it; if not, it stops after each photo has been shown once.

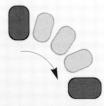

6. To stop the slideshow before it finishes, tap the screen. The photo controls appear, and the slideshow stops at the current photo.

7. To move to the next or previous photo, tap the Forward button or tap the Back button.

8. To perform various actions on a photo, such as using it as wallpaper, tap the Action button. This is covered in the next section.

9. When you're done with the slideshow, tap the return button, which is labeled with the album's name.

Deleting Photos or Video from an iPhone

You can only delete photos and videos in the Camera Roll album from your iPhone. (To remove photos that are loaded onto iPhone via syncing with a computer, you must change the sync settings so those photos are excluded and then resync.) To delete a photo or video you've taken with iPhone's camera, captured as a screenshot, or downloaded from email, take the following steps.

1. Move to the Photos application and open the Camera Roll source.

2. Tap the photo you want to delete.

3. Tap the Trash icon.

4. Tap Delete Photo. The Trash icon opens and "swallows" the photo, at which point it is deleted. You see the next photo in the Camera Roll source.

Emailing a Photo

You can email photos via iPhone's
Mail application starting from the
Photos application.

1. View the photo you want to send
   in an email.

2. Tap the Action button.

3. Tap Email Photo. A new email
   message is created, and the photo
   is added as an attachment.

4. Use the email tools to address the
   email, add a subject, type the
   body, and send it. (See Chapter 7,
   "Emailing," for detailed information about using your iPhone's
   email tools.) After you send the
   email, you move back to the
   photo.

Images from Email

As you learned in Chapter 7, when
you save images attached to
email, they are stored in the
Camera Roll photo album just like
photos you take with the iPhone.

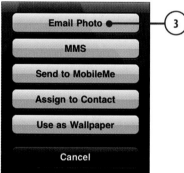

Texting a Photo

Sending a photo stored on the iPhone to someone via a text message is fast and easy. Here's how.

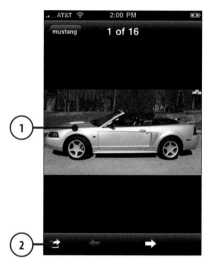

1. View the photo you want to send in an email.

2. Tap the Action button.

3. Tap MMS. A new text message is created, and the photo is added to it.

4. Use the texting tools to create the message and send it. (See Chapter 8, "Texting," for detailed information about sending text messages.) After you send the message, you move back to the photo.

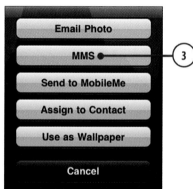

Not So Fast

Not all cell providers support text messages with photos. If yours doesn't, you won't see the MMS button.

Sending a Photo to MobileMe

If you have a MobileMe membership, you can post photos from the iPhone directly to your MobileMe galleries on the web, where they can viewed or downloaded.

1. View the photo you want to move to the web.

2. Tap the Action button.

3. Tap Send to MobileMe.

4. Add a title and description for the photo. (The description is optional.)

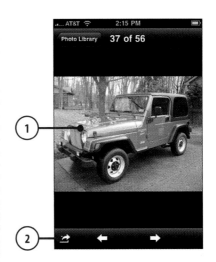

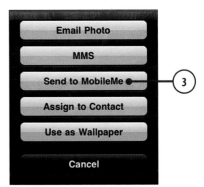

5. Scroll down the screen until you see the albums on your MobileMe website.

6. Tap the album to which you want the photo posted.

7. Tap Publish. The photo is posted to the album you selected.

8. Tap the action you want to perform, such as Tell a Friend, which sends a message inviting someone to visit your published photo, or View on MobileMe to view the published photo.

iPhone photo posted on the web.

Assigning a Photo to a Contact

You can assign photos on your iPhone to your contacts. When you assign a photo to a contact, you see that photo when the contact calls you, when you receive email from the contact, and so on. You can assign any photo to a contact, but you get the best results when you use a photo that you've taken with iPhone because it will scale to full screen when the person calls you; other kinds of photos appear as thumbnails instead.

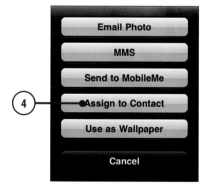

1. Take the photo you want to assign to a contact. If the photo you want to use already exists on iPhone, skip this step.

2. View the photo you want to associate with a contact.

3. Tap the Action button.

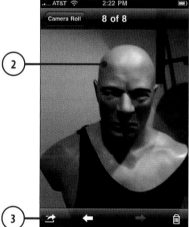

4. Tap Assign to Contact. The All Contacts screen appears. (For more information on working with contacts, see Chapter 5, "Managing Contacts.")

5. Tap the contact with which you want to associate the photo.

6. Drag and pinch or unpinch the image until the part you want to add to the contact shows on the screen the way you want to see it.

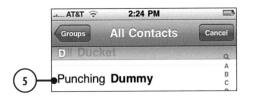

7. Tap Set Photo. The photo is saved to the contact; when iPhone interacts with that contact, such as when you receive a call, the photo is displayed on iPhone's screen. You return to the photo.

Deleting Contact Photos

When a photo is associated with a contact, even if you delete the original photo taken with iPhone, the photo remains with the contact. (You can only delete photos taken with iPhone; photos that are transferred from a computer must be removed from the sync to be removed from iPhone.) Contact photos are quite small, so don't worry about them using lots of iPhone's memory.

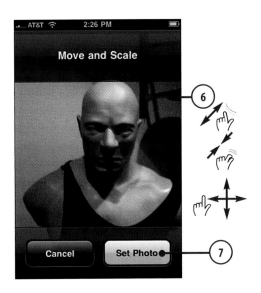

Sharing Photos

You can share a group of photos with others as easily as you can email an individual photo. Check this out.

1. Open the album (or the Camera Roll source) containing the photos you want to share.

2. Tap the Action button.

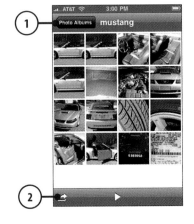

3. Tap the first photo you want to share. It is marked with a red check mark and the Share and Copy buttons are incremented by 1.

4. Tap the other photos you want to share.

5. Tap Share.

6. Tap Email to attach the selected photos to an email message or MMS to send them via a text message.

7. Complete and send the email or text message.

Copy (or Delete) 'Em

If you tap the Copy button, the images you selected are copied to the iPhone's clipboard. You can then move into another application and paste them in. When you are working with the Camera Roll source, you can delete selected photos by tapping the Delete button.

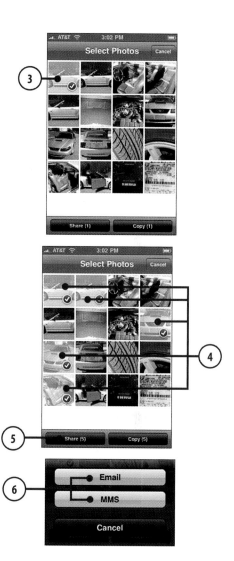

Viewing, Editing, and Working with Video on an iPhone 3GS

As you learned earlier, if you have an iPhone 3GS, you can capture video clips. Once captured, you can view clips stored there, edit them, and share them.

Watching Video

Watching videos you've captured
with your iPhone is simple.

1. Move to the Photos application
   and open the Camera Roll source.
   Video clips have a camera icon
   and running time at the bottom
   of their icons.

2. Tap the clip you want to watch.

3. Tap either Play button. The video
   plays. After a few moments, the
   toolbars disappears.

Rotation Works with Video, Too
Just like photos, you can rotate the
iPhone to change its orientation.

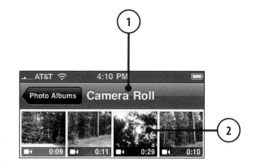

Playhead   Thumbnails

4. Tap the video. The toolbars reappear.

5. To pause the video, tap Pause.

6. To view the next video clip (or photo if that's what's next in the source you are working with), tap the Next button.

7. To view the previous clip (or photo if that's what's next in the source you are working with), tap the Previous button.

8. To jump to a specific point in a clip, drag the playhead to where you want to starting playing it; if you hold your finger in one place for a period of time, the thumbnails expand so your placement of the playhead can be more precise. When you lift your thumb, the playhead remains at its current location; if the clip is playing, it resumes playing from that point.

Editing Video

You can trim a video clip to remove unwanted parts. Here's how you do it.

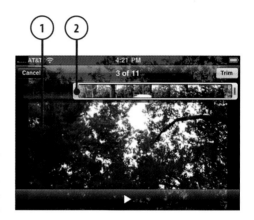

1. View the video you want to edit.

2. Drag the left crop marker to where you want the edited clip to start. As soon as you move the crop marker, the part of the clip that is inside the selection is high-lighted in the yellow box; the Trim button also appears.

3. Drag the right crop marker to where you want the edited clip to end.

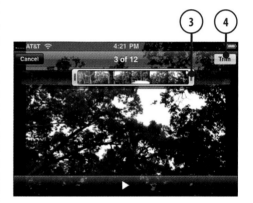

4. Tap Trim.

5. Tap Trim Original to keep an edit-ed version of the original clip or Save as New Clip to create a new clip containing only the frames between the crop markers. The frames outside the crop markers are removed from the clip. The clip is trimmed and replaces the original clip or a new clip is creat-ed depending on the option you selected.

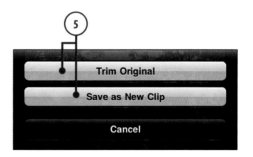

Deleting Video

To remove a video clip from your iPhone, tap the Trashcan icon and then tap the Delete Video button at the prompt.

Sharing Video

You can share videos you've taken on your iPhone by email, text message, MobileMe, or YouTube. Sharing videos via email, text message, or MobileMe is just like sharing photos. Move to the clip, tap the Action button, and tap Email, Video, MMS, or Send to MobileMe (see the steps to perform these tasks with photos earlier in this chapter for details).

You can share your videos on YouTube by performing the following steps.

1. View the video you want to share.

2. Tap the Action button.

3. Tap Send to YouTube. The video is compressed for YouTube.

4. Enter your YouTube username and password, and tap Sign In. You don't have to do this every time; it depends if you've signed out of your account. If you aren't prompted to log in, you already are.

5. Enter a title and description of the video clip.

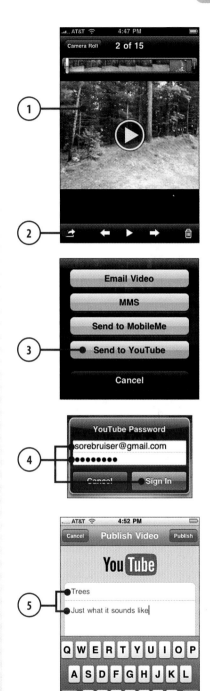

6. Enter one or more tags.

7. Associate the clip with a category.

8. Tap Publish. The clip is posted to YouTube.

9. Tap the action you want, which can be View on YouTube to immediately view your posted clip or Tell a Friend to send a message that contains a link to your video.

Moving Video from iPhoto (on Macs) to iTunes

When you transfer video from your iPhone 3GS to iPhoto, the iPhoto application can't play the video clips. When you double-click a clip, it opens in the QuickTime Player application where you can watch it. If you want to add your clips to iTunes, click the Action button on the QuickTime Player toolbar and choose iTunes. Select the format for the clip and it is added to your iTunes Library. Select the Movies source and you can watch your videos in iTunes. You can also include them in the sync settings to move them back to the iPhone.

Moving Photos from Your iPhone to a Computer

As you use iPhone to take photos or screenshots, you're going to want to move some of the photos you capture to your computer. How you do this depends on the kind of computer and photo application you use.

Moving Photos from iPhone to a Windows PC

How you move photos from iPhone to a Windows PC depends on the specific application you use to manage your digital photos. Most applications designed to import photos from a digital camera should also work with iPhone. One example is Adobe Photoshop Elements.

1. Connect your iPhone to the computer. If new photos are detected, the Apple iPhone dialog appears.

2. Select Photoshop Elements.

3. Check the Always use this program for this action check box.

4. Click OK. The Photoshop Elements Photo Downloader appears.

5. To create subfolders for each photo session on iPhone, open the Create Subfolders menu and choose how you want to name the subfolders.

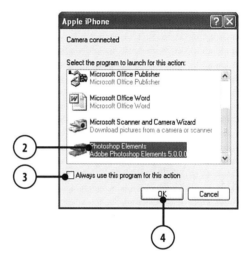

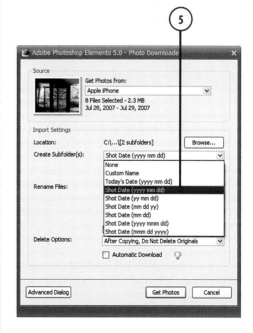

6. If you want to rename the files, use the Rename Files menu.

7. Check the Open Organizer when Finished check box.

8. Use the Delete Options menu to determine what happens to the photos on the iPhone after they are imported. The best option is After Copying, Verify and Delete Originals because it frees up space on the iPhone while ensuring the photos have been imported successfully.

9. Click Get Photos. Photos move from the iPhone into Photoshop Elements, and the application opens.

10. Use Photoshop Elements to work with the photos you imported.

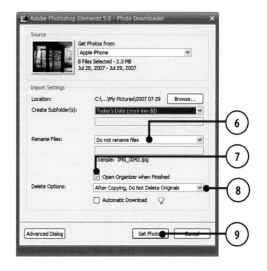

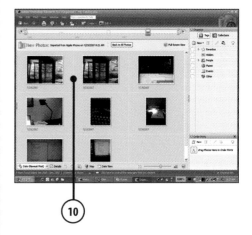

Moving Photos from iPhone to a Mac

iPhone is designed to move its photos into your iPhoto Library easily.

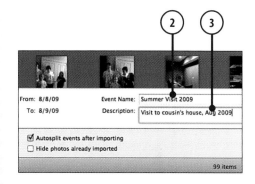

1. Connect your iPhone to a Mac. If there are photos or videos on your iPhone, iPhoto opens automatically and moves into Import mode. The iPhone is selected as the import source.

2. Enter an event name for the photos you want to import in the Event Name field.

3. Enter a description of the photos you want to import in the Description field.

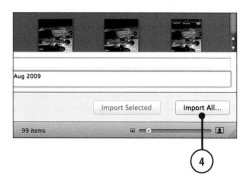

4. Click Import All. Photos and videos are copied from the iPhone into iPhoto.

5. Click Delete Photos if you want to delete the photos and videos from the iPhone or Keep Photos if you want them to remain on the iPhone.

6. Use iPhoto to work with the photos and videos you imported from iPhone.

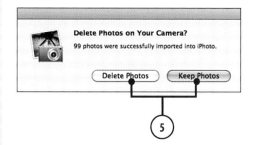

Tap here to map your way.

Tap here to use these apps.

In this chapter, you'll explore how to use one of the iPhone's best preinstalled applications, Maps. The topics include the following:

→ Finding your way with Maps
→ Understanding other preinstalled iPhone applications

14

Using Preinstalled Applications

You've already learned enough great iPhone tricks that you're probably convinced iPhone is one of the most useful, not to mention one of the coolest, gadgets ever. Here's where you get some icing on that nice iPhone cake.

iPhone comes with a powerful set of applications that you can use out-of-the-box, such as Mail, Safari, Calendar, Contacts, and so on. However, these are really only the starting point for your iPhone; there are a number of other applications preinstalled on your iPhone for you to use.

One of the most useful is Maps, which you can use to create custom maps and then track your movement using the iPhone's GPS. Some of the other preinstalled applications are pretty useful, too.

This Is Only the Beginning

While the preinstalled applications are a great start, there are literally thousands and thousands of iPhone applications you can download, install, and use. In Chapter 15, "Installing and Maintaining iPhone Applications," you'll get the details on how to take advantage of these.

Finding Your Way with Maps

Maps just might be one of the most useful iPhone applications, especially if you are directionally challenged like I am. Using the Maps application, you can find the location of addresses using Google Maps. You can also get directions from one address to another. Even better, in most cases, you can use GPS or cell network data to show your current location on the map and on the routes you generate. Also maps are linked to your contacts, so you can quickly show the location of any address in your contacts on a map and then get directions.

A number of ways exist to find locations on the map, such as by searching or by using a contact's address. After you find a location, you can use that location for different purposes, such as to create driving directions.

>>>*step-by-step*

Finding a Location by Searching

You can search for locations in many ways. Your search can be specific, such as an address, or your search can be more general, such as a search for gas stations or restaurants.

Tap Maps to find your way.

1. Tap in the Search bar. (If you don't see the Search bar, tap the Search button at the bottom of the screen.)

Easy Searching

As you enter a search, iPhone attempts to match what you type with recent searches. As it finds matches, it presents the list of matches to you. Tap a search on the list to perform it.

2. Type your search. You can enter an address, city, category, or just about anything else. The more specific your search term, the more likely it is that you'll find the location. But general searches can be helpful, such as a search for gas stations.

iPhone remembers the context of your last search, so if you want to change the general area of the search item, you should include a state or zip code in the search term. For example, if you search for an address in one state and then perform a general search (such as for libraries), iPhone searches in the area of the address for which you previously searched. To change that context, enter the state or zip code where you want to search (such as *libraries Indiana* to find libraries in Indiana).

Spelling Counts

As you type a search, iPhone attempts to identify typos; if it finds one, it presents a prompt that enables you to change the term to iPhone's recommendation.

3. Tap Search. The map appears, and the locations that meet your search criteria are marked with push pins; the location that iPhone thinks is most likely to be the one you are looking for has the Info bar above it. Your current location is shown in the blue circle if it is identified by the cell network or by the blue dot if the iPhone is using GPS.

4. To see information about a location, tap the Info button.

5. Use the information in the "Working with Maps" task later in this chapter to work with the location.

Clear a Search

To clear a search, tap the Clear button, which is the gray circle containing an "x," located at the right end of the Search bar.

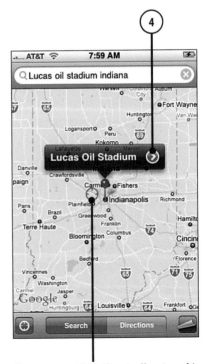

Your current location (cell network)

Finding a Location with Bookmarks

Bookmarks enable you to save locations and return to them easily. (See the "Working with Maps" task later in this chapter to learn how to set bookmarks.)

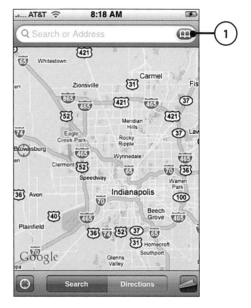

1. Open the Search screen and tap the Lists button in the Search bar.

2. Tap Bookmarks.

3. Browse up or down the list to see all the bookmarks available to you.

4. Tap the bookmark you want to see on the map. You move back to the map, and the bookmarked location is shown.

5. Use the information in the "Working with Maps" task later in this chapter to work with the location.

One Very Useful Bookmark
At the top of the Bookmarks list, you see Current Location. This is useful when you are creating directions; when you tap it, your current location is selected if you are generating directions, or you move to the map and your current location is shown (via GPS or a cell network).

Deleting or Changing Bookmarks

You can remove bookmarks from the list, and you can change their information as shown in the following steps.

1. Move to the Bookmarks screen.

2. Tap Edit. Unlock and Order buttons appear for each bookmark.

3. To change the order of bookmarks, tap a bookmark's Order button and drag it up or down the list of bookmarks.

4. To delete a bookmark, tap its Unlock button.

5. Tap Delete. The bookmark is deleted from the list.

6. To change a bookmark's name, tap it.

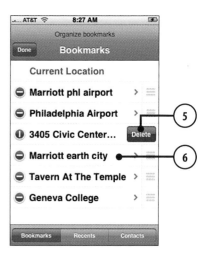

7. Use the keyboard to make changes to the bookmark's name.

8. Tap Bookmarks. You return to the Bookmarks screen, and the changes you made to the bookmark's name are shown.

9. When you're done making changes, tap Done. You exit the Edit mode and can work with bookmarks again—or tap Done again to return to the map.

Other Ways to Find Locations

You can also find a location by opening a contact and tapping an address; you move to the map showing the location of the address you tapped. To do this, tap the Lists button in the Search bar and then tap Contacts. Use the All Contacts screen to find the contact with the address you want to see on the map. You can also repeat a recent search by tapping the Lists button and then tapping Recents; tap the recent search you want to perform again.

Finding Your Current Location

When you are using a map, knowing your current location is very important. Your iPhone has two ways to identify your location, via GPS or via a cell network. GPS locations are more accurate, so iPhone uses a GPS signal if it is available; if not, it uses the current cell network to identify you. The steps you use to find your location are the same; iPhone chooses the method automatically.

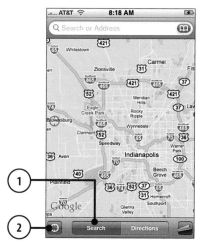

1. Tap the Search tab.

2. Tap the My Location button. What you see depends on the method iPhone uses to locate you.

   If iPhone uses a cell network, you see a large blue circle to show your general location.

   If iPhone can make your location more specific, the map zooms in, and the location circle gets smaller until iPhone has your location shown as precisely as possible.

   If iPhone can use GPS for your location, you see the blue GPS locator dot on the map. The dot pulses to show you that it is a dynamic display, meaning the dot moves as you do. Because GPS is more accurate, iPhone uses it first. GPS signals are usually blocked by buildings, so if you are inside, it's unlikely GPS will be available.

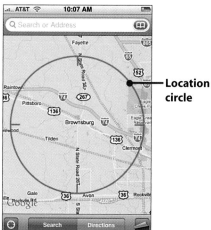

Location circle

GPS location

Working with Maps

After you find locations on a map, you can work with them for a variety of purposes.

1. Using the techniques (such as searching for a location) explained in the previous sections, find locations in which you are interested.

2. To zoom in on a location, double-tap the map near the location or unpinch the map to zoom in.

3. To scroll the map, drag your finger up or down and left or right.

4. Double-tap to zoom out by a set amount or pinch your fingers together on the screen to zoom out.

5. Tap a location's push pin. You see the name of the location and the Info button.

6. Tap the Info button.

7. Use the information on the Info screen to call the location, view its website, or see it on the map.

8. Scroll down the screen.

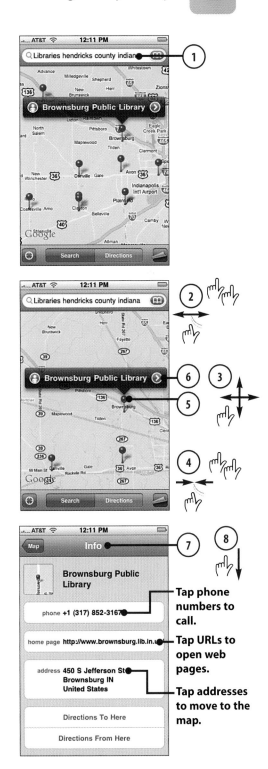

Tap phone numbers to call.

Tap URLs to open web pages.

Tap addresses to move to the map.

Show Them All

When your search has found more than one location on the map, tap the Options button (the page with upturned corner) and then tap List to see a listing of all the locations shown. Tap a location to jump to it on the map. This is helpful when you've done a more general search, and you want to see all the results easily.

---

9. To set a bookmark for the location, tap Add to Bookmarks. The Add Bookmarks screen appears.

10. Use the keyboard to make changes to the bookmark's name.

11. Tap Save. The location is added to your bookmarks, and you return to the Info screen.

12. Tap Map. You move back to the map and can work with other locations.

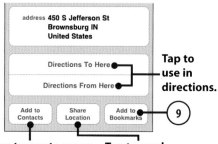

Tap to use in directions.

Tap to create a new contact with the location's information or add it to an existing contact.

Tap to send an email with a link to the location.

Buttons Change

The buttons you see on a location's Info screen depend on the status of that location. For example, if you've already added the location as a bookmark, the Add to Bookmarks button doesn't appear.

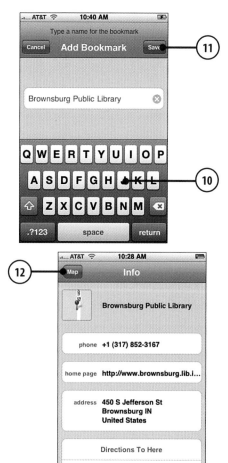

It's Not All Good

In its current release, iPhone's GPS functionality is pretty good, but it's not a full-fledged turn-by-turn navigation system with audible driving instructions. The Map's GPS shows you your location on a map and tracks your motion with GPS. However, the GPS indicator on the screen isn't linked to the route you are following, and Maps does little to keep you on track; you have to watch the GPS marker and keep yourself on track visually (not the safest thing to do while you are driving). You have the option to keep the GPS marker centered on the screen, but because it isn't linked to the route, if you get too far off track, you might see the route or the indicator, but not both. And the iPhone doesn't generate new routes for you automatically, you have to manually reset your current location and generate a new route. That's not good to do while you're driving either. You have to add an application (AT&T, the iPhone's cell provider in the United States, offers one, but it includes a monthly service fee) to get more advanced GPS functionality.

>>>*step-by-step*

Getting Directions

The Maps application can generate directions between two locations along with an estimate of how long the trip will take. Using Location services (GPS or cell network), you can see where you are along a route or how to get back to a route if you get off it.

1. Tap Directions.

Can't Tell if You're Coming or Going?

You can start the direction process from a location's Info screen by tapping the Directions To Here or Directions From Here button to set that location as the starting point or endpoint.

2. Find the start location by searching for it or by using the Lists button to select it from a list. Finding a start or end location works just like finding any location. For example, you can use a bookmark, recent item, or contact information to set a location along with searching for a location.

3. Find the end location by searching for it or by using the Lists button to select it from a list.

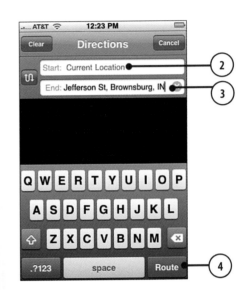

Your Permission Please?

When the iPhone needs to access your location, you might see a prompt. Tap OK to allow it or Don't Allow to block it.

4. Tap Route. A path from the start location to the end location is generated and appears on the map in a purple line. The start point is shown as a green pushpin, while the end point is a red pushpin. If GPS location is available, you see your position on the map. If GPS isn't available, but iPhone can determine your location using the cell network, you see the blue circle to show your location.

5. Tap the Car icon for driving directions, the Bus icon for public transit routes, or the Person icon for walking directions. The route is updated to reflect your choice. The rest of the steps show driving directions, but because of how the Maps GPS works, it is more useful for walking because the slower speed makes it easier to manipulate the iPhone as you walk.

6. Zoom or scroll the map as needed to view the entire route.

7. When you're ready to start moving along the route, tap Start. You see the first leg of the route. Instructions and information about the leg appear at the top of the screen.

Going Back Again

To quickly reverse the current route, tap Edit. Then tap the Reverse button, which is located to the left of the Start and End fields.

8. Follow your location along the first leg of the route. As you approach the next segment of the route, you see a circle on the route.

Keeping Centered

To keep the GPS indicator on your screen (the map moves as you do instead of the indicator moving), tap the My Location button located in the lower left corner of the screen. The buttons turns dark and the GPS indicator stays in the center of the screen while the map moves "under it." As long as you remain on or near the route, you continue to see both the dark purple route line and the blue GPS indicator on the screen. If you get too far off the route, you might not see it on the screen. You can zoom out to see the route again, but you have to manually generate another route and choose Current Location as the starting point to get back on course.

Start point

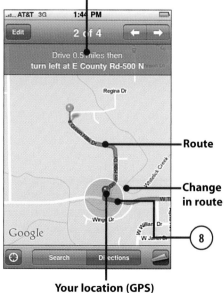

**Your location Route   End point
(GPS)**

Information about the current leg

Route

**Change
in route**

Your location (GPS)

9. After you've made the change to get onto the next segment of the route, tap the Forward button to move to the next segment on the map. If the next leg isn't visible on the current map, the GPS indicator might move off the map; tap the My Location button to center the map on the indicator again.

10. To move to a previous segment, tap the Back button.

11. To change the route while en route, tap Edit.

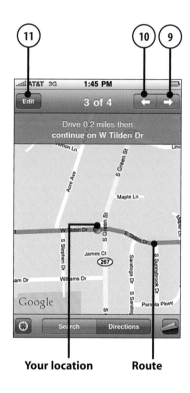

Your location   **Route**

Be Careful

As I mentioned earlier, it takes some manual manipulation and looking at iPhone's screen to move through a route on iPhone. This can distract you if you are driving a car, so be very careful. Remember that driving safely is more important than keeping on a route.

12. Use the Edit screen to make changes in the same way you set the route originally.

MORE ON MAPS

>> Go Further

Maps does more than I have room in this chapter to show. When you are viewing a map, tap the Options button, which is the sheet with a folded corner located in the lower right corner of the screen. On the resulting menu, you see various tools. You can use the Drop Pin command to place your own pushpins on the map (useful for creating directions when you don't know the exact address of where you want to go). You can use the Show Traffic to see traffic conditions. You can show a satellite view by tapping Satellite or show the map and a satellite view by tapping Hybrid. Tapping List shows you a route in list form; tap segment to see it on the map.

Understanding Other Preinstalled iPhone Applications

There are number of other preinstalled applications that you might find to be useful or entertaining:

- **YouTube**   You can watch YouTube videos via a Wi-Fi or cellular data connection. In addition to viewing them, you can share them, rate them, and other tasks you can do from the YouTube website.

- **Stocks**   Use this one to track stocks in which you are interested. You can add any index, stock, or fund as long as you know the symbol for it, and you can even use the application to find a symbol if you don't know it. You can see current performance and you can view historical performance for various time periods. Rotate the iPhone to see a more focused view when you are examining a specific item.

- **Weather**   See high-level weather conditions and a forecast for any number of locations. You can use the defaults, and if you tap the Info button, you add, remove, and organize the locations you want to track. Flip through the pages to see each area's forecast.

- **Voice Memos**   Record your verbal notes. Play them back, and through a sync, move them onto your computer. You can record through the iPhone's microphone or via the mic on the earbud headset.

- **Notes**   Create and edit text notes. You can view the notes on the iPhone, and you can move them onto a computer through a sync.

- **Calculator**   In portrait orientation, the Calculator is the equivalent of one you'd get at the local dollar store. Rotate the iPhone to move up in the calculating world.

- **Compass**   Transform your iPhone into a compass. You can see your current location on the analog-looking compass and with precision in degree latitude and longitude. Tap the My Location button to see your location on a map in the Maps application.

Third-party iPhone applications

In this chapter, you explore how to install, maintain, and manage third-party applications on your iPhone. The topics include the following:

→ Using iTunes to find and install iPhone applications

→ Using the App Store application to find and install iPhone applications

→ Using iPhone applications you install

→ Maintaining iPhone applications

Installing and Maintaining iPhone Applications

Your iPhone is quite a powerful device and supports a full suite of programming tools. That's a good thing because this capability has unleashed the creativity of developers around the world, and there are thousands of applications available to you. Apple's marketing campaign for the iPhone states that if you want to do something, there is an app for it. That is quite a claim, but it also happens to be pretty accurate.

With all these applications available to you, there's a potential for complexity in finding and installing applications that interest you. Fortunately, iTunes, with its easy access to the iTunes Store on your computer and the App Store application on your iPhone, makes it easy to find and install applications. The tools you need to maintain your applications are also built-in, so you don't have to spend much time or effort making sure you are using the latest versions of your favorite apps. Using applications you install is similar to using the default applications such as Maps, Mail, Safari, and so on. Managing the applications on your iPhone isn't hard either, but there are a few things you should know.

Using iTunes to Find and Install iPhone Applications

The iTunes Store has many applications that you can download and install on your iPhone. Many of these are free, while others have a license fee (which you pay through your iTunes Store account). Downloading applications from the iTunes Store is similar to downloading audio and video content. (That topic is covered in detail in Chapter 3, "Moving Audio, Video, and Photos onto Your iPhone.")

Like moving other kinds of content onto iPhone from the iTunes Store, there are two steps to this process. The first is to download applications to your iTunes Library. The second is to move those applications onto iPhone by syncing it with iTunes.

>>>step-by-step

Downloading Applications from the iTunes Store

You can use the iTunes Store to browse for and download applications.

1. Open iTunes and select iTunes Store on the Source list.

2. In the iTunes Store section, click App Store. You move to the App Store Home page. You can click the various links you see to find applications, or you can browse for applications using the Categories section. The rest of these steps demonstrate using the Categories section.

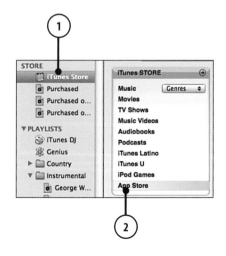

3. Scroll down to see the Categories section.

4. Click the category of the application in which you are interested, such as Social Networking. The applications within that category appear.

5. Select how you want applications to be sorted using the Sort By drop-down list. The options are Name, Most Popular, or Release Date.

6. Use the browsing tools to move through other pages within the category you are browsing.

7. When you find an application in which you are interested, click its icon. You move to the application's description screen, where you can read about the application (including user reviews) and look at screenshots.

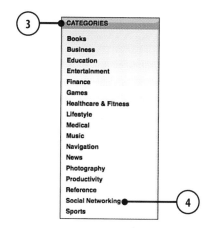

Just Download It

You don't have to view an application's details to download it. Just click the GET APP (for free applications) or BUY APP (for applications that have a license fee) button next to the application's icon while you are browsing to start the download process.

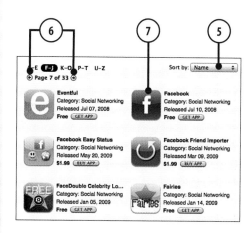

8. Check the requirements to make sure the application is compatible with your iPhone. (See Chapter 17, "Maintaining an iPhone and Solving Problems," to learn how to update your iPhone's software.)

9. When you're ready to download the application, click the GET APP button if it is a free application or the BUY APP button if it has a license fee.

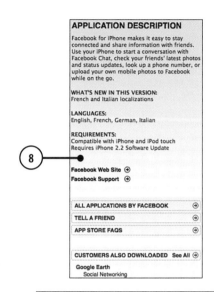

10. If you aren't signed into your iTunes Store account, do so at the prompt by entering your Apple ID and password (or AOL screen name and password) and then clicking Get. The application is downloaded to your iTunes Library. (You can view the applications you have downloaded by clicking Applications on the Source list.)

Searching for Apps in All the Right Places

You can also search for iPhone applications. Click the Power Search link located in the Quick Links section in the top-right side of the iTunes Store Home page. Choose Applications on the Power Search drop-down list and then enter a title or description, developer name, or category. On the Device Compatibility drop-down list, choose iPhone. If you want to limit the results to include only free applications, check the Search for free applications check box. Click Search. Any applications that meet your criteria are shown.

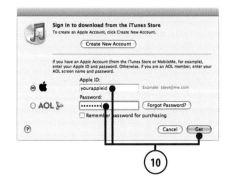

Moving Applications from Your iTunes Library onto iPhone

After applications have been downloaded to your iTunes Library, you can move them onto iPhone.

1. Connect your iPhone to your computer and select it on the Source list.

2. Click the Applications tab.

3. Check the Sync applications check box.

4. To move all the applications you've downloaded onto the iPhone, click All applications and skip to step 7.

5. To move just some of your applications onto iPhone, click Selected applications.

6. Check the check box next to each application you want to move onto the iPhone; uncheck the check boxes for applications you don't want to install on your iPhone.

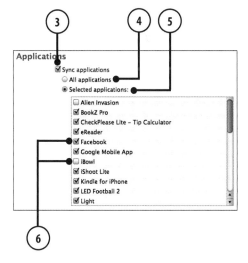

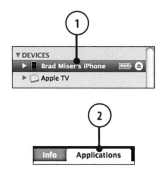

Bonus Task

Please go to this book's website at www.informit.com/title/9780789742315 and click the Downloads tab to find an additional task titled, "Removing Applications from an iPhone."

7. Click Apply. The applications you selected are copied onto and installed on the iPhone. If you selected All applications, each time you sync, all your applications are moved onto the iPhone. If you chose Selected applications instead, you'll need to repeat these steps to change the configuration of applications on your iPhone, such as to install an application whose check box was previously not checked.

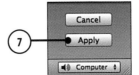

Removing Applications

If you unselect any applications in step 6 that are currently installed on your iPhone, you see a warning dialog explaining that those applications and any data they store will be deleted from the iPhone when you sync it. Click Remove if that's okay, or click Cancel and check the application's check box before completing the sync if you want to keep the application and its data on your iPhone.

Using the App Store to Find and Install iPhone Applications

The App Store, which is an iPhone application in itself, enables you to find applications and download them directly onto iPhone without going through iTunes on a computer. When you use the App Store, you can find applications using any of the following options:

- The Featured button takes you to applications that are being featured in the iTunes Store. This screen has two tabs. New shows you applications that are new to the store. What's Hot lists applications that have been downloaded most frequently.

- The Categories button shows you various categories of applications that you can browse. (This works similarly to browsing categories in the iTunes Store.)

- Top 25 takes you to a list of the top 25 iPhone applications. This screen has two tabs: Top Paid shows you the top applications for which you have to pay a license fee, whereas Top Free shows you a similar list containing only free applications.

- The Search button enables you to search for applications. You can search by name, developer, and other text.

>>>*step-by-step*

1. Move to the Home screen and tap App Store. At the bottom of the screen, you see the buttons you can use to choose a method to find applications. These steps show you how to find applications by category; the other options are similar.

2. Tap Categories.

3. Browse the list until you see a category of interest.

4. Tap a category in which you are interested.

5. If the application has subcategories, browse the subcategories; if you move directly to applications, skip to step 7.

6. Tap a subcategory in which you are interested.

7. Tap the Top Paid tab to see the most frequently downloaded applications that require a license fee; tap Top Free to see the most popular free applications; or tap Release Date to see the applications most recently added to the store.

8. Browse the applications. For each application, you see its icon, developer, name, user ranking, number of user reviews, and its cost (a price or Free).

9. Tap an application in which you are interested. You move to the application's Info screen.

10. Read the application's description.

11. To read reviews and see screen-shots, scroll down the screen.

12. Browse the screenshots.

13. Scroll up.

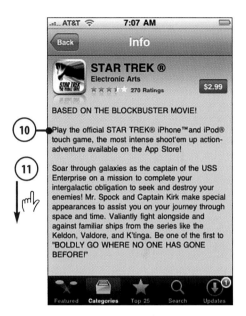

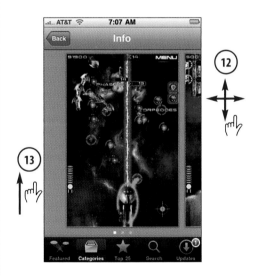

14. Tap the Ratings link, which is labeled with the average user rating and the number of ratings received. You move to the application's Reviews screen where you see user reviews for the application.

15. Scroll the screen to read reviews.

Make Your Voice Known

After you have used an application, you can add your own review by moving back to its Reviews screen and tapping Write a Review. You move to the Submit Review screen where you have to enter your iTunes Store account information before you can write and submit a review.

16. Tap Info. You move back to the Info screen.

17. Scroll to the top of the screen.

18. To download the application, tap FREE if it is a free application or tap the price to download the application if it has a license fee. The button becomes INSTALL if it is a free application or BUY NOW if it has a license fee.

Gotta Share?

If you decide an application is one someone should know about, move to the application's Info screen and tap Tell a Friend. An email message is created with a link to the application. Complete and send the email.

19. Tap INSTALL or BUY NOW.

20. If prompted to do so, enter your iTunes Store password and tap OK.

The application is downloaded to the iPhone. You move to the Home screen where you see the application's icon with the word "Loading" under it.

After the application is downloaded, it installs, and you see the progress bar and "Installing" under the application's icon.

When the installation is complete, you see the application's icon, and it is ready for you to use. (The next time you sync your iPhone, the application is also added to your iTunes Library.)

Keep the Home Screen Organized

As you add application icons to the Home screen, you can organize your icons on the pages of the Home screen in a way that makes the screen layouts the most efficient for you to use. To learn how, see Chapter 16, "Customizing an iPhone."

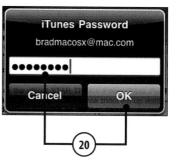

Application being downloaded

Application being installed

Application ready to use

Using iPhone Applications You Install

After you've installed applications, you use them just like iPhone's default applications. Tap the application's icon on the Home screen, and it opens. At that point, how you use the application depends on the specific one you are using.

Button for an installed application

Running application

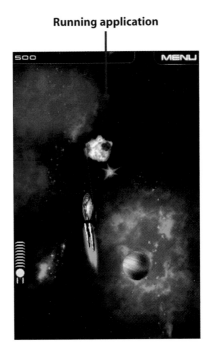

Some applications enable you to configure preferences using iPhone's Settings tool. To see which of your applications provide settings, open the Settings screen and scroll to the bottom. If you see an application, the application has settings and you can tap its name to access its settings.

Tap to configure an installed application's settings.

Maintaining iPhone Applications

Like applications you use on a computer, iPhone applications are regularly updated. When updates are available for applications installed on your iPhone, you see a counter on the App Store icon that indicates updates for some or all of your installed applications are available. To update your applications, perform the following steps.

>>>*step-by-step*

1. Move to the Home screen and tap App Store.

2. Tap Updates. On the Updates screen, you see all the installed applications for which an update is available. For each application, you see its developer, name, the version number of the update, and the release date.

3. Scroll the screen to see all the updates available.

All at Once

To download and install all available updates, tap Update All on the Updates screen.

4. Tap the application you want to update. You move to the Update screen.

Number of updates for installed applications

Number of updates available

5. Read about the update.

6. If the update is free (most are), tap FREE; if it isn't, tap the button showing the cost of the update. The button becomes the INSTALL button for a free update or BUY NOW for an update that has a fee.

7. Tap INSTALL or BUY NOW.

8. If prompted to do so, enter your iTunes Store password and tap OK.

The update begins to download to iPhone. You move back to the Home screen, where you see the updated application's icon with the word "Loading" under it.

When the download process is complete, you see the progress of the installation process under the icon.

When the update is complete, the status information disappears. The next time you run the application, you use the updated version.

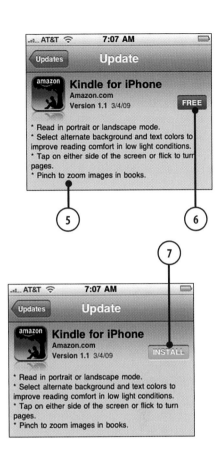

Using iTunes to Check for Updates

You can also update applications via iTunes. Select the Applications source on the Source list. Click the Check for Updates link or the *X* Updates Available link (where *X* is the number of updates available if you've already checked for updates) at the bottom of the iTunes window. iTunes checks the versions of applications in your iTunes Library versus the current versions that are available. If newer versions are found, you can download them. The next time you sync iPhone, the updates are moved from your iTunes Library onto the iPhone.

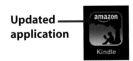

Updated application

Customize the icons that appear on your Home screens.

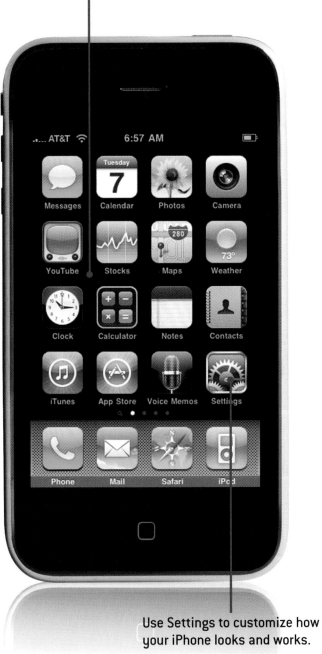

Use Settings to customize how your iPhone looks and works.

In this chapter, you explore ways you can make your iPhone more your own. The topics include the following:

→ Customizing your Home screens
→ Accessing iPhone settings
→ Running in Airplane mode
→ Configuring general sound settings
→ Setting screen brightness
→ Setting wallpaper
→ Configuring other general settings

Customizing an iPhone

When you read earlier chapters that explained various iPhone functions, such as listening to music or emailing, you've experienced customizing an iPhone by using its Settings tools. Many of those settings relate directly to functionality discussed in other chapters, which is why they are covered there. However, a number of an iPhone's settings are more general in nature, which is where this chapter comes into play.

Some examples include sound settings, screen brightness, and so on. While you might not use these functions everyday, they enable you to make your iPhone work more the way you want it to.

One of the most useful customizations is to configure your iPhone's Home screens so they are the most convenient for you (which doesn't actually involve using the Settings application, but this chapter seems like the best place to tell you about it).

Customizing Your Home Screens

The iPhone's Home screens are the starting point for anything you do because these screens contain the icons you tap to access the functions you want to use. The Home screens come configured with icons in default locations. You can change the location of these icons to be more convenient for you. As you add applications and create your own webpage icons, it becomes even more important that you organize your Home screens so you can quickly get to the items you use most frequently. You can move icons around on the same screen and between the pages of the Home screen.

>>>step-by-step

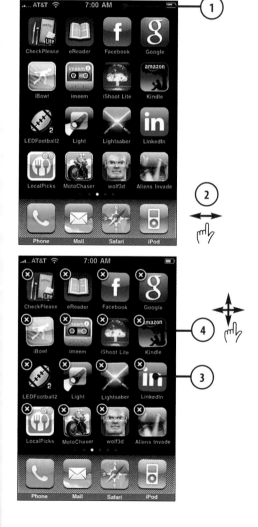

1. Move to the Home screen.

2. Drag across the Home screen until the page containing an icon you want to move appears. (If you drag all the way to the left, the iPhone's Search screen appears.)

3. Tap and hold any icon. After a moment, the icons begin jiggling, and you also see delete buttons (x) next to certain icons. This jiggling indicates you can move icons around the Home screens. The delete button indicates you can remove the icon.

4. Tap and hold down on an icon you want to move and drag it to a new location, or to move the icon onto a different page of the Home screen, drag it to the right or left side of the screen until the page changes to be the page on which you want to place the icon. When you drag an icon to a position already occupied by icons, the icons slide apart to allow you to place the icon you are moving in the new location. If the page is already full, the icon in the lower-right corner moves to the page to the right.

5. When the icon is in the position you want, lift your finger up. The icon is placed in that location.

6. To remove an application or webpage bookmark, tap its delete button.

Icons You Can Delete and Those You Can't

You can only delete icons for things you've added to your iPhone, which are either applications you've installed or bookmarks to webpages you've added; when you delete an icon, you also delete the application or bookmark, and it is no longer on your iPhone. You can't delete any of the default applications, which is why their icons don't have delete buttons. If you don't use some of these applications, move their icons to pages of your Home screen that you don't use very much so they don't get in your way.

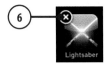

7. Tap Delete. If you are deleting an application, you are prompted to rate it. When you delete a webpage icon, skip step 8 because those icons are deleted immediately.

8. To rate the application, tap the number of stars you want to rate it with and tap Rate (you might have to log in to your iTunes Store account); to skip rating it, tap No Thanks instead. The application's icon is removed from the Home screen, and the content is removed from your iPhone.

9. Continue organizing the pages of your Home screen until they are what you want them to be. When you are happy with the Home screen layout, press the Home button. The icons are locked into place, which is indicated when they stop jiggling.

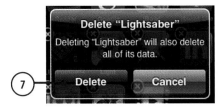

Accessing iPhone Settings

To configure the rest of the options explained in this chapter, first move to the Home screen and tap the Settings button. The Settings screen appears; scroll to see and use all the settings available. The following sections describe various setting options and show you how to configure them. In all cases, start by moving to the Settings screen and then performing step 1.

(If a setting isn't explained in this chapter, it is covered in the chapter about the related topic. For example, the Network setting is explained in Chapter 2, "Connecting to the Internet, Bluetooth Devices, and iPhones/iPods.")

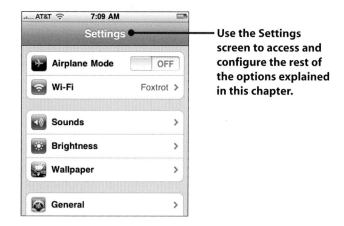

Use the Settings screen to access and configure the rest of the options explained in this chapter.

Using Airplane Mode

Although there's a debate whether devices such as iPhones pose any real danger to the operation of aircraft, there's no reason to run any risk by using iPhone while you are on an airplane. (Besides, not following crew instructions on airplanes can lead you to less-than-desirable situations.) When you place iPhone in Airplane mode, its transmitter and receivers are disabled so it poses no threat to the operation of the aircraft. While it is in Airplane mode, you can't use the phone, email, the web, or any other functions that require communication between iPhone and other devices or networks. Of course, when you have permission to do so, you can use iPhone for iPod functions as well as all the other features that don't require connections to networks or other devices.

To put iPhone in Airplane mode, move to the Settings screen and press the OFF button next to Airplane Mode. The OFF button becomes ON to show you that Airplane mode is enabled; all connections to network servers and the cell network stop, and iPhone goes into quiet mode in which it doesn't broadcast or receive any signals.

Indicates iPhone is in Airplane mode

Airplane mode button

In Airplane mode, you can use your iPhone for various functions, such as iPod, photos, games, and so on. To turn Airplane mode off, move to the Settings screen and press the Airplane Mode ON button, which then becomes the OFF button to show you Airplane mode is disabled. The iPhone resumes transmitting and receiving signals, and all the functions that require a connection starting working again.

Wi-Fi in Airplane Mode

Some airplanes are now supporting Wi-Fi onboard. To access this without violating the requirement not to use a cell network, put the iPhone in Airplane mode, which turns Wi-Fi OFF. Move to the Settings screen, tap Wi-Fi, and then tap OFF next to Wi-Fi. Wi-Fi starts up and you can select the network you want to join (see Chapter 2). You can use this configuration at other times, too, such as when you want to access the Internet, but you don't want to be bothered with phone calls.

>>>step-by-step

Configuring General Sound Settings

You learned about most of an iPhone's sound settings in earlier chapters. Two sound settings are more general, and the following steps describe how to access and change them.

1. Tap Sounds.

2. Scroll down to the bottom of the screen.

3. If you don't want your iPhone to make a sound when you lock it, tap Lock Sounds ON. Its status becomes OFF to show you that the sound when you lock an iPhone is disabled, and the iPhone no longer makes this sound when you press the Sleep/Wake button to put it to sleep and lock it. Tap OFF to re-enable this sound.

4. If you don't like the audible feedback when you tap keys on the iPhone's virtual keyboard, tap Keyboard Clicks ON to disable that sound. Its status becomes OFF, and an iPhone's keyboard is silent as you type on it. Tap OFF, and the audible feedback returns.

Setting Screen Brightness

Because you're continually looking at an iPhone's screen, it should be the right brightness level for your eyes. However, the screen is also a large user of battery power, so the less bright an iPhone's screen is, the longer its battery lasts. You have to find a good balance between viewing comfort and battery life. Fortunately, your iPhone has a brightness feature that adjusts for current lighting conditions automatically.

1. Tap Brightness.

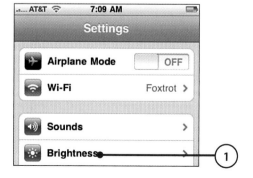

2. Tap the ON button to disable the
   Auto-Brightness feature; its status
   becomes OFF. Tap OFF to enable
   this feature again; when enabled,
   an iPhone's screen dims automatically when you are in low-level
   lighting conditions.

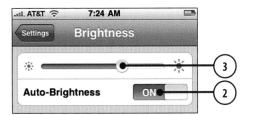

3. Drag the slider to the right to raise
   the base brightness or to the left
   to lower it. A brighter screen uses
   more power but is easier to see.

A Bright Idea

The Auto-Brightness feature adjusts
the screen brightness based on the
lighting conditions in which you are
using the iPhone. You'll get more
battery life with Auto-Brightness on,
but you might not be comfortable
with the screen at a lower brightness. Try using your iPhone with this
feature enabled to see if the automatic adjustment bothers you. You
can always set the brightness level
manually to increase it if needed.

Setting Wallpaper

When an iPhone is awake but locked, you see its wallpaper. You can set the wallpaper for an iPhone using either the default wallpaper collection or by choosing a photo you've taken with or moved onto your iPhone. To use one of iPhone's default images as your wallpaper, perform the following steps.

1. Tap Wallpaper. If you don't have any photos stored on the iPhone, you move directly to default wallpaper images and can skip to step 3. If you have added images to the iPhone, the Wallpaper screen appears, and you see the sources of wallpaper available to you.

2. Tap Wallpaper. The default wallpaper images appear.

Using Your Photos as an iPhone Wallpaper

To learn how to use photos you've taken with or moved onto your iPhone as wallpaper, see Chapter 13, "Working with Photos and Video."

---

3. Tap the image you want to use as wallpaper. You see a preview of the image you selected.

4. Tap Set. The next time your iPhone is awake but locked, you see the wallpaper you selected.

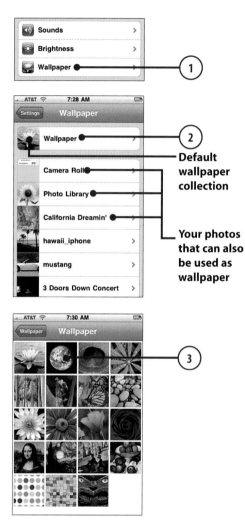

Default wallpaper collection

Your photos that can also be used as wallpaper

Configuring Other General Settings

An iPhone has a large number of other general settings you can use to tweak how it works. These are explained in the following sections. For all the following tasks, move to the General settings screen by tapping General on the Settings screen and then perform step 1.

>>>step-by-step

Getting Information about an iPhone

The About function provides lots of information about your iPhone. Some of this can be useful for troubleshooting or other purposes.

1. Tap About.

2. Scroll up and down the screen to view information about your iPhone, such as the cell network you use; the number of songs, videos, photos, and applications stored on it; its memory; software version number; its serial number; and so on.

3. Tap General.

4. Tap Usage.

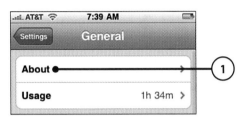

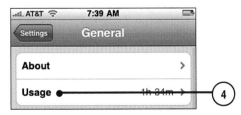

5. Scroll the screen to see various usage information, such as the the last full charge, call times, cell network data, and so on.

6. To reset the phone's statistics, scroll to the bottom of the screen.

7. Tap Reset Statistics.

8. Tap Reset at the prompt. Some of the statistics, including current period call time and the cell network data, are set to zero and begin tracking again.

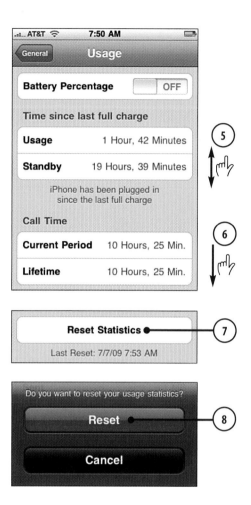

Configuring Location Services

If you don't want applications, such as Maps, to access your iPhone's current location, tap the Location Services ON button. The status becomes OFF to indicate that an iPhone won't be able to access the services it uses to identify where it is. To re-enable these services, tap OFF so the status becomes ON.

Securing Your iPhone

Your iPhone has a number of ways to protect it, which is important considering the information it can store. Using its General settings, you can secure your iPhone in a number of ways, and you can also limit the functions and type of content available on it. Using the Find My iPhone feature, you can locate your iPhone and erase its contents if necessary.

Securing Your iPhone with General Settings

To secure your iPhone, perform the following steps.

1. Tap Auto-Lock.

2. Tap the amount of idle time you want to pass before the iPhone automatically locks and goes to sleep. You can choose from 1 to 5 minutes; choose Never if you want to manually lock your iPhone. I recommend you keep Auto-Lock set to a relatively small value to conserve your iPhone's battery.

3. Tap General.

4. If you want to secure the content on your iPhone with a passcode, tap Passcode Lock.

5. Enter a four-digit passcode.

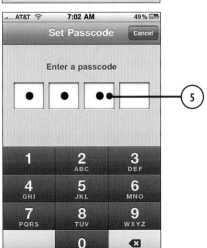

6. Re-enter the passcode. If the two passcodes match, you see the Passcode Lock screen.

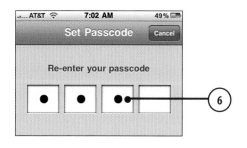

Passcode Lock

With passcode lock enabled, you must enter the passcode to unlock your iPhone, so make sure you don't forget your passcode.

7. To disable the passcode, tap Turn Passcode Off and enter the passcode. You move back to the General screen, and the passcode is removed from the iPhone; if you want to set it again, you need to repeat steps 4 through 6.

8. To change your passcode, tap Change Passcode. You then enter your current passcode and enter your new passcode twice. You return to the Passcode Lock screen, and the new passcode takes effect.

9. To set the amount of time an iPhone is locked before a passcode is required to unlock it, tap Require Passcode.

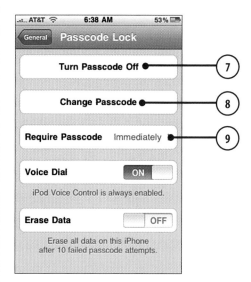

10. Tap the amount of time your iPhone is locked before the passcode takes effect (this assumes you've set a passcode as described in step 4). The shorter this time is, the more secure an iPhone is, but also the more times you'll have to enter the passcode if you lock/put your iPhone to sleep frequently.

11. Tap Passcode Lock.

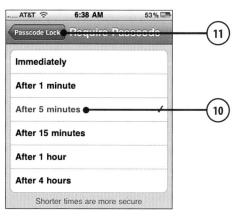

12. To prevent phone numbers from being dialed through voice commands, tap Voice Dial ON so its status becomes OFF. You'll still be able to speak commands for iPod functions, but won't be able to dial numbers with voice commands until you re-enable Voice Dial by tapping OFF so its status becomes ON again.

13. If you want your iPhone to automatically erase all your data after an incorrect passcode has been entered 10 times, tap Erase Data OFF.

14. Tap Enable. The status of Erase Data becomes ON. Should you or anyone else enter in the correct passcode on the eleventh try, your data (basically any changes you've made to the contents of the iPhone) will be erased from the iPhone.

15. Tap General.

16. To limit the kind of content or functions that can be used on your iPhone, tap Restrictions.

17. Tap Enable Restrictions.

18. Create a restrictions passcode. You have to enter this passcode to change content restrictions.

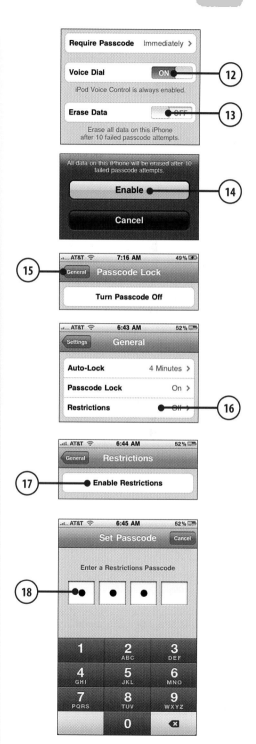

Dueling Passcodes

There are two passcodes: the Auto-Lock passcode and the Restrictions passcode. Each controls access to their respective functions. You can use different passcodes for each or use the same passcode so that you only have to remember one.

---

19. Re-enter your restrictions passcode. You return to the Restrictions screen, and the Allow buttons and Allowed Content functions are enabled.

20. Tap the ON button next to each function you want to disable. Its status becomes OFF to show you that content or function can't be accessed. For example, to prevent web browsing, tap ON next to Safari; the status becomes OFF, and the Safari icon is removed from the Home screen and can't be used. With the other controls, you can prevent access to YouTube videos, the iTunes Store application, the App Store application, the camera, and Location Services.

21. Scroll down to see the Allowed Content controls.

22. To prevent purchases from being made within applications, tap ON next to In-App Purchases. Its status becomes OFF, and purchases can't be made from within applications. This is a good way to prevent unintended purchases, particularly when someone else is using your iPhone.

23. Tap Ratings For.

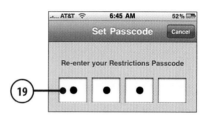

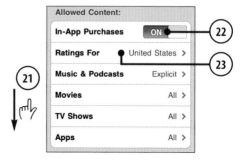

24. Tap the country whose rating system you want to use for content on your iPhone.

25. Tap Restrictions.

26. Tap Music & Podcasts.

27. To prevent content tagged as explicit in the iTunes Store from being played, tap ON so its status becomes OFF. Any explicit content will not be able to be played.

28. Tap Restrictions.

29. Tap Movies.

Whose Ratings?

The country you select in step 24 determines the options you see in steps 30, 33, and 36. The steps show the U.S. rating systems; if you select a different country, you'll see rating options for that country instead.

---

30. Tap the highest (or lowest depending on your point of view) rating of movies that you want to be playable (for example, tap PG to prevent R and NC-17 movies from playing); tap Allow All Movies to allow any movie to be played; or tap Don't Allow Movies to prevent any movie content from playing. Movie ratings that are prevented are highlighted in red.

31. Tap Restrictions.

32. Tap TV Shows.

33. Tap the highest rating of TV shows that you want to be playable (for example, tap TV-14 to prevent TV-MA shows from playing); tap Allow All TV Shows to allow any show to be played; or tap Don't Allow TV Shows to prevent any TV content from playing. Ratings that are prevented are highlighted in red.

34. Tap Restrictions.

35. Tap Apps.

36. Tap the highest rating of application that you want to be available (for example, tap 12+ to prevent 17+ applications from working); tap Allow All Apps to allow any application to be used; or tap Don't Allow Apps to prevent all applications.

Where's My Good Stuff?

When you change content settings, such as allowing explicit content after it was prevented, you might have to resync your iPhone for those changes to take effect.

37. Tap Restrictions.

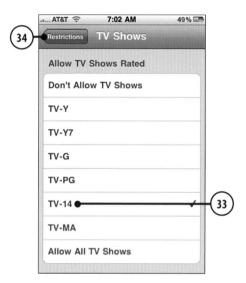

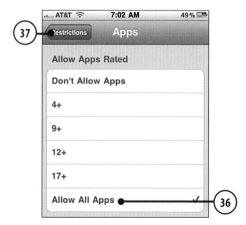

When you try to perform an action that requires a passcode, you are prompted to enter the required passcode. When you do so successfully, you are able to perform the action, such as unlocking your iPhone or changing its restrictions (if you set the passcodes to be different, make sure you enter the appropriate one).

Enter your Auto-Lock passcode to use your iPhone.

Automatic Erase

When you have enabled the Erase Data function and you enter an incorrect passcode when unlocking your iPhone, you see a counter showing the number of unsuccessful attempts. When this reaches 10, all the data on your iPhone will be erased on the next unsuccessful attempt.

Securing Your iPhone with Find My iPhone

If you have a MobileMe account (to learn how to get one, see Chapter 1, "Getting Started with Your iPhone,"), you can use the Find My iPhone feature to locate your iPhone should you ever lose track of it. If someone who isn't known to you has your iPhone, you can protect its data by erasing its contents.

To use this feature, turn Push on and enable Find My iPhone on the iPhone.

1. On the Settings screen, tap Mail, Contacts, Calendars.

2. Tap your MobileMe account.

3. If OFF is displayed next to Find My iPhone, tap it; if ON is displayed, skip to step 5.

4. Tap Allow at the prompt.

5. Tap Mail.

6. Scroll down until you see Fetch New Data.

7. Tap Fetch New Data.

8. If Push is set to OFF, tap OFF to enable push so its status becomes ON.

9. Scroll down until you see Advanced.

10. Tap Advanced.

11. Tap your MobileMe account.

12. Tap Push.

___

Keep It Secure

For better security, you should configure a passcode lock as described earlier in this chapter. If you don't, anyone who picks up your iPhone can use it. At least with a passcode, someone has to enter the correct passcode to access your information.

___

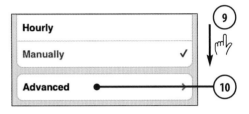

Once activated on the iPhone, you can access your iPhone's location via the MobileMe website.

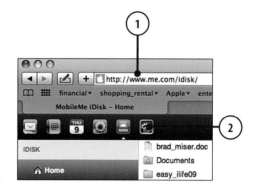

1. Use Safari or Firefox to move to and log in to your MobileMe website.

2. Click the Account button.

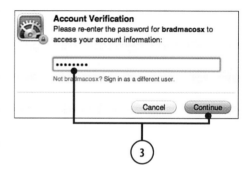

3. Enter your MobileMe password and click Continue.

4. Click Find My iPhone. You see the status of your iPhone and after a few moments, you see a map with a circle showing the location of your iPhone. Initially, the circle will be large, but the tool continues to try to refine the location; as it does, the circle gets smaller. The precision of the location shown depends on a number of factors, including whether the phone can be located via GPS, the cell network, and so on.

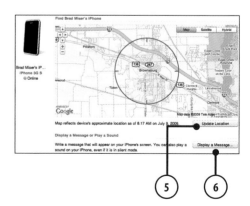

5. To update the phone's location, click Update Location.

6. To display a message and play a sound on the iPhone, click Display a Message.

7. Type the message you want to display.

8. If you want a sound to play, check the Play a sound for 2 minutes with this message check box.

9. Click Send. The message is sent to the iPhone. You also receive a confirmation email to your MobileMe account that shows the message that was sent.

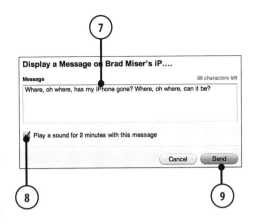

Make it Stop!

To stop the sound playing on the iPhone, unlock it and tap the OK button on the message prompt. (If you don't require a passcode, anyone who has the phone can do this, which is one reason requiring a passcode is more secure.)

10. If you decide you've lost control of your iPhone and want to erase its contents, click Remote Wipe.

11. Read the text and check the check box.

12. Click Erase All Data. All the data on your iPhone is erased and it is restored to factory settings.

The message you created is displayed on the iPhone, and a sound plays if you selected that option.

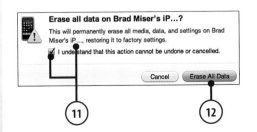

Remote Wiping

Remote wiping is a bit of a two-edged sword. It protects your data by erasing your iPhone, which also means you can't use Find My iPhone to locate it anymore. You should only use this if you're pretty sure that someone has your phone because after you wipe it, there's no way to try to track the phone's location. How fast you move to a wipe also depends on if you've required a passcode or not. If you do require a passcode, you know that your phone's data can't be accessed without that code so it will take a little time to crack it, and you might be slower on the Erase All Data trigger. If your phone doesn't have a passcode, you might want to pull the trigger faster. If you do recover your phone after a wipe, go through the restore process to return your iPhone to its condition as of your most recent backup. (See Chapter 17, "Maintaining an iPhone and Solving Problems," for information about restoring an iPhone.)

Configuring the Home Button and Search Options

You can configure properties relating to your Home screens with the following steps.

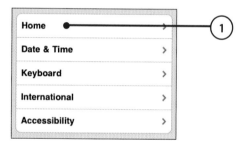

1. Tap Home.

2. Tap the action that you want to happen when you press the Home button twice: Tap Home to move to the Home screen (same as a single press); tap Search to move to the Search screen; tap Phone Favorites to move to your favorites list; tap Camera to move into the camera; or iPod to show the iPod control bar.

3. If you always want the iPod controls to appear when you press the Home button twice while music is playing, leave the iPod Controls setting to ON; if you always want the action you set in step 2 to happen instead, tap ON so it becomes OFF.

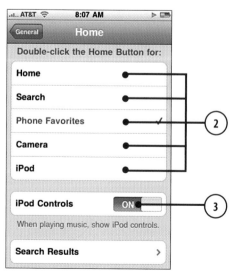

4. Tap Search Results.

5. Tap any category of content that you don't want to be included in searches. When a category has a check mark, it will be included; when a category doesn't have a check mark, it is ignored when you search.

6. Drag the list button next to a category up or down the screen to move it up or down on the list. Categories that are higher on the Search Results screen will be higher in search results. For example, if Mail is the top item on the list, emails will appear at the top of the results screen when you search.

7. Repeat steps 5 and 6 until you've configured searches so only categories you want to search are included and the results appear in the order you prefer.

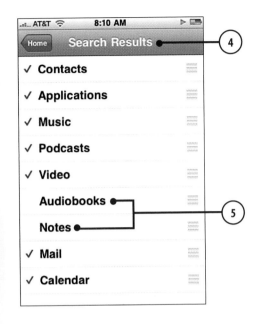

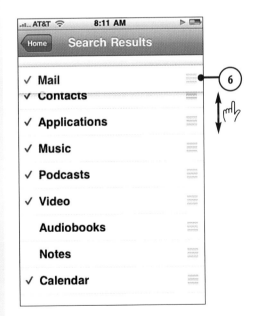

Configuring the Keyboard

As you've seen, you use the iPhone's keyboard for lots of things, such as emailing, surfing the web, and so on. There are a number of settings that determine how the keyboard works.

1. Tap Keyboard.

2. To disable the automatic spell checking/correction, tap Auto-Correction ON so its status becomes OFF. Your iPhone will no longer suggest spelling as you type.

3. To prevent your iPhone from automatically capitalizing as you type, tap Auto-Capitalization ON. Its status becomes OFF, and the iPhone no longer changes the case of letters as you type them.

4. To enable the Caps Lock key, tap Enable Caps Lock OFF. The status becomes ON, and when the keyboard appears, you can use the Caps Lock key.

5. To disable the shortcut that types a period followed by a space when you tap the space bar twice, tap "." Shortcut ON. Its status becomes OFF, and you must tap a period and the space bar to type these characters.

6. To change the keyboard's configuration, tap International Keyboards (covered in the next section).

Setting International Options

You can configure various aspects of the iPhone to reflect the countries and standards you want to use.

1. Tap International.

2. Tap Language.

3. Tap the language you want to use. The selected language is marked with a check mark.

4. Tap Done. Your iPhone starts using the language you selected.

5. Tap Voice Control.

6. Tap the language you want to use when you speak voice commands.

7. Tap International.

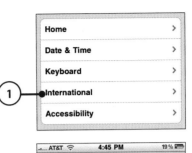

8. Tap Keyboards.

9. Tap the OFF button next to the keyboard languages you want to enable so their status becomes ON; turn off any keyboards that you want to disable by tapping their ON buttons so their status becomes OFF. You must have at least one keyboard enabled, but you can have multiple keyboards active at the same time. (Some languages have submenus you use to choose the keyboard layouts you want for that language.)

10. Tap International. The number of keyboards you have enabled is shown on the right side of the screen in the Keyboards option.

11. Tap Region Format.

12. Tap the region whose formats you want to use. Some regions have alternate format choices; you can choose from among the format options that are used in those regions.

13. Tap International. At the bottom of the International screen, you see examples of the format you selected.

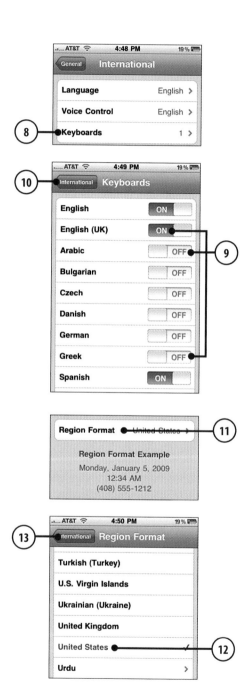

Tap to change keyboards

When you have more than one language enabled, a Globe button appears on an iPhone's keyboard to the left of the space bar. Tapping this button cycles through each of the enabled keyboards; each keyboard's name appears briefly as you tap the button. When you reach the language you want to use, you can type using the characters for that language.

Reset

Mostly for troubleshooting purposes, you can reset various aspects of your iPhone using the Reset command at the bottom of the General screen. This is explained in Chapter 17.

CUSTOMIZING FOR ACCESSIBILITY

The iPhone is designed to be accessible to as many people as possible. Using the Accessibility settings, you can customize the iPhone for people with specific needs. With VoiceOver, the iPhone will read onscreen elements, such as text and buttons. Using the Zoom settings, you can set the entire screen to zoom, and you also see pointers on how the revised zoom settings work. You can use the White on Black setting to swap light with dark so the screen's background becomes dark and text becomes light. Use the Mono Audio setting to change all sound to mono. Turn Speak Auto-text on to have the iPhone speak automatic text corrections it makes. To configure these settings, tap Accessibility on the General settings screen.

An iPhone is easy to maintain and isn't likely to give you much trouble.

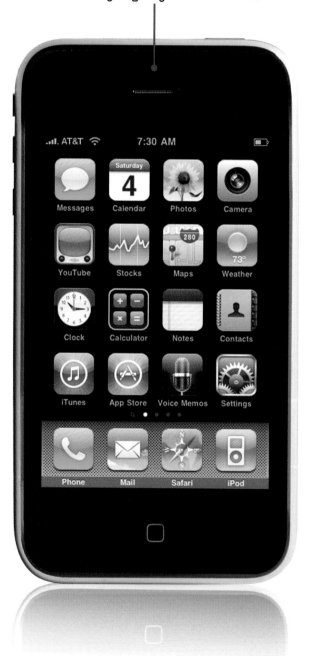

In this chapter, you learn how to keep an iPhone in top shape and to know what to do should problems happen. Topics include the following:

→ Maintaining an iPhone
→ Solving iPhone problems

Maintaining an iPhone and Solving Problems

You probably noticed this is a short chapter, and there is a good reason for that: An iPhone works very well, and you are unlikely to have problems with it, especially if you keep iTunes and the iPhone's software current. When problems do occur, you can usually solve them with a few simple steps. If that fails, there's lots of help available for you on the Internet.

Maintaining an iPhone

Some basic maintenance tasks keep an iPhone in top working condition. Even better, you can do most of these tasks with just a couple of mouse clicks because you can configure iTunes to do most of the work for you.

Maintaining iTunes

As you've learned in this book, iTunes is a vital partner for your iPhone. You should keep iTunes current to ensure that you have the latest bug fixes, new features, and so on. Fortunately, you can configure iTunes to maintain itself.

>>>*step-by-step*

Maintaining iTunes on Windows PCs

You can easily update iTunes on a Windows PC, but it's even better to have iTunes update itself automatically.

1. In iTunes, choose Edit, Preferences.

2. Click the General tab.

3. Check the Check for updates automatically check box.

4. Click OK. The dialog closes. iTunes checks for updates automatically. When it finds an update, it prompts you to download and install it.

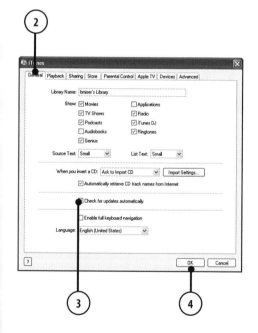

Check for Updates Now Windows

To check for updates at any time, choose Help, Check for Updates. iTunes checks for updates immediately. If you are using the current version, you see a message telling you so. If an update is available, iTunes prompts you to download and install it.

Maintaining iTunes on Macs

You can easily update iTunes on a Mac, but it's even better to have iTunes update itself automatically.

1. Open the System Preferences application.

2. Click Software Update.

3. Check the Check for updates check box.

4. Choose the frequency that Software Update checks for updates on the pop-up menu, such as Weekly.

5. Check the Download important updates automatically check box. The Mac checks for updates for iTunes, along with all the other Apple software on your Mac according to the timeframe you selected. When it identifies an update, it downloads the update automatically and prompts you to install it or prompts you to download and install it, depending on the kind of update it is.

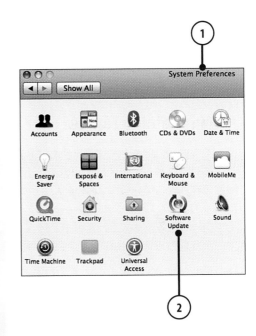

Check for Updates Now Mac

To check for updates at any time, open the Apple menu and choose Software Update. The Software Update application runs. If it finds an iTunes or other updates, the application prompts you to download and install them.

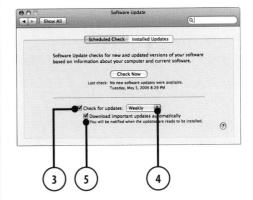

Maintaining an iPhone's Software

One of iTunes' functions is to maintain an iPhone's software, which is one of the reasons you should keep iTunes current. Periodically, iTunes checks for updates to the iPhone operating system software. When iTunes finds an update, it downloads it for you. The next time you connect your iPhone to your computer, you are prompted to install the update. You can allow the update when you are prompted about it and follow the onscreen instructions to install it, or you can update your iPod's software manually by performing the following steps.

1. Connect your iPhone to your computer.

2. Select your iPhone on the Source list.

3. Click the Summary tab. You see the current version of the iPhone's software.

4. If a newer version of the iPhone software is available, click Update or click Check for Update to manually check for an update. (If you manually check for an update and you're using the current version of the iPhone's software, you see a dialog telling you so, and you can skip the rest of these steps. If you aren't using the current version, the button becomes Update.)

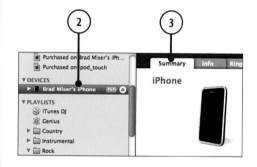

5. Read information about the update and follow the onscreen instructions to download and install it onto an iPhone.

6. Agree to the license agreement. iTunes begins to download and install the update on the iPhone.

When the software has been downloaded and installed, the iPhone is automatically restarted. As the process proceeds, you see various status messages in iTunes. Eventually, the iPhone disappears from iTunes, is restarted, and becomes available in iTunes again, and you see that your software is current.

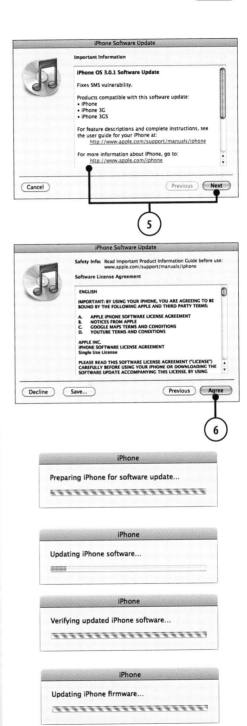

Maintaining an iPhone's Power

Obviously, an iPhone with a dead battery isn't good for very much. As you use an iPhone, you should keep an eye on its battery status. As long as the battery status is green, you're okay. As an iPhone gets low on power, the battery on the status icon becomes empty and eventually turns red. Two separate warnings will alert you when the battery lowers to 20% and then again at 10%. If you keep going from there, the iPhone runs out of power and shuts down. Of course, it gives you plenty of warning through onscreen messages before this happens.

By default, the iPhone displays only the battery icon. For a more precise indication of battery status, enable the Battery Percentage display by moving to the Settings screen, tapping General, tapping Usage, and tapping OFF next to Battery Percentage. Its status becomes ON and you see the percentage of battery power remaining next to the icon.

Battery status

Sync Regularly

You should sync your iPhone frequently to keep its information backed up on your computer. (You can set syncing to happen whenever you connect your iPhone to your computer, as explained in Chapter 4, "Configuring and Synchronizing Information on an iPhone.") In the event you run into a major problem that requires restoring or erasing your iPhone, you can recover its data from the backup. If you wait a long time between syncs/backups and encounter a problem, you could lose data. Syncing frequently also keeps your iPhone's battery charged.

The obvious way to avoid running out of power is to keep your iPhone charged. The good news is that all you have to do is to connect the iPhone to your computer, and its battery charges. While this is occurring, you see the charging icon in the upper-right corner of the screen, and if you wake an iPhone up, a large battery icon showing the relative state of the battery appears on its screen. When charging is complete, the battery status icon replaces the charging icon in the upper right corner of the screen, the large battery icon disappears, and you see an iPhone's wallpaper if it's locked, or you see whatever screen you happen to be using if it isn't locked.

You can also connect an iPhone to an external charger if your computer isn't handy.

This iPhone is charging.

Keeping an iPhone Topped Off

It's a good idea to keep your iPhone's battery topped off; this type of battery actually does better if you keep it charged rather than letting it run down all the way before recharging. Periodically, say every month or two, you might want to let an iPhone run completely out of power to maximize its life.

In addition to keeping your iPhone's battery charged, consider the following recommendations to maximize the amount of time you can use it between charges:

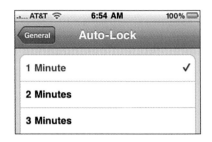

- Put your iPhone to sleep when you aren't using it by pressing the Sleep/Wake button.

- Set Auto-Lock to a small interval, such as 1 Minute. When an iPhone locks, it goes to sleep immediately, which puts it in low-power mode (Settings, General, Auto-Lock).

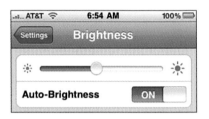

- Set the brightness of the screen to a low but comfortable level and leave Auto-Brightness turned on (Settings, Brightness).

- Use a Wi-Fi connection to the Internet whenever you can (see Chapter 2, "Connecting to the Internet, Bluetooth Devices, and iPhones/iPods"). Wi-Fi uses less power than the cellular data network, and you'll also have a faster connection (Settings, Wi-Fi).

- Disable features you don't use, especially those that communicate with other devices. Specific suggestions follow.

- If you don't use Bluetooth devices, make sure Bluetooth is turned off (Settings, General, Bluetooth OFF).

- If you don't need the speed offered by the higher-speed cellular data network, turn it off (Settings, General, Network, Enable 3G OFF, if you use the AT&T network).

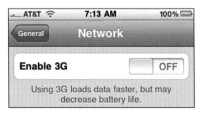

- If you don't need email to be pushed to any email accounts, disable email push (Settings; Mail, Contacts, Calendars; Fetch New Data; Push OFF).

- If you do need email pushed to some accounts, disable push for the accounts you don't need email pushed to by setting them to Fetch (Settings; Mail, Contacts, Calendars; Fetch New Data; Advanced; email account; Fetch).

- Set email to be manually fetched instead of automatically fetched (Settings; Mail, Contacts, Calendars; Fetch New Data; Manually).

- Inactivate email accounts you don't need to use at all (Settings; Mail, Contacts, Calendars; email account; Account OFF).

- Disable functions for email accounts you don't need to use (Settings; Mail, Contacts, Calendars; email account; Account OFF).

- Run in Airplane mode when you can. When iPhone is in Airplane mode, all the features that require connections to the Internet or other devices are disabled, which are also the features that use power most quickly. It's fast and easy to move in and out of Airplane mode (Settings, Airplane mode OFF or ON). So, when you want to conserve battery power and don't need the functions that connect to the Internet or the cell network, enable Airplane mode, whether you happen to be on an airplane or not.

Wi-Fi in Airplane Mode

Interestingly, you can turn Wi-Fi on while your iPhone is in Airplane mode. This is useful if you happen to be somewhere where you don't want to use the cell network, but do want to use Wi-Fi to access the Internet. For example, if you are on a plane that has a Wi-Fi network, you can enable Wi-Fi while leaving the cell functions disabled.

Cleaning an iPhone's Screen

The iPhone's onscreen controls are amazing. But because you use them by tapping and dragging your fingers on the screen, the screen gets smudged. You can clean the screen by rubbing it carefully using the cloth included with the iPhone. You should never spray any cleaners directly onto an iPhone's screen. However, you can apply a slight amount of glass cleaner to a very soft cloth and gently wipe an iPhone's screen to clean it. In most cases though, you can get the screen clean with the provided cloth by itself.

Keeping a Clean Screen

If the smudges on an iPhone screen bother you, consider adding a clear plastic protector to the screen. There are many kinds of these available (some cases include a screen protector), but they all work in the same way in that they have a side that clings to the screen. You touch the other side, which is more resistant to smudges than is an iPhone's glass screen. Using a protector sheet does change the feel of using and the look of an iPhone so you might or might not like to use one. However, even if the look and feel of a protector sheet isn't ideal, it can also help guard against scratches. While an iPhone's screen is pretty tough, it can be scratched, so you might want to trade-off the slight degradation of a protector sheet against the possibility of a permanent scratch on the screen.

Solving iPhone Problems

Even a device as reliable as your iPhone can sometimes run into problems. Fortunately, the solutions to most problems you encounter are simple. If a simple solution doesn't work, there is a great deal of detailed help available from Apple, and there's even more available from the community of iPhone users.

The problems that you can address with the simple steps described in this section vary and range from such issues as the iPhone hanging (won't respond to commands) to the iPhone not being visible in iTunes when connected to your computer (and so it can't be synced). No matter which problem you experience, try the following steps to solve them.

Restarting an iPhone

If an iPhone starts acting up or an application stops responding, restart the iPhone.

1. Press and hold the Sleep/Wake button until the red slider appears on the screen.

2. Drag the red slider to the right. The iPhone powers down.

3. Press and hold the Sleep/Wake button until you see the Apple logo on the screen. The iPhone restarts. When the Home screen appears, try using the iPhone again. If the problem is solved, you're done.

Restarting the Computer and iTunes

If iTunes can no longer see your iPhone, restart the computer and open iTunes again.

1. Disconnect the iPhone from the computer.

2. Restart the computer.

3. After the computer restarts, connect your iPhone to it. iTunes should open, and the iPhone should be selected on the Source list. If so, all should be well. If not, you need to try something else.

All USB Ports Are Not Created Equal

If your computer can't see your iPhone when it's connected, try a different USB port. You should use a USB port on the computer itself rather than one on a keyboard or USB hub.

Resetting an iPhone

If restarting an iPhone or the computer doesn't help, try resetting an iPhone using the following escalation of steps.

1. If you are using an application and it freezes, restart the iPhone using the previous steps. If the problem goes away, you're done. If not, continue to the next step.

2. If you can't restart the iPhone normally, press and hold down both the Home and the Sleep/Wake buttons for at least ten seconds. You should see the Power Off slider; if you do, shut down and then restart the iPhone. If you don't see the slider, the iPhone should turn itself off and then restart; you can release the buttons when you see the Apple logo on the screen. If the problem goes away, you're done. If not, continue.

3. If you can use an iPhone's controls, proceed with the following steps. If you can't use any of its controls, you need to restore the iPhone, which is explained in the next section.

4. On the Home screen, tap Settings.

5. Tap General.

6. Scroll down until you see the Reset command.

7. Tap Reset.

8. Tap Reset All Settings.

9. Tap Reset All Settings at the prompt. All settings on the iPhone reset to their defaults, and the iPhone restarts. If the problem goes away, you're done—except for reconfiguring your settings, of course. If not, continue.

10. Repeat steps 4 through 7 to move back to the Reset screen.

Reset Specific Areas

If you are experiencing problems in a specific area, such as connecting to a network, try resetting just that area (for example, Reset Network Settings) before you pull out the big gun by erasing the iPhone.

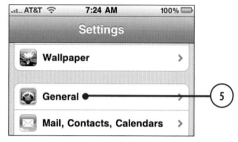

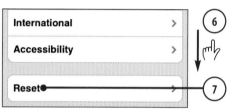

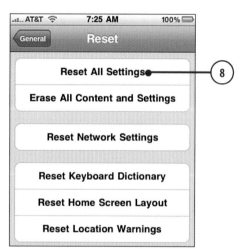

11. Tap Erase All Content and Settings. When you do this, you lose all the content on your iPhone. Make sure you have that content elsewhere before you erase an iPhone. If the content is in your iTunes Library, you're fine. But if you've added information that you have not synced to iTunes, such as contacts, directly onto the iPhone, you lose that information when you erase ithe iPhone.

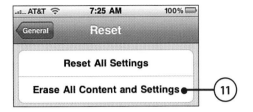

Go Home Again

In Chapter 16 you learn that you can organize the pages of your Home screen by moving icons around. To return the pages to their default state, tap Reset Home Screen Layout. Tap Reset Home Screen at the prompt. The icons on your Home screen are returned to their default locations.

12. Tap Erase iPhone at the prompt. The iPhone is erased, and it should return to like-new condition. You have to sync it again, reconfigure its settings, and so on. If the problem recurs, you must restore the iPhone.

Restoring an iPhone

The most severe action you can take on your iPhone is to restore it. When this happens, the iPhone is erased, so you lose all its contents, and its current software is overwritten with the latest version. If you have added information to your iPhone since it was last backed up (when you last connected it to the computer), that information is lost when you restore your iPhone—so be careful before doing this. If none of the other steps corrected the problem, restoring the iPhone should.

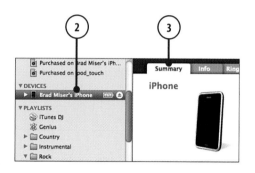

1. Connect the iPhone to your computer.

2. Select the iPhone on the Source list.

3. Click the Summary tab.

4. Click Restore. Remember you lose everything on your iPhone when you restore it, so make sure you have all its data stored elsewhere, such as in your iTunes Library before you do this.

5. Click Restore in the dialog.

6. Read the information about the current version of the iPhone's software and click Next.

7. Click Agree. The current version of the iPhone's software is downloaded to your computer, and iTunes reinstalls it on your iPhone. You see several progress indicators along the way. The iPhone will be restarted and iTunes begins reinstalling its software. When the process is complete, you see a message explaining what has happened.

8. Click OK. The iPhone is restarted and you see the Set Up Your iPhone screen.

9. Click the Restore from the backup radio button.

10. On the pop-up menu, choose your iPhone's name.

11. Click Continue. iTunes restores the iPhone from the backup.

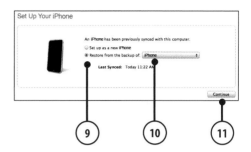

Starting Over

If you want to start at the beginning, select the Set up as a new iPhone radio button in step 9 instead. Follow the onscreen prompts. When that process is complete, you're prompted to name and reconfigure the iPhone as you did when you first starting using it.

12. Click OK in the completion dialog. The iPhone is synced according to the settings stored in the backup. When the sync process is complete, the iPhone should be back in working condition with all your content restored to it. If you have a lot of content, this process can take a while because the sync is done starting with the iPhone's memory being "empty."

How Does It Remember?

You might wonder how an iPhone can be restored. It's because iTunes backs up critical iPhone data and settings on your computer. Each time you sync, this information is backed up on the computer so it is available again when it is needed, such as when you restore your iPhone. You should connect your iPhone to your computer regularly even if the content you sync doesn't changed much. This ensures the iPhone's backup is current.

Reinstalling iTunes

If iTunes is unable to see your iPhone and the iPhone appears to be working normally, reinstall iTunes on your computer. (This is much more likely to be required on a Windows PC than on a Mac.) See Chapter 1, "Getting Started with Your iPhone," for instructions on downloading and installing iTunes on your computer.

No iTunes Content Worries as Long as You Back Up

iTunes stores content, such as music and video, in a different location than the application itself. You can reinstall iTunes without disturbing your iTunes content. Of course, you should always have your iTunes content backed up, such as storing it on DVD or an external hard drive, in case something happens to your computer. If a problem with your computer causes you to lose content you've purchased from the iTunes Store, you have to pay for it again. So be sure you back up your iTunes content regularly.

Trouble Sending Email from an iPhone?

If you are sure you've configured an email account correctly and you can receive email to that address but you can't send any from that address, the provider of the account probably doesn't allow sending email from any IP address except those it provides. This is most common when the email account is provided through an Internet Service Provider, such as a cable company. You have a couple of solutions. One is to access your email through the provider's web email interface. The other is to add a second email account (such as a Gmail account) to an iPhone and use that account when you want to send email. See Chapter 7, "Emailing," for information about choosing the account through which you are sending email.

Getting Help with iPhone Problems

If none of the previous steps solved the problem, you can get help in a number of ways:

- **Apple's website**   Go to www.apple.com/support/. On this page, you can access all kinds of information about iPhones, iTunes, and other Apple products. You can browse for help, and you can search for answers to specific problems. Many of the resulting articles have detailed, step-by-step instructions to help you solve problems as well as links to more information.

- **Provider's website.** If you visit the website for your cellular provider, you can get help with problems you're having with your connection to its network, and you can log in to your account to get information about it. For example, if your provider is AT&T, visit www.wireless.att.com.

- **Web searches** One of the most useful ways to get help is to do a web search for the specific problem you're having. Just open your favorite search tool, such as Google, and search for the problem. You are very likely to find many resources to help you, including websites, forums, and such. If you encounter a problem, it's likely someone else has, too, and they've probably put the solution on the web.

- **Me** You're welcome to send email to me for problems you're having with your iPhone. My address is bradmiser@me.com. I'll do my best to help you as quickly I can.

Index

NUMBERS

24-hour clock feature, 224

A

About function, 413
accepting cookies, 265
accessibility settings, customizing, 431
accessing
    Home screen toolbar, 5
    Settings screen, 408
    websites via URL (Safari web browser), 270
accounts
    AT&T Services feature, 132
    email accounts, configuring, 162
        advanced configuration, 170-175
        Exchange accounts, 165-169
        Fetch New Data settings, 176-177
        global settings, 179-181
        Gmail accounts, 163-164
        SMTPserver settings, 175
        troubleshooting, 169
    email accounts, syncing, 86-87, 91
adding
    caller information to Favorites list, 148
    information fields to contacts, 114
    songs to On-the-Go playlists, 325-326
Address Book, syncing with, 83-84, 88-89

Airplane mode, 408-409, 442
alarms (Clock)
    configuring, 253, 257
    deleting, 258
    disabling, 256, 259
    dismissing, 259
    editing, 258
    managing, 259
    naming, 256
    snooze function, 256
    sound of, choosing, 255
albums
    Albums tool, finding music via, 305-307
    artwork
        finding, 297
        importing into iTunes, 54
    covers
        Album Cover view (Now Playing screen), 317-319
        text labels in Cover Flow Browser, 296
    viewing, 319
alerts
    Calendar events
        configuring for, 243
        dismissing, 249
    invitation alerts (Calendar), turning on/off, 227
    MobileMe sync alerts, managing, 26
    sound, turning on/off, 243
    text messaging alerts, turning on/off, 209-210
    voicemail alerts, 129, 153
all-day events (Calendar), 239
answering calls, 143
    during in-process calls, 145
    earbuds, 145

muting music/video during, 146
AOL AIM instant messaging application, downloading, 208
App Store, downloading applications from, 394
    applications
        emailing links to, 398
        installing, 399
        rating, 398
        reading about, 396
        reviewing, 397-398
        sorting, 395
    license fees, 398
    screenshots, 397
Apple website, 451
applications
    App Store, downloading from, 394
        emailing links to applications, 398
        installing applications, 399
        license fees, 398
        rating applications, 398
        reading about applications, 396
        reviewing applications, 397-398
        screenshots, 397
        sorting applications, 395
    configuring, 400
    deleting, 407
    iTunes Store, downloading from, 390
        directly to iPhone, 76-79
        directly to iPod Touch, 75-76
        license fees, 392
        reading about applications, 391

sorting applications, 391
viewing application
requirements, 392
maintaining, 401-403
managing, 399
moving from iTunes Library
onto iPod Touch, 393
organizing, 399
P2P connections, 48-49
rating, 407
removing, 394
running, 400
updating, 401-403
artists (musicians), finding
music via, 300-303
AT&T Services feature, 132
AT&T website, 452
attachments (email)
.ics files, 247
photos as, 357, 363
viewing, 187
audio
audiobooks, downloading, 76
CDs, importing into iTunes,
52-53
configuring settings, 409
iTunes Music Store application, purchasing from,
78-79
playlists
creating in iTunes, 63
smart playlists, 64-65
podcasts, 60-62
purchasing music from
iTunes Store, 55-57, 75-79
transferring from iTunes to
iPhone, 67-71
volume control, 294
audiobooks, 324. **See also**
music; podcasts
Auto-Brightness feature, 411
Auto-Capitalization feature, 428
Auto-Correction feature, 428
Auto-Lock feature, 415
Autofill feature (Safari web
browser), 263, 287-288
automatic logins, webpages, 288

B

backups, iTunes content, 451
batteries
life of, monitoring, 14
maintaining, 438-441

maximizing life of, 440-441
saving, Fetch New Data
feature, 230
BCC (blind copies) of email
messages, 180
blocking explicit content. **See**
Restrictions feature
Bluetooth Internet connections, pairing, 45
bookmarks
Map bookmarks,
377-378, 382
Safari web browser
creating on Home
screen, 284
deleting, 283
editing names of, 278, 281
organizing, 278-282
saving, 277-278
syncing, 85, 90, 268
brightness (screens), setting,
410-411
browsing. **See also** finding;
searches
applications in
App Store, 395-396
iTunes Store, 391
contacts, 116-117
iTunes Store, 56
locations via
bookmarks, 377
contact information, 379
searches, 374-376
music via
Albums tool, 305-307
artists, 300-303
Cover Flow Browser, 294
More menu, 308
playlist, 298
Songs tool, 304
voicemail messages, 154
business/finance
company contacts, creat-
ing, 108-109
Stocks application, 387
buying content from iTunes
Store application, 78-79

C

caches (web browsers),
clearing, 267
Calculator application, 387
Calendar

clearing, 235
date/time settings
configuring, 223, 226-228
Time Zone support fea-
ture, 228-229
Day view, 236-237
Default Calendar,
selecting, 230
events
adding by accepting
invitations, 246-248
adding manually, 237,
240, 243-245
all-day events, 239
configuring alerts for, 243
deleting, 235
dismissing alerts for, 249
editing, 235, 237
managing invitations, 246
repeating events, 241-243
setting duration of,
238-240
syncing, 228
turning on/off invitation
alerts, 227
viewing, 234-237
Fetch New Data feature,
230-231
invitations
accepting, 246-248
ics files, 247
managing, 246
turning on/off alerts, 227
Month view, 234-236
moving information to,
230-231
syncing, 84-85, 89-90, 228,
232, 245
viewing, 233
calendars (iCal), syncing, 84-85,
89-90
calls
adding information to
Favorites list, 148
answering, 143
during in-process calls, 145
earbuds, 145
muting music/video dur-
ing, 146
Call Failed screen, 138
Call Forwarding feature, 130
Call Waiting feature, 131
caller ID information, hiding, 131

clearing recent calls list, 147
conference calls, 140-141
    ending, 143
    private conversations
        during, 142
    removing callers from, 142
    time usage during, 143
dialing via
    contacts, 134
    Favorites list, 135
    keypad, 133
    recent calls list, 136
    Voice Control feature,
        149-150
in-process calls
    answering calls during, 145
    conference calls, 140-142
    entering numbers
        during, 139
    managing, 138
    merging calls, 141
    swapping calls, 142
merging, 141
sending to voicemail, 145
silencing the ringer, 145
swapping, 142
using headsets during, 149
voicemail, 150
    alerts, 153
    changing greetings, 152
    changing passwords, 158
    contact names associated
        with, 153
    deleting messages, 156
    fast-forwarding mes-
        sages, 155
    finding messages, 154
    listening to messages, 154
    lost/forgotten passwords,
        159
    passwords, 152
    pausing messages, 155
    recording greetings, 151
    returning calls, 157
    rewinding messages, 155
cameras, 4
    deleting photos, 348, 356
    deleting video, 356
    previewing video, 349
    recording video in land-
        scape mode, 349
    taking photos
        flashes, 348
        focusing, 347
        framing subjects, 347

GPS tags, 348
landscape mode, 346
screenshots, 350
shutter sounds, 348
viewing photos, 348
capitalizing text
automatically, 428
Caps Lock feature, 428
Categories button (App
    Store), 395
CDs, importing into iTunes,
    52-53
cell phone providers, Wi-Fi net-
    work Internet connections, 41
cellular data networks, Internet
    connections, 41-44
changing
    greetings (voicemail), 152
    voicemail passwords, 132
    Wi-Fi network Internet con-
        nections, 38-39
chapters (video), moving to, 337
check boxes (iTunes), 66
cities, associating with
    clocks, 252
cleaning screens, 443
clearing
    caches (web browsers), 267
    Calendar, 235
    cookies, 266
    location searches, 376
    music searches, 310
    recent calls list, 147
    text messages, 220
    website histories, 266, 276
Clock
    24-hour clock feature, 224
    alarms
        choosing sound of, 255
        configuring, 253, 257
        deleting, 258
        disabling, 256, 259
        dismissing, 259
        editing, 258
        managing, 259
        naming, 256
        snooze function
            (alarms), 256
    cities, associating with, 252
    current time, viewing, 250
    deleting, 253
    editing, 252
    multiple clocks, creating, 251
    renaming, 253

reordering, 253
time zones, configuring, 225
time/date settings
    configuring, 223, 226-228
    Time Zone support fea-
        ture, 228-229
    viewing current time, 250
    World Clock, 251-252
Closed Captioning (video),
    enabling, 343
closed network Wi-Fi Internet
    connections, 36-37
closing webpages (Safari web
    browser), 291
.com key, 271
commercial network Wi-Fi
    Internet connections, 35
company contacts, creating,
    108-109
Compass application, 387
computers
    restarting, 444
    USB ports, 445
condition monitoring, 14
conference calls, 140-141
    ending, 143
    private conversations
        during, 142
    removing callers from, 142
    time usage during, 143
configuring
    Accessibility settings, 431
    applications, 49, 400
    Auto-Lock feature, 415
    Calendar
        alerts, 243
        all-day events, 239
        event durations, 238
        repeating events, 241-243
    Clock, alarms, 253-257
    date/time settings, 223,
        226-228
    email accounts, 162
        advanced configuration,
            170-175
        Exchange accounts,
            165-169
        Fetch New Data settings,
            176-177
        global settings, 179-181
        Gmail accounts, 163-164
        SMTP server settings, 175
    Home button, 426

iPhone, restoring settings, 448-449
iPod Control Bar, 320
iPod settings, 329-331
iPod toolbar, 327-328
iPod Touch
 Safari settings, 262-266
 video settings, 342-343
iTunes Store application toolbar, 77
Location Services, 414
MobileMe, 21-24
Passcode Lock feature, 415, 423
phone settings
 AT&T Services feature, 132
 Call Forwarding feature, 130
 Call Waiting feature, 131
 hiding caller ID information, 131
 International Assist feature, 130
 ringer volume, 128
 selecting ringtones, 129
 SIM PIN feature, 132
 TTY support, 132
 Vibrate feature, 128
 voicemail alerts, 129
 voicemail passwords, 132
Restrictions feature, 417-420
Safari settings, 262-266
screen brightness settings, 410
slideshows, 352, 355
sound settings, 409
time/date settings, 223, 226-228
confirming deleted email messages, 180
connections (Internet)
Bluetooth, pairing, 45
cellular data networks, 41-44
roaming fees, 44
tethering, 45
Wi-Fi networks
 automatic prompts to join, 30
 cell phone providers, 41
 closed networks, 36-37
 commercial networks, 35
 forgetting, 39-40
 open networks, 30-34
 switching networks, 38-39
connections (P2P), 47-49

contacts
Address Book, syncing with, 83-84, 88-89
browsing, 116-117
company contacts, 108-109
Contacts application, navigating, 116-117
creating via
 email, 104-105
 manual creation, 106
 recent calls, 102-103
 syncing, 101
custom labels, 109-113
deleting manually, 121
dialing via, 134
displaying, 100
editing, 119-120
email addresses, adding to contacts, 105
finding locations via, 379
information fields, adding, 114
information on
 adding additional information, 120
 deleting, 119
 viewing, 116-118
organizing, 100
photos
 assigning to, 361
 associating with contacts, 107
 deleting from, 362
Safari web browser, using in, 263-264
sending email messages to, 190
sorting, 100
syncing, 101
text messaging, 211
conversing via text messaging, 216-217
deleting conversations, 221
photos and, 218-219
cookies, 265-266
copying
applications from iTunes Library onto iPod Touch, 393
text, 10-11
Cover Flow Browser, 299
finding music via, 294
text labels for album covers, 296
current locations, finding, 380

custom labels (contacts), 109-113
customizing
Accessibility settings, 431
Home screen, 406-407
iPhone, restoring settings, 448-449
iTunes Store application toolbar, 77
keyboards, 428-430
screen brightness settings, 410
searches, 426-427
sound settings, 409
wallpaper, 412

D

date/time settings
24-hour clock feature, 224
configuring, 223, 226-228
current date/time, viewing, 15, 250
time zones
 associating clocks with cities, 252
 configuring, 225
 creating multiple clocks for, 251
 Time Zone support feature, 228-229
Day view (Calendar), 237
Debug Console, 267
Default Calendar (Calendar), selecting, 230
default email accounts, setting, 181
deleting
alarms (Clock), 258
applications, 407
bookmarks (Safari web browser), 283
Calendar events, 235
clocks, 253
contacts
 contact information, 119
 manually deleting, 121
conversations, 221
email messages, 180, 199
Genius playlists, 313
icons, 407
Map bookmarks, 378
photos, 348, 356, 362
songs from On-the-Go playlists, 326

text messages, 220-221
video, 341, 356, 366
voicemail messages, 156
dialing via
contacts, 134
Favorites list, 135
keypad, 133
recent calls list, 136
Voice Control feature, 149-150
disabling
alarms (Clock), 256, 259
Call Waiting feature, 131
email sounds, 182
JavaScript, 265
plug-ins, 265
pop-up blocking, 265
text messaging alerts, 209-210
dismissing
alarms (Clock), 259
alerts, Calendar events, 249
Docking port, 4
downloading
applications from
App Store, 394-396
iTunes Store, 390-392
audiobooks, 76
iTunes, 17
movies from iTunes Store, 55-57, 75-79
music from iTunes Store, 55-57, 75-79
podcast episodes, 61
purchased iTunes Store application content to iPhone, 75-79
TV shows from iTunes Store, 55-57, 75-79
dragging (touch control), 26
driving directions, getting from Maps, 383
editing directions, 386
reversing directions, 385
Drop Pin command (Maps application), 386
duplicate information, syncing and, 83

E

earbuds, 145, 149. **See also** headsets
editing
alarms (Clock), 258
bookmark names (Safari web browser), 278, 281

Calendar events, 235-237
clocks, 252
contacts
adding additional information, 120
manually, 119
custom labels (contacts), 110-113
driving directions, 386
Map bookmarks, 378
music searches, 310
On-the-Go playlists, 326
text, 8
video, 366
email
accounts, configuring, 162
advanced configuration, 170-175
Exchange accounts, 165-169
Fetch New Data settings, 176-177
global settings, 179-181
Gmail accounts, 163-164
SMTPserver settings, 175
accounts, syncing, 86-87, 91
accounts, troubleshooting, 169
Address Book, syncing with, 83-84, 88-89
addresses
adding to contacts, 105
hiding information, 186
removing from email messages, 191
typing for sending email messages, 190-191
viewing information, 186-188
application links from App Store, 398
attachments
.ics files, 247
photos as, 187, 357, 363
viewing, 187
contacts
adding email addresses to, 105
creating from email, 104-105
Entourage, syncing with, 85
folders, creating, 202
messages
attachments, viewing, 187
BCC (blind copies) of, 180

checking for new, 197
deleting, 180, 199
determining status of, 198
forwarding, 195-196
HTML email messages, 188
organizing, 200-201
receiving/reading, 183-188
removing email addresses from, 191
replying to, 194
saving images attached to, 203
saving without sending, 193
sending, 189-194, 451
viewing in folders, 202
viewing photos in, 187, 357, 363
searching, 204-205
spam filtering, 205
webpage links, 285
ending conference calls, 143
Entourage, syncing with, 85
equalizer settings, 329
erasing data, 447. **See also** resetting iPhone
Erase Data feature, 417, 421
remote wiping, 426
events (Calendar)
adding
accepting invitations, 246-248
managing invitations, 246
manually, 237, 240, 243-245
alerts
configuring, 243
dismissing, 249
invitation alerts, 227
all-day events, 239
deleting, 235
duration of, setting, 238-240
editing, 235-237
repeating events, 241-243
syncing, 228
viewing, 234-237
Exchange accounts, configuring, 165-169
explicit content, blocking, 417-420

F

fast-forwarding through voicemail messages, 155
Favorites list
  caller information, adding to, 148
  dialing via, 135
Featured button (App Store), 394
fees
  license fees
    App Store applications, 398
    iTunes Store applications, 392
  roaming fees, 132
Fetch New Data feature
  Calendar, 230-231
  email accounts, 176-177
finance/business
  company contacts, creating, 108-109
  Stocks application, 387
Find My iPhone feature, 421-424
finding. *See also* browsing; searches
  album artwork, 297
  applications
    App Store, 394-395
    iTunes Store, 390
  applications in iTunes Store, Power Search link, 392
  contacts, 116-117
  help, 452
  Home screen searches, 13-14
  iPhone statistical information, 413
  iTunes Store application searches, 76-79
  locations
    bookmarks, 377
    contact information, 379
    current locations, 380
    searches, 374-376
  music via
    Albums tool, 305-307
    artists, 300-303
    Cover Flow Browser, 294
    Genius, 310-313
    More menu, 308
    playlists, 298
    Shuffle option, 314
    shuffling by shaking, 314
    Songs tool, 304

  speaking (voice command), 315
  specific searches, 309
podcasts, 61
video, 334
voicemail messages, 154
Firefox web browser, syncing, 86, 90
flashes (cameras), 348
focus (cameras), 347
folders
  email folders, creating, 202
  iTunes management, 63
  viewing email messages in, 202
forgetting Wi-Fi network Internet connections, 39-40
forms (Safari web browser), completing
  AutoFill feature, 287-288
  manually completing, 286
forwarding
  calls, turning on/off, 130
  email messages, 195-196
  text messages, 220
framing subjects (taking pictures), 347

G

Genius
  finding music via, 310-313
  playlists
    creating based on current song, 310-311
    creating based on selected song, 312
    deleting, 313
    refreshing, 313
global email settings, configuring, 179-181
Gmail account configuration, 163-164
Google
  Address Book contacts, syncing with iPod Touch, 84
  search engine, 262
GPS functionality
  current locations, finding, 380
  GPS indicator (Maps), keeping centered, 385
  GPS tags (photos), 348
greetings (voicemail), recording, 151-152

H

hanging up, conference calls, 143
HD movies/TV, 56
Headphone port, 4
headsets, 149
hearing-impaired functionality (TTY support), 132
help, troubleshooting iPhone, 451-452
hiding
  caller ID information, 131
  email address information, 186
histories (website)
  clearing, 266, 276
  returning to previous websites, 275-276
Home button, 4, 426
Home screen
  bookmarks, creating, 284
  customizing, 406-407
  icons
    deleting, 407
    organizing, 406
  navigating, 12
  searches, 13-14
  toolbar, accessing, 5
HTML email messages, 188
Hybrid view (Maps application), 386

I

iCal calendars, syncing, 84-85, 89-90
icons
  deleting, 407
  organizing, 406
.ics files, 247
IM (instant messaging), downloading AOL AIM application, 208
images
  album artwork
    finding, 297
    importing into iTunes, 54
  contacts
    assigning to, 361
    associating with, 107
    deleting from, 362
  deleting, 348, 356, 362
  emailing, 357, 363

GPS tags, 348
MobileMe accounts, 359-360
moving to
   Macs, 371
   Windows PCs, 369-370
orientation, changing, 346
saving images attached to
   messages, 203
sharing, 362-363
slideshows
   configuring, 352, 355
   landscape mode, 355
   music and, 354
   viewing, 354
taking photos
   flashes, 348
   focusing, 347
   framing subjects, 347
   landscape mode, 346
   screenshots, 350
   shutter sounds, 348
text messaging, 210, 218-
   219, 358
transferring to iPhone via, 75
   Mac, 74
   Windows PC, 72-73
viewing, 348
   individually, 350-351
   landscape mode, 351
wallpaper, changing, 412
importing CDs into iTunes,
   52-53
in-process calls
   answering calls during, 145
   conference calls, 140-143
   entering numbers
      during, 139
   managing, 138
   merging calls, 141
   swapping calls, 142
information fields, adding to
   contacts, 114
installing
   applications from App
      Store, 399
   iTunes, 17
International Assist feature, 130
International Keyboards configuration, 428-430
international options, setting,
   429-430
Internet connections
   Bluetooth, pairing, 45
   cellular data networks, 41-44

roaming fees, 44
tethering, 45
Wi-Fi networks
   automatic prompts to
      join, 30
   cell phone provider con-
      nections, 41
   closed networks, 36-37
   commercial networks, 35
   forgetting networks, 39-40
   open networks, 30-34
   switching networks, 38-39
invitations (events)
   accepting, 246-248
   alerts, turning on/off, 227
   .ics files, 247
   managing, 246
iPhone
   customizing, restoring set-
      tings, 448-449
   maintaining
      batteries, 438-441
      cleaning screens, 443
      software updates, 436-437
   P2P connections, 47-49
   resetting, 445-446
   restarting, 444
   restoring, 448-449
   statistical information,
      viewing, 413
   troubleshooting, help,
      451-452
iPhoto, moving video to
   iTunes, 368
iPod
   iPod Control Bar, 319-321
   iPod toolbar, 327-328
   settings, configuring,
      329-331
iPod Touch
   applications
      moving onto iPod Touch
         from iTunes Library, 393
      removing, 394
   batteries, saving, 230
   configuring
      Safari settings, 262-266
      video settings, 342-343
   P2P connections, 47-49
   power-saving techniques,
      Fetch New Data
      feature, 230
   screen orientation,
      rotating, 27

syncing with iTunes on
   Macs, 82
transferring iTunes content
   to, 67
iTunes, 16
   backing up content, 451
   check boxes in, 66
   downloading, 17
   installing, 17
   maintaining, 434-435
   managing, 63
   movies, purchasing from
      iTunes Store, 55-57, 75-79
   moving video from iPhoto
      to iTunes, 368
   music
      importing album art-
         work, 54
      importing audio CDs,
         52-53
      purchasing from iTunes
         Store, 55-57, 75-79
      tagging, 54
   organizing, 63
   podcasts, 60-62
   reinstalling, 451
   restarting, 444
   ringtones, creating, 124-127
   smart playlists, 64-65
   syncing on Macs, 82
      Address Book contacts,
         83-84
      duplicate information, 83
      Entourage, 85
      iCal calendars, 84-85
      Mail accounts, 86-87
      Notes, 85-86
      Safari bookmarks, 85
   syncing on Windows PCs
      Address Book contacts,
         88-89
      Advanced options, 92
      iCal calendars, 89-90
      mail accounts, 91
      Notes, 90
      web browser
         bookmarks, 90
   transferring content to
      iPhone, 67-68, 71-72
      iPod Touch, 67
   TV shows, purchasing from
      iTunes Store, 55-57, 75-79
   updating, 18

iTunes Library
  moving applications onto
    iPod Touch, 393
  saving On-the-Go playlists
    to, 327
iTunes Store
  account creation/sign in,
    18-19
  audiobooks, purchasing, 76
  browsing, 56
  downloading applications
    from, 390
      license fees, 392
      reading about applica-
        tions, 391
      sorting applications, 391
      viewing application
        requirements, 392
  movies
    purchasing, 55-57, 75-79
    renting, 58-60
  music, purchasing, 55-57
  podcasts, 60-62
  previewing content in, 78-79
  purchasing content from,
    78-79
  ringtones, creating, 124-127
  searching in, 76-79
  signing in, 55
  toolbar, reconfiguring, 77
  TV shows, purchasing, 55-
    57, 75-79

J - K - L

JavaScript, disabling, 265

key indexes for Wi-Fi network
  connections, 34
keyboard, 7
  .com key, 271
  customizing
    Auto-Capitalization fea-
      ture, 428
    Auto-Correction feature,
      428
    Caps Lock feature, 428
    International Keyboards
      configuration, 428-430
    Shortcut text feature, 428
  text
    copying/pasting, 10-11
    editing, 8
    selecting, 9
  word suggestions, 7
keypad, dialing via, 133

labels (custom)
  contact labels
    creating, 109
    editing, 110-113
  viewing in email headers, 180
landscape mode
  photos, 346, 351
  slideshows, 355
  video, 349
languages, selecting for
  video, 336
license fees
  App Store applications, 398
  iTunes Store applications, 392
links (webpages)
  emailing, 285
  moving to, 273
List view (Calendar), 236
listening to. **See also** playing
  podcasts, 321-324
  ringtones, 129
  voicemail messages, 154
loading additional email messages, 184
Location Services,
  configuring, 414
locations
  clearing searches, 376
  finding
    bookmarks, 377
    contact information, 379
    current locations, 380
    searches, 374-376
  viewing information on, 381
locking
  iPhone, 14-15
  volume limit settings,
    330-331
logins (automatic),
  webpages, 288
lyrics (music), viewing, 316

M

Macs
  iTunes
    installing, 17
    updates, 435
  MobileMe, configuring, 24
  photos
    moving to, 371
    transferring to iPhone, 74
  syncing information
    iTunes, 82-87
    MobileMe, 24

Mail accounts, syncing, 86-87, 91
maintaining
  applications, 401-403
  batteries, 438-439, 441
  iPhone, software updates,
    436-437
  iTunes
    Macs, 435
    Windows PCs, 434
  screens, cleaning, 443
managing
  alarms (Clock), 259
  applications, 399
  in-process calls, 138
  iTunes, 63
  Map bookmarks, 378
  MobileMe synch alerts, 26
  transferal of iTunes content
    to iPhone, 68
Maps
  bookmarks
    deleting, 378
    editing, 378
    finding locations via, 377
    naming, 382
    setting, 382
    sorting, 378
  driving directions, 383
    editing, 386
    reversing, 385
  Drop Pin command, 386
  GPS indicator, keeping cen-
    tered, 385
  Hybrid view, 386
  locations
    clearing searches, 376
    finding current locations,
      380
    finding via bookmarks,
      377
    finding via contact infor-
      mation, 379
    finding via searches, 374-
      376
    viewing information on,
      381
  scrolling in, 381
  Show Traffic command, 386
  zooming in/out, 381
merging
  calls, 141
  synchronized contacts, 87
messages (email). **See** email
messaging (text)

AOL AIM application,
downloading, 208
clearing all messages, 220
conversing via, 216-217
*deleting conversa-
tions, 221*
photos and, 218-219
deleting messages, 220
determining number of
messages, 216
enabling/disabling alerts,
209-210
forwarding messages, 220
MMS, 210
network plan costs, 207-208
photos and, 210, 218-219
previewing messages, 210
receiving messages, 214
replying to messages, 214
sending, 211-213
video and, 210
microphones, 149. **See also**
headsets
Microsoft Exchange, account
configuration, 165-169
MMS (Multimedia Messaging
Service), 210
MobileMe
account creation, 21
configuring, 21-24
fees, 20
free trial, 20
photos, 359-360
syncing, 21-26, 92-97
monitoring
battery life, 14
iPhone condition, 14
Month view (Calendar), navigating, 236
More menu, finding music
via, 308
movies
explicit content,
blocking, 419
HD movies, 56
iTunes, purchasing from
iTunes Store, 55-57, 75-79
rented movies, 58-60,
338-339
transferring from iTunes to
iPhone, 67-69

moving
applications from iTunes
Library onto iPod
Touch, 393
iTunes content to
iPhone, 67-68, 71-72
iPod Touch, 67
photos to
iPhone, 72-75
Macs, 74, 371
*Windows PCs, 72-73,
369-370*
ringtones to iPhone, 127
video from iPhoto to
iTunes, 368
multi-touch interface, iPhone
as, 5
music. **See also** audiobooks;
podcasts
albums, viewing, 319
finding via
Albums tool, 305-307
artists, 300-303
Cover Flow Browser, 294
Genius, 310-313
More menu, 308
playlists, 298
Shuffle option, 314
shuffling by shaking, 314
Songs tool, 304
*speaking (voice com-
mand), 315*
specific searches, 309
iPod Control Bar, 319-321
iTunes
*importing album art-
work, 54*
*importing audio CDs
into, 52-53*
*purchasing from iTunes
Store, 55-57, 75-79*
tagging music in, 54
lyrics, viewing, 316
Now Playing screen, mov-
ing, 303
On-the-Go playlists, 324-327
playing, 316-319
rating songs, 318
slideshows and, 354
smart playlists, 64-65
transferring from iTunes to
iPhone, 67-68
videos, watching, 342

N

naming
alarms (Clock), 256
bookmarks (Safari web
browser), 278, 281
Maps bookmarks, 382
navigating Home screen, 12
network connections (Internet)
Bluetooth, pairing, 45
cellular data networks, 41-44
roaming fees, 44
tethering, 45
Wi-Fi networks
*automatic prompts to
join, 30*
cell phone providers, 41
closed networks, 36-37
commercial networks, 35
forgetting, 39-40
open networks, 30-34
switching networks, 38-39
network coverage, 132
new email messages
checking for, 197
determining status of, 198
Notes application, 85-86, 90, 387
Now Playing screen
Album Cover view, 317-319
lyrics, viewing, 316
moving, 303
Timeline Bar, 316-318
Track List view, 317-319
NTSC format (video),
enabling, 343

O

On-the-Go playlists, 324-327
online resources, iPhone support, 451-452
open network Wi-Fi Internet
connections, 31
access fees, 30
passwords, 32
security key indexes, 34
troubleshooting, 33
opening multiple webpages, 289
organizing
applications, 399
bookmarks (Safari web
browser), 278-282
contacts, 100
email messages, 200-201

icons on Home screen, 406
iTunes, 63
Map bookmarks, 378
orientation (screen)
  photo orientation,
    changing, 346
  rotating, 27
  video orientation,
    changing, 364

P

P2P (Peer-to-Peer) connections,
  47-49
pairing (Bluetooth Internet
  connections), 45
PAL format (video),
  enabling, 343
parental controls, 417-420
Passcode Lock feature, 415, 423
passwords
  lost/forgotten
    passwords, 159
  Safari web browser, using
    with, 264
  voicemail, 132, 152, 158
  webpages, automatic
    logins, 288
  Wi-Fi network
    connections, 32
pausing
  video, 365
  voicemail messages, 155
PCs
  iTunes
    downloading, 17
    installing, 17
    syncing with iPhone, 89-92
    syncing with iPod Touch,
      88-89
    updates, 434
  MobileMe, configuring,
    21-22
  photos
    moving to, 369-370
    transferring to iPhone,
      72-73
phone calls
  adding information to
    Favorites list, 148
  answering, 143
    during in-process calls, 145
    earbuds, 145
    muting music/video dur-
      ing, 146

Call Failed screen, 138
clearing recent calls list, 147
conference calls, 140-143
dialing via
  contacts, 134
  Favorites list, 135
  keypad, 133
  recent calls list, 136
  Voice Control feature,
    149-150
in-process calls
  answering calls during, 145
  conference calls, 140-142
  entering numbers
    during, 139
  managing, 138
  merging calls, 141
  swapping calls, 142
silencing the ringer, 145
swapping, 142
U.S. prefixes, 130
using headsets during, 149
voicemail, 150
  alerts, 153
  changing greetings, 152
  changing passwords, 158
  contact names associated
    with, 153
  deleting messages, 156
  fast-forwarding mes-
    sages, 155
  finding messages, 154
  listening to messages, 154
  lost/forgotten
    passwords, 159
  passwords, 152
  pausing messages, 155
  recording greetings, 151
  returning calls, 157
  rewinding messages, 155
  sending to, 145
phone settings, configuring
  AT&T Services feature, 132
  Call Forwarding feature, 130
  Call Waiting feature, 131
  hiding caller ID
    information, 131
  International Assist
    feature, 130
  ringer volume, 128
  selecting ringtones, 129
  SIM PIN feature, 132
  TTY support, 132
  Vibrate feature, 128

voicemail alerts, 129
voicemail passwords, 132
photos
  contacts
    assigning to, 361
    associating with, 107
    deleting from, 362
  deleting, 348, 356, 362
  email messages
    sending via, 357, 363
    viewing in, 187
  GPS tags, 348
  MobileMe accounts, 359-360
  moving to
    Macs, 371
    Windows PCs, 369-370
  orientation, changing, 346
  sharing, 362-363
  slideshows
    configuring, 352, 355
    landscape mode, 355
    music and, 354
    viewing, 354
  taking
    flashes, 348
    focusing, 347
    framing subjects, 347
    landscape mode, 346
    screenshots, 350
    shutter sounds, 348
  text messaging, 210, 218-
    219, 358
  transferring to iPhone via, 75
    Mac, 74
    Windows PC, 72-73
  viewing, 348
    individually, 350-351
    landscape mode, 351
  wallpaper, changing, 412
PIN (personal ID numbers), associating with SIM cards, 132
pinching/unpinching (touch
  control), 6, 27
playing. *See also* listening to
  music, 316, 318-319
  video, 336
    Closed Captioning, 343
    music videos, 342
    NTSC format, 343
    PAL format, 343
    podcasts, 340
    rented movies, 338-339
    Where Left Off feature,
      337, 343
    Widescreen format, 343

playlists
    creating in iTunes, 63
    finding music via, 298
    Genius playlists, 310-313
    On-the-Go playlists, 324-327
    smart playlists, 64-65
plug-ins, disabling, 265
podcasts. **See also** audiobooks;
    music
    listening to, 321-323
    new episodes, download-
        ing, 61
    searching for, 61
    subscribing to via iTunes
        Store, 60-62
    transferring from iTunes to
        iPhone, 70-71
    video podcasts, 323, 340
pop-up blocking, disabling, 265
Power Search link (iTunes
    Store), 392
power-saving techniques,
    Fetch New Data feature, 230
previewing
    content from iTunes Store
        application, 78-79
    text messages, 210
    video, 349
private conversations during
    conference calls, 142
problem-solving. **See** trou-
    bleshooting
purchasing
    audiobooks, 76
    content from iTunes Store
        application, 78-79

Q - R

rating
    applications, 398, 407
    songs, 318
reading email messages,
    183-188
receiving
    calls, 143
        during in-process
            calls, 145
        earbuds, 145
        muting music/video dur-
            ing, 146
    email messages, 183-188
    text messages, 214

recent calls list
    clearing, 147
    contacts, creating from,
        102-103
    dialing via, 136
reconfiguring iTunes Store
    application toolbar, 77
recording
    greetings (voicemail), 151
    video in landscape
        mode, 349
refreshing
    Genius playlists, 313
    webpages, 273
reinstalling iTunes, 451
remote wiping, 426
removing
    applications, 394
    callers from conference
        calls, 142
    email addresses from email
        messages, 191
renaming clocks, 253
rented movies, 58-60, 338-339
reordering
    clocks, 253
    songs in On-the-Go
        playlists, 326
repeating events (Calendar),
    241-243
replying to
    email messages, 194
    text messages, 214
requirements (applications),
    viewing in iTunes Store, 392
resetting iPhone, 445-446. **See
    also** erasing data
restarting
    computers, 444
    iPhone, 444
    iTunes, 444
    video, 337, 343
restoring iPhone, 448-449
Restrictions feature, configur-
    ing, 417-420
reversing driving directions, 385
reviewing applications from
    App Store, 397-398
rewinding voicemail
    messages, 155
ringers
    silencing, 145
    volume, adjusting, 128

ringtones
    creating, 124-127
    headsets and, 149
    listening to, 129
    moving to iPhone, 127
    viewing, 128
roaming fees, 44, 132
rotating screen orientation, 27

S

Safari web browser
    Autofill feature, 263, 287-288
    bookmarks
        creating on Home
            screen, 284
        deleting, 283
        editing names of, 278, 281
        organizing, 278-282
        saving, 277-278
        syncing, 85, 90, 268
    caches, clearing, 267
    configuring settings,
        262-266
    contact information, using,
        263-264
    cookies, 265-266
    JavaScript, disabling, 265
    passwords, using with, 264
    plug-ins, 265
    search engines
        Google, 262
        Yahoo!, 263
    URL, accessing websites
        via, 270
    user names, using with, 264
    web forms, completing
        AutoFill feature, 287-288
        manually completing, 286
    web searches, 274-275
    websites
        accessing via
            bookmarks, 268
        accessing via URL, 270
        automatic logins, 288
        clearing histories, 266, 276
        closing webpages, 291
        Debug Console, 267
        emailing webpage
            links, 285
        moving between multiple
            webpages, 290-291
        moving to previous/later
            webpages, 273

moving to webpage
links, 273
opening multiple web-
pages, 289
refreshing webpages, 273
returning to previous
websites, 275-276
scrolling webpages, 272
viewing, 272-274
viewing Address bar, 274
webpage landscape
mode, 273
zooming in/out of web-
pages, 272
saving
bookmarks (Safari web
browser), 277-278
email messages without
sending, 193
images attached to email
messages, 203
On-the-Go playlists, 327
scaling video, 336
screens
brightness, setting, 410-411
cleaning, 443
orientation, rotating, 27
screenshots, 350, 397
scrolling
Maps, 381
webpages, 272
searches. *See also* browsing;
finding
album artwork, 297
application searches
App Store, 394-395
iTunes Store, 390-392
contacts, 116-117
customizing, 426-427
email, 204-205
Home screen, 13-14
iTunes Store application
searches, 76-79
location searches, 374-376
music searches, 309-310
podcasts, 61
Search button (App
Store), 395
search engines
Google, 262
Yahoo!, 263
videos, 334
voicemail messages, 154
web searches, 274-275, 452

security
Auto-Lock feature, 415
Erase Data feature, 417, 421
Find My iPhone feature,
421-424
Passcode Lock feature,
415, 423
passwords, Wi-Fi network
connections, 32
remote wiping, 426
Restrictions feature, configuring, 417-420
Voice Dial feature, 417
security key indexes, Wi-Fi network connections, 34
selecting text, 9
sending email, 189-194, 451
Settings screen
Accessibility settings, customizing, 431
accessing, 408
phone settings, configuring
AT&T Services feature, 132
Call Forwarding
feature, 130
Call Waiting feature, 131
hiding caller ID informa-
tion, 131
International Assist fea-
ture, 130
ringer volume, 128
selecting ringtones, 129
SIM PIN feature, 132
TTY support, 132
Vibrate feature, 128
voicemail alerts, 129
voicemail passwords, 132
shaking, shuffling music by, 314
sharing
photos, 362-363
video, 367
Shortcut text feature, 428
Show Traffic command (Maps
application), 386
shuffling music, 314
shutter sounds (cameras), 348
shutting down iPhone, 15
signatures (email), 181
silencing ringers, 145
SIM cards, associating PIN
numbers with, 132
Sleep mode, 4, 14-15

slideshows
configuring, 352, 355
landscape mode, 355
music and, 354
viewing, 354
smart playlists, creating in
iTunes, 64-65
SMTP servers, email account
configuration, 175
snooze function (Clock), 256
songs
On-the-Go playlists
adding to, 325-326
deleting from, 326
reordering in, 326
rating, 318
Songs tool, finding music
via, 304
sorting
applications in
App Store, 395
iTunes Store, 391
contacts, 100
Map bookmarks, 378
sound
configuring settings, 409
email settings, 182
shutter sounds
(cameras), 348
Volume control, 4, 294
spam filtering, 205
speaking (voice commands)
finding music via, 315
Voice Control feature,
149-150
special needs users, customizing accessibility settings, 431
spell checking, 428
statistical information,
viewing, 413
status of email messages,
determining, 198
Stocks application, 387
stopping video, 337, 343
storage capacity (iPhone), 67
subscribing to podcasts via
iTunes Store, 60-62
support, iPhone troubleshooting, 451-452
swapping calls, 142
switching Wi-Fi network
Internet connections, 38-39

syncing, 438
  applications from iTunes
    Library onto iPod
    Touch, 393
  bookmarks (Safari web
    browser), 268
  Calendar, 228, 232, 245
  contacts, 101
  duplicate information, 83
  Entourage, 85
  iTunes on iPhone, 67-68,
    71-72
  iTunes on Macs, 82
    Address Book contacts,
      83-84
    duplicate information, 83
    Entourage, 85
    iCal calendars, 84-85
    Mail accounts, 86-87
    Notes, 85-86
    Safari bookmarks, 85
  iTunes on Windows PCs, 88
    Advanced options, 92
    iCal calendars, 89-90
    mail accounts, 91
    Notes, 90
    web browser
      bookmarks, 90
  MobileMe, 92-97
    alert management, 26
    first time syncing, 25
    Macs, 24
    Windows PC, 21-22
  photos to iPhone, 75
    Mac, 74
    Windows PC, 72-73

T

tagging music in iTunes, 54
tapping (touch control), 27
tethering Internet
  connections, 45
text
  Auto-Capitalization
    feature, 428
  Auto-Correction feature, 428
  Caps Lock feature, 428
  copying/pasting, 10-11
  editing, 8
  International Keyboards
    configuration, 428-430
  selecting, 9
  Shortcut feature, 428

text messaging, 207
  AOL AIM application,
    downloading, 208
  clearing all messages, 220
  conversing via, 216-217
    deleting
      conversations, 221
    photos and, 218-219
  deleting messages, 220
  determining number of
    messages, 216
  enabling/disabling alerts,
    209-210
  forwarding messages, 220
  MMS, 210
  network plan costs, 208
  photos and, 210,
    218-219, 358
  previewing messages, 210
  receiving messages, 214
  replying to messages, 214
  sending, 211-213
  video and, 210
time limits, rented movies, 339
time/date settings
  24-hour clock feature, 224
  configuring, 223, 226, 228
  current time/date, viewing,
    15, 250
  time zones
    associating clocks with
      cities, 252
    configuring, 225
    creating multiple clocks
      for, 251
    Time Zone support
      feature, 228-229
Timeline Bar, 316-318
toolbars
  Home screen toolbar,
    accessing, 5
  iTunes Store application
    toolbar, reconfiguring, 77
top 25 button (App Store), 395
touch controls, 6, 26
Track List view (Now Playing
  screen), 317-319
traffic conditions. *See* Show
  Traffic command (Maps
  application)
transferring
  iTunes content to
    iPhone, 67-68, 71-72
    iPod Touch, 67

photos to iPhone, 75
  Mac, 74
  Windows PC, 72-73
troubleshooting
  computers, restarting, 444
  email, 451
  email accounts, 169
  iPhone
    help, 451-452
    resetting, 445-446
    restarting, 444
    restoring, 448-449
  iTunes
    reinstalling, 451
    restarting, 444
  Wi-Fi network
    connections, 33
TTY support, turning on/off, 132
turning on/off
  alarms (Clock), 259
  Auto-Capitalization
    feature, 428
  Auto-Correction feature, 428
  Call Forwarding feature, 130
  Call Waiting feature, 131
  Caps Lock feature, 428
  Erase Data feature, 417
  International Assist
    feature, 130
  International Keyboards
    configuration, 428-430
  iPhone, 15
  Shortcut text feature, 428
  text messaging alerts,
    209-210
  TTY support, 132
  Vibrate feature, 128
  Voice Dial feature, 417
  voicemail alerts, 129
TV shows
  explicit content,
    blocking, 420
  HD TV shows, 56
  iTunes Music Store applica-
    tion, purchasing from,
    55-57, 75-79
  transferring from iTunes to
    iPhone, 67
typing
  Auto-Capitalization
    feature, 428
  Auto-Correction feature, 428
  Caps Lock feature, 428
  copying/pasting text, 10-11

editing text, 8
International Keyboards
configuration, 428-430
selecting text, 9
Shortcut text feature, 428
word suggestions, 7

U

unlocking
iPhone, 14-15
volume limit settings,
330-331
unpinching/pinching (touch
control), 6, 27
unread email messages, 184
updates
applications, 401-403
iPhone software, 436-437
iTunes, 18
Macs, 435
Windows PCs, 434
URL (uniform resource
locators)
.com key, 271
websites, accessing via
(Safari web browser), 270
U.S. phone number prefixes, 130
USB ports, 445
usernames
Safari web browser, using
with, 264
webpages, automatic
logins, 288

V

Vibrate feature, turning
on/off, 128
video
chapters, moving to, 337
deleting, 341, 356, 366
editing, 366
iTunes Music Store application, purchasing from,
78-79
jumping through, 365
language selection, 336
movies
*blocking explicit
content, 419*
HD movies, 56

*purchasing from iTunes
Store, 55-57, 75-79*
*renting from iTunes Store,
58-60*
moving from iPhoto to
iTunes, 368
orientation, changing, 364
pausing, 365
playing, 336
Closed Captioning, 343
music videos, 342
NTSC format, 343
PAL format, 343
podcasts, 340
rented movies, 338-339
*Where Left Off feature,
337, 343*
Widescreen format, 343
playlists
creating in iTunes, 63
smart playlists, 64-65
podcasts, 323
previewing, 349
recording in landscape
mode, 349
restarting, 337, 343
scaling, 336
searching for, 334
settings, configuring,
342-343
sharing, 367
stopping/restarting, 337, 343
text messaging, 210
transferring from iTunes to
iPhone, 67, 69
TV shows
*blocking explicit
content, 420*
HD TV shows, 56
*purchasing from iTunes
Store, 55-57, 75-79*
viewing, 364-365
watching, 336
Closed Captioning, 343
music videos, 342
NTSC format, 343
PAL format, 343
podcasts, 340
rented movies, 338-339
*Where Left Off feature,
337, 343*
Widescreen format, 343
YouTube, 367, 387

viewing
albums, 319
attachments in email mes-
sages, 187
Calendar
events, 234-237
specific calendars, 233
contact information,
116-118
current time, 250
email address information,
186-188
email messages in
folders, 202
iPhone statistical information, 413
labels in email headers, 180
location information, 381
photos, 348, 365
in email messages, 187
individually, 350-351
landscape mode, 351
slideshows, 354
ringtones, 128
slideshows, 354
time/date, 15
video, 364-365
websites in Safari web
browser, 272-274
virtual keyboard. **See** keyboard
visual voicemail. **See** voicemail
voice command, finding music
via, 315
Voice Control feature, 149-150
Voice Dial feature, 417
Voice Memos application, 387
voicemail, 150
alerts, 129, 153
contact names associated
with, 153
deleting messages, 156
fast-forwarding
messages, 155
finding messages, 154
greetings, recording,
151-152
listening to messages, 154
passwords, 152
changing, 132, 158
*lost/forgotten
passwords, 159*
pausing messages, 155
returning calls, 157

rewinding messages, 155
sending calls to, 145
volume control, 4, 294
iPod settings, 329-331
ringer volume, adjusting, 128

W

Wake/Sleep button, 4, 14-15
wallpaper, changing, 412
watching video, 336
Closed Captioning, 343
music videos, 342
NTSC format, 343
PAL format, 343
podcasts, 340
rented movies, 338-339
Where Left Off feature,
337, 343
Widescreen format, 343
Weather application, 387
web browsers, syncing. **See
also** Safari web browser
Firefox, 86, 90
Safari, 85, 90
web caches, clearing, 267
web forms (Safari web browser), completing
AutoFill feature, 287-288
manually completing, 286
web resources, iPhone support,
451-452
web searches, 274-275, 452
webpages
automatic logins, 288
landscape mode, 273
links
emailing, 285
moving to, 273
multiple webpages
closing webpages, 291
moving between, 290-291
opening, 289
previous/later pages, moving to, 273
refreshing, 273
scrolling, 272
zooming in/out of, 272
websites
accessing via URL (Safari
web browser), 270
Address bar, viewing, 274
automatic logins, 288
.com key, 271

Debug Console, 267
histories
clearing, 266, 276
returning to previous
websites, 275-276
iPhone/iPod Touch-format-
ted websites, 270
Safari web browser
automatic logins, 288
closing webpages, 291
emailing webpage links,
285
moving between multiple
webpages, 290-291
moving to previous/later
webpages, 273
moving to webpage links,
273
opening multiple web-
pages, 289
refreshing webpages, 273
scrolling webpages, 272
viewing in, 272-274
webpage landscape
mode, 273
zooming in/out of web-
pages, 272
Wi-Fi network connections
Airplane mode, 409, 442
automatic prompts to
join, 30
cell phone provider con-
nections, 41
closed networks, 36-37
commercial networks, 35
forgetting networks, 39-40
open networks, 31
access fees, 30
passwords, 32
security key indexes, 34
troubleshooting, 33
switching networks, 38-39
Widescreen format (video),
enabling, 343
Windows PCs
iTunes
downloading, 17
installing, 17
syncing with iPhone,
89-92
syncing with iPod Touch,
88-89
updates, 434

MobileMe, configuring,
21-22
photos
moving to, 369-370
transferring to iPhone,
72-73
World Clock, 251-252
wrong numbers, Voice Control
feature, 150

X - Y - Z

Yahoo! search engine, 263
YouTube, 367, 387

zooming in/out
Maps, 381
webpages, 272
zoom feature, 6, 27

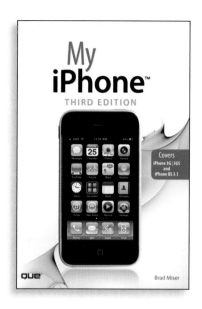

FREE Online Edition

Your purchase of **My iPhone** includes access to a free online edition for 45 days through the Safari Books Online subscription service. Nearly every Que book is available online through Safari Books Online, along with more than 5,000 other technical books and videos from publishers such as Addison-Wesley Professional, Cisco Press, Exam Cram, IBM Press, O'Reilly, Prentice Hall, and Sams.

SAFARI BOOKS ONLINE allows you to search for a specific answer, cut and paste code, download chapters, and stay current with emerging technologies.

Activate your FREE Online Edition at
www.informit.com/safarifree

> **STEP 1:** Enter the coupon code: FPSEREH.

> **STEP 2:** New Safari users, complete the brief registration form. Safari subscribers, just log in.

If you have difficulty registering on Safari or accessing the online edition, please e-mail customer-service@safaribooksonline.com